Pagan Religions in Five Minutes

Religion in 5 Minutes

Series Editors
Russell T. McCutcheon
University of Alabama
Aaron W. Hughes
University of Rochester

Published

Religion in Five Minutes
Edited by Aaron Hughes and Russell T. McCutcheon

Atheism in Five Minutes
Edited by Teemu Taira

Buddhism in Five Minutes
Edited by Elizabeth J. Harris

Hinduism in Five Minutes
Edited by Steven W. Ramey

Indigenous Religious Traditions in Five Minutes
Edited by Molly Bassett and Natalie Avalos

The Old Testament Hebrew Scriptures in Five Minutes
Edited by Philippe Guillaume and Diana V. Edelman

Forthcoming

African Diaspora Religions in Five Minutes
Edited by Emily D. Crews and Curtis J. Evans

Ancient Religion in Five Minutes
Edited by Andrew Durdin

Christianity in Five Minutes
Edited by Robyn Faith Walsh

Islam in Five Minutes
Edited by Edith Szanto

Jainism in Five Minutes
Edited by Steven M. Vose

Judaism in Five Minutes
Edited by Sarah Imhoff

Mormonism in Five Minutes
Edited by Daniel O. McClellan

Yoga Studies in Five Minutes
Edited by Theodora Wildcroft and Barbora Sojková

Pagan Religions in Five Minutes

Edited by
Suzanne Owen and Angela Puca

SHEFFIELD UK   BRISTOL CT

Published by Equinox Publishing Ltd.

UK: Office 415, The Workstation, 15 Paternoster Row, Sheffield, South Yorkshire S1 2BX

USA: ISD, 70 Enterprise Drive, Bristol, CT 06010

www.equinoxpub.com

First published 2024

© Suzanne Owen, Angela Puca and contributors 2024

All rights reserved. No part of this publication may be reproduced or transmitted in any form or by any means, electronic or mechanical, including photocopying, recording or any information storage or retrieval system, without prior permission in writing from the publishers.

British Library Cataloguing-in-Publication Data

A catalog record for this book is available from the British Library.

ISBN-13	978 1 80050 524 7	(hardback)
	978 1 80050 525 4	(paperback)
	978 1 80050 526 1	(ePDF)
	978 1 80050 611 4	(ePub)

Library of Congress Cataloging-in-Publication Data

Names: Owen, Suzanne, 1965- editor. | Puca, Angela, editor.
Title: Pagan religions in five minutes / edited by Suzanne Owen and Angela Puca.
Description: Sheffield, South Yorkshire ; Bristol, CT : Equinox Publishing Ltd., 2024. | Series: Religion in 5 minutes | Includes bibliographical references and index. | Summary: "Pagan Religions in Five Minutes provides an accessible set of essays on questions relating to Pagan identities and practices, both historically and in contemporary societies as well as informative essays on different Pagan groups, such as Druidry, Wicca, Heathenry and others. Each essay is by a leading scholar in the field, offering clear and concise answers along with suggestions for further reading. The book is ideal for both the curious and as an entry book for classroom use and studying Paganism"--Provided by publisher.
Identifiers: LCCN 2024020258 (print) | LCCN 2024020259 (ebook) | ISBN 9781800505247 (hardback) | ISBN 9781800505254 (paperback) | ISBN 9781800505261 (epdf) | ISBN 9781800506114 (epub)
Subjects: LCSH: Paganism. | Religions.
Classification: LCC BL432 .P33 2024 (print) | LCC BL432 (ebook) | DDC 200--dc23/eng/20240531
LC record available at https://lccn.loc.gov/2024020258
LC ebook record available at https://lccn.loc.gov/2024020259

Typeset by Scribe Inc.

Contents

Foreword   xi
Ronald Hutton

Preface   xvii
Suzanne Owen and Angela Puca

Paganism

1. What is Paganism?   3
   Angela Puca
2. Is Paganism a religion?   6
   Suzanne Owen
3. What is the difference between "Pagan," "pagan," "Paganism," and "neo-Paganism"?   9
   Graham Harvey
4. How did modern Paganism begin?   12
   Sabina Magliocco
5. What is the relationship between ancient and contemporary Paganism?   15
   Caroline Tully
6. How many Pagans are there?   18
   Vivianne Crowley
7. Are most Pagans solitary practitioners?   21
   Helen A. Berger
8. What is a Pagan worldview?   24
   Graham Harvey
9. Is there anything common to all Pagan religions?   27
   Jennifer Uzzell
10. Is Paganism a nature religion?   30
    Ethan Doyle White

11. How do Pagans view nature and the environment? 33
    Chas S. Clifton

12. Do Pagans have sacred sites? 37
    Ethan Doyle White

13. Do all Pagans follow the same festivals? 40
    Douglas Ezzy

14. Do Pagans have a holy book like the Bible? 43
    Denise Cush

15. What is the relationship between Theosophy and Paganism? 46
    Yves Mühlematter

Pagan religions

16. Can a Pagan follow more than one path or tradition? 51
    Caroline Tully

17. What is the difference between hard and soft polytheism? 54
    Jefferson Calico

18. What is the difference between an eclectic and a traditional Pagan or witch? 57
    Angela Puca

19. Are all witches Pagan? 60
    Mary Hamner

20. Can anyone be called a "witch"? 63
    Francesca Po

21. What is the difference between Wicca and witchcraft? 66
    Mary Hamner

22. What is Heathenry? 69
    Jefferson Calico

23. What is the difference between Druidism and Druidry? 72
    Jennifer Uzzell

24. Is Druidry the Indigenous religion of Europe? 75
    Suzanne Owen

25. What are Technopagans? 78
    Chris Miller

26. What was ancient Slavic "paganism"? *Giuseppe Maiello*	81
27. What is Romuva in Lithuania? *Milda Ališauskienė*	84
28. Is Romuva an official religion in Lithuania? *Rasa Pranskevičiūtė-Amoson*	88
29. How has Paganism developed in Brazil? *Karina Oliveira Bezerra*	91

Pagan beliefs and practices

30. How do Pagans conceive of gods? *Vivianne Crowley*	97
31. Is there salvation in paganism? *Michael York*	100
32. Can a person have Pagan beliefs without being Pagan? *Alessandro Testa*	103
33. Are some Pagans atheist? *Sarah Best*	106
34. Do Pagans worship Ancestors? *Jennifer Uzzell*	109
35. What are pagan ethics? *Michael York*	112
36. How do Pagans interact with deities and spirits? *Jenny Butler*	115
37. What does a Pagan minister do? *Holli S. Emore*	118
38. What does the pentacle symbol mean to Pagans? *Angela Puca*	121
39. Do Pagans believe in reincarnation or life after death? *Jennifer Uzzell*	124
40. Do Pagans practice ritual sex? *Angela Puca*	127
41. Are astrology and the tarot part of Paganism? *Francesca Po*	129

42.	How do Pagans view magic? *Karina Oliveira Bezerra*	132
43.	Is there a difference between magic and magick? *Caroline Tully*	135
44.	What is Chaos Magic? *Isis Mrugalla-Kalmbacher*	138
45.	Do Pagans use the internet for their religion? *Franz Winter*	142
46.	Is Christmas a pagan festival? *Alessandro Testa*	145
47.	Is Carnival a pagan festival? *Alessandro Testa*	148
48.	Are Halloween and Easter pagan festivals? *Jenny Butler*	151

Pagan discussions

49.	Do Pagans practice sacrifice? *Jefferson Calico*	157
50.	Are Satanism and Paganism the same? *Ethan Doyle White*	160
51.	What explains the enduring bias against Pagans? *Franz Winter*	163
52.	Is there antipathy between Pagans and Christians? *Denise Cush*	166
53.	Can a Christian also be a Pagan? *Rhiannon Grant*	169
54.	Can Paganism be applied to non-European religions, such as Shinto? *Douglas Ezzy*	172
55.	Can witch doctors and Africana spiritual traditions be regarded as Pagan? *Mary Hearns-Ayodele*	175
56.	How much of Paganism is based on cultural appropriation? *Sabina Magliocco*	178

57.	Do Pagans have particular political views? Ethan Doyle White	181
58.	Is there a problem with fascism in contemporary Paganism? Amy Hale	184
59.	Are Pagans involved in the war in Ukraine? Giuseppe Maiello	187
60.	Why do some polytheists reject the term "Pagan"? Angelo Nasios	189
61.	Is Paganism empowering for women and LGBTQI+? Giovanna Parmigiani	192
62.	Is Paganism "queer"? [M] Dudeck	195
63.	Why is witchcraft popular among teenagers? Denise Cush	198
64.	Do Pagans avoid technology? Chris Miller	201
65.	What is WitchTok? Mary Hamner	204
66.	How do Pagans use fiction and film? Carole M. Cusack	207
67.	Is Paganism make-believe? [M] Dudeck	210

Studying and teaching Pagan religions

68.	How do scholars study Paganism? Chris Miller	215
69.	Should Pagan religions be taught in schools? Denise Cush	218
70.	Are contemporary Pagan religions indicative of a new form of religiosity? Denise Cush	221
	Index	225

Foreword

Ronald Hutton

To write an afterword for a valuable collection such as this is relatively easy, as what is needed for that is to comment on the contributions and show how they add to existing knowledge and resources. To provide a foreword is more difficult because it involves introducing the contents without claiming an editor's sense of the purpose and context of the book and without prejudging the reader's experience of it. What I propose to do, therefore, is to explain why I think what follows is important and what I deem to be its implications.

It is worth asking at the beginning what the intended audience for the work is, as the contributors imply different instinctual answers to that question among them. All, beyond doubt, write with a clarity and simplicity that makes their entries perfectly intelligible to any intelligent person. Some, however, are more obviously addressing a general readership, while others are considering questions and issues more relevant to fellow scholars studying and teaching the subject. What can be suggested, therefore, is that the whole collection is admirably suited to readers who are concerned with modern Paganism at all levels of educational systems while also having real value to anybody with a general interest in it and a desire to be further informed.

In satisfying that desire, it has admirable breadth in terms of both coverage and geographical range, not only spanning, as it does, virtually any issue comprehended within the subject area but drawing on examples from the whole of Europe and English-speaking nations overseas. The authors are assembled from an equivalently broad catchment area and from both inside and outside of academic institutions. Despite this large assemblage of experience, personality, and viewpoint, common themes and conclusions strongly emerge from the collection. One is the apparently unanimous consensus that there is no direct continuity between ancient paganism and modern Paganism. Instead, the latter is viewed as a set of modern developments that draw on images and ideas from the pagan ancient world, some of which have survived continuously within Christian society without being recombined into a coherent and enduring system until recently. There is also an equally comprehensive acceptance that what defines and unites the various traditions of Paganism today is that they are all religious or spiritual frameworks that are primarily inspired and informed by the religions of ancient Europe and the Near East. This characteristic begets others that are as comprehensively recognized—namely, an acceptance that divinity (and so human celebrants) can be female as well as or instead of male, that there is divinity inherent in the natural world, and that the divine does not give commandments to humans and monitor their performance but permits and encourages people to develop responsibly their own individual potential. There is also a general acknowledgment that there are strong resemblances between modern Paganism and traditional religions in the non-European world, notably forms of Hinduism and Shinto, and the beliefs and practices of many Indigenous peoples. This is generally accompanied, however, by an equal acceptance that to label these extra-European systems unproblematically as Pagan is fraught with national, ethnic, and cultural sensitivities.

Beyond this, differences of attitude and emphasis set in. One of these is centered on how Pagans should be characterized and described and manifests in a twofold division of approaches. The first of these is simply to accept that a Pagan is anybody who identifies with that label and then to describe the people who assemble under it. The second is to consider those people and then to suggest frameworks and concepts by which they can be better understood and characterized, so providing definitions that can be helpful in discussing Paganism as a whole. Both approaches run through scholarly disciplines, and the second will be adopted in this foreword henceforth. One immediate and obvious conclusion to result from it, given the findings of this book, is that Pagans divide most clearly into two different groups. One consists of those who seek to reconstruct specific forms of ancient religion, representing particular cultures and ethnic groups, such as Egyptian, Greek, Roman, Anglo-Saxon, Norse, Lithuanian, or Russian. These traditions tend to have emerged in recent decades, although some, especially those concerned with Germano-Scandinavian forms of paganism, are longer established. They represent a minority among Pagans in English-speaking lands but are the majority or sole tradition in several European countries. The other grouping comprises those traditions that share characteristics of a more eclectic, generalized, and distinctively modern Paganism mainly derived from Wicca. Those characteristics include an annual cycle of eight seasonal festivals located at the solstices and equinoxes and the quarter days that open the seasons; the use of the circle, formed and consecrated anew for each ceremony, as the standard unit of sacred space; and the honoring or acknowledgment of a goddess and/or god who represents the natural world and combines qualities and aspects of various different ancient deities, often from different pantheons. This kind of Paganism is dominant in the English-speaking world but also has a strong presence in continental Europe.

Beyond this straightforward twofold distinction, however, it is obvious from this collection, as it is from the most cursory inspection of the field, that Paganism is remarkably heterogenous, unregulated, decentralized, and constantly developing. It has no controlling clergy, no fixed set of sacred texts (although bodies of ancient and medieval literature provide common source material for particular traditions), and no public institutional existence. In part, these qualities result from the fragmented and spontaneous way in which it has emerged, but also, they act as a reminder that ancient paganism itself was heterogenous and dispersed. Moreover, it embodied some major differences within itself. One of the greatest of these, which has shaped the nature of religion and politics ever since, lay on either side of a geographical boundary running through the eastern Mediterranean and Near East. To the south of this were large and closely centralized kingdoms and empires such as Egypt, Babylonia, Assyria, and Persia, with absolute rulers who were regarded as having a special relationship with the divine and even to be in some respects divine themselves. These states tended to have forms of religion in which deities were owed automatic obedience and wielded unlimited power over humanity. They were normally addressed in terms signifying masters and mistresses, high social superiors, or sovereigns. These cultures often had creation myths by which the deities being revered brought about the existence of the cosmological order and assigned humans a place in it. By contrast, ancient Europeans emerged into history divided into tribes or cities, often occupying small polities, between which movement was possible. These cultures tended to have deities as localized as those communities, among whose service people could choose. They were addressed in the terms employed for fellow humans to whom courtesy and respect were owed rather than subservience. Where creation myths existed, they normally represented the cosmos as coming into existence as the result of a series of accidents, with humans and deities being different kinds of beings rather than the one being the intended creation of the other. With such profound differences existing within ancient paganism (and this has been just what is probably the most striking example), it is hardly surprising that modern equivalents display considerable variation.

It is hoped that these reflections may provide a helpful context within which readers may approach the entries that follow, or else an encouragement for them to reject that context and draw different conclusions of their own. The same hope applies to a yet wider set of considerations that are embedded in this book, surrounding the nature of "religion" itself. That is a term that recurs throughout the book, rarely defined in the process and, where it is defined, implicitly or explicitly, with no clear agreement over the result. This is hardly surprising, as it is also ubiquitous in modern societies without having any greater agreement about its meaning, even (or especially) among professional scholars. The ancient Romans originally invented it and are no help in the matter because they themselves could not agree on what it actually meant. Some sense of a common usage, however, does emerge, both from a study of ancient and traditional cultures and from the contributions to this book: it has generally been used to signify respectful relationships made between humans and presumed superhuman beings (or a superhuman being or entity). If this is the case, then the same observation of usage suggests that the term "philosophy" is commonly used to refer to explanations of the cosmos that make no reference to such beings or do not emphasize them. Likewise, "spirituality" is most frequently employed to indicate a sense of the world as numinous and meaningful, which again does not center on such beings.

These suggestions are not intended to constrain readers. Those who reject the term "religion" because for them it carries connotations of structure, hierarchy, dogma, and obedience may fairly do so, though those connotations are not objectively inherent in it. Likewise, those who feel that it is time to "move beyond" the definition that centers on superhuman beings are entitled to argue a need for this, although to do so, they should also suggest a plausible and generally acceptable alternative. Rightly or wrongly, the assumed presence of such beings tends to feature in the discourse of those who discuss religion, both in this book and in general. It also reflects not only ancient usage and practice but also beliefs and practices across the current world. In itself, for example, Buddhism may be a cosmic philosophy to explain the nature of existence, but where it is the dominant faith system of peoples, it always has the trappings of "religion." The Buddha himself and the ascended sages of the tradition, or bodhisattvas, are treated with reverence and given temples, icons, and rites equivalent to deities and ascended saints in other faiths. To make these observations is not to establish a boundary to the terminology that can then be policed—for example, it must remain a matter of opinion and debate whether those who self-define as atheist or humanist Pagans practice a form of Paganism or a form of atheism or humanism with some features shared with Paganism.

This has been quite an abstract, analytical discussion, and probably a lot drier or stodgier than the contents of the book that follows. Nevertheless, it may have served to not only highlight some of the major issues that this book throws up, and what it contributes to them, but convey some sense of their overall coherence and importance. For those who want to know about Paganism today, as far in the round as it is possible swiftly to get, this book should be a first port of call.

Ronald Hutton, professor of history, University of Bristol

Preface

Suzanne Owen and Angela Puca

We had organized a public event at Leeds Trinity University called "Everything You Want to Know about Paganism (but Were Afraid to Ask)." We were going to collect questions from members of the audience, give a short presentation on Pagan Religions, and then try to answer the questions we'd collected. The date for this was March 24, 2020. However, when it became clear that COVID-19 was becoming prevalent, we canceled the event, and on March 17, 2020, staff and students at the university were told to return home, which delayed our plans for this volume. We are therefore grateful to Jane Emmett, our then line manager, and Chloe, a student volunteer, for providing some of the questions that appear in this volume. We would also like to thank the Patrons of Angela's Symposium for providing many more. Angela and I added other questions to fill the gaps, and some were suggested by scholars who had responded to our call.

The next stage was to solicit contributors, which we did primarily through three academic email lists—the Pagan studies list of the American Academy of Religion, the Dolmen list of the European Association for the Study of Religions, and the British Association for the Study of Religions list. We also asked a few scholars we knew personally to discuss specific topics based on their interests or expertise. We tried to include a wide range of views from different geographical regions as far as we were able. Special thanks to Andrew Reitemeyer, who transcribed the discussion from Angela's Symposium and did an initial edit of the contributions for style.

There are two critical points to address about this volume. The first was our decision to capitalize "Pagan" for contemporary usages, unless an author states reasons for doing otherwise, and use the lowercase for premodern and pejorative uses of the term (see chapter 3 by Graham Harvey). As for the title "Pagan Religions," this was chosen partly because it is in the Equinox Publishing Ltd. book series Religion in Five Minutes, edited by Russell T. McCutcheon and Aaron W. Hughes. Also, for many centuries, "pagan" was a term used by others to mean having no religion. The alternative—Paganism—we thought was too ambiguous, as some readers might think the book was about the "others" of early Christianity when, for the most part (with a couple of exceptions), we wanted to focus on contemporary Pagans: "Pagan" as a self-identity. However, we are aware that many contemporary Pagans would not regard what they're doing as a religion, and we respect this view.

In constructing this volume, our aim was to present a comprehensive yet concise overview of contemporary Pagan religions, addressing Paganism's multifaceted practices, beliefs, and traditions. The book's structure, which consists of a question and a scholar's response for each chapter, aims to make the content interesting and simple to understand. Our hope was to bridge the gap between academic discourse and the general public's curiosity, making the world of Pagan studies more accessible to those outside the realm of academia.

It's worth noting that the questions curated here are not just random inquiries; they reflect the genuine uncertainties, misconceptions, and curiosities that individuals, both within and outside the Pagan community, grapple with. By addressing these questions, we wanted to provide clarity, dispel myths, and foster a deeper understanding of Paganism in its myriad forms.

Once we got an idea of the list of questions we would include, we divided the volume into three broad areas:

- Paganism—questions on Paganism as a category or broadly across different traditions.
- Pagan religions—questions on different Pagan groups.
- Pagan discussions—questions on debates, misconceptions, and topics Pagans might reflect on themselves.

And finally, there is a shorter section, "Studying and teaching Pagan religions."

We also recognize that the landscape of Paganism is continually evolving, with new traditions and practices emerging alongside ancient ones. Hence while this book captures the essence of Paganism as it stands today, it is by no means an exhaustive or final account. It is, however, a starting point and a primer for those keen to delve deeper into this rich and diverse subject area.

Lastly, we wish to reiterate our gratitude to all contributors, supporters, and readers who have made this project possible. Through collective effort and understanding, we can promote a world where diverse spiritual beliefs and practices are respected and celebrated. As scholars, our ultimate goal is to foster knowledge and understanding as well as critical engagement with the topics. We hope this volume serves as a valuable resource in that endeavor.

Suzanne Owen and Angela Puca, Leeds Trinity University

Paganism

1
What is Paganism?

Angela Puca

Paganism is an umbrella term that was used in the past to describe a diverse range of religious practices, beliefs, and traditions that are not part of the major monotheistic religions such as Christianity, Islam, and Judaism. Although the term has been in use since the time of the Roman Empire, its meaning has evolved over the years, and it now encompasses a wide array of spiritual systems that share certain common characteristics.

One of the primary characteristics of Paganism is its polytheistic nature, which means that Pagans can worship multiple gods and goddesses. These deities are often associated with various aspects of nature, such as the sun, moon, or specific elements (water, earth, air, and fire), as well as with human attributes like love, wisdom, and war. Additionally, Paganism is often characterized by animistic beliefs, which assert that nonhuman entities (such as animals, plants, or even inanimate objects) possess a spiritual essence or consciousness.

Paganism can be further divided into different categories based on specific traditions or geographical regions. Some of the more well-known Pagan traditions are Wicca, a modern religious movement with roots in pre-Christian European beliefs; Druidry, which draws inspiration from the spiritual practices of the ancient Celtic peoples; and Hellenism, which aims to revive the ancient Greek religious tradition.

Another defining feature of Paganism is its focus on the sanctity and interconnectedness of all life, often expressed through the veneration of nature and the belief in the divine presence in the natural world. This spiritual connection to the environment is commonly expressed through rituals and ceremonies that celebrate the cycles of the seasons and the various stages of life (birth, death, and rebirth). Many Pagan practices emphasize the importance of living in harmony with nature, respecting the earth, and recognizing the interdependence of all living beings.

It is important to note that Paganism is not a monolithic religious tradition but rather an umbrella term that encompasses a wide variety of beliefs and practices. Consequently, there is a great deal of variation among Pagans in terms of their specific beliefs, practices, and rituals. While some Pagans may identify primarily with a particular tradition (such as Wicca or Druidry), others may draw on elements from multiple traditions or create their own eclectic spiritual path.

Despite the diversity within Paganism, several core principles tend to be shared across different traditions. These include a reverence for nature, a belief in the interconnectedness of all things, and an emphasis on personal spiritual growth and self-discovery. Many Pagans also place a high value on individual freedom, creativity, and autonomy, rejecting dogma and hierarchical structures in favor of a more egalitarian and inclusive approach to spirituality.

In recent years, Paganism has experienced a resurgence of interest and popularity, particularly in Western countries. This revival has been attributed to several factors, including an increasing awareness of environmental issues, a desire for a more personal and experiential approach to spirituality, and a growing interest in exploring alternative religious traditions beyond the confines of mainstream monotheism.

In summary, Paganism is a diverse and complex religious phenomenon that encompasses a wide range of beliefs, practices, and traditions. While it is difficult to provide a comprehensive definition of Paganism that applies to all its adherents, it is generally characterized by a polytheistic worldview, a reverence for nature, and an emphasis on personal spiritual growth and self-discovery. As a highly varied and adaptable spiritual path, Paganism offers a wealth of opportunities for individuals to explore their own unique relationship with the divine, the natural world, and their fellow human beings.

About the author

Angela Puca, PhD (2021), is an independent religious studies scholar and university lecturer. She is bridging the gap between academia and the general public with her social media project Angela's Symposium, where she disseminates peer-reviewed research to a wide audience engagingly. She's the author of the forthcoming *Italian Witchcraft and Shamanism*, to be published by Brill, and coeditor of *Pagan Religions in Five Minutes* for Equinox Publishing Ltd.

Suggestions for further readings

In this book

See also chapters 4 (How did modern Paganism begin?), 8 (What is a Pagan worldview?), and 70 (Are contemporary Pagan religions indicative of a new form of religiosity?).

Elsewhere

Berger, Helen A. *A Community of Witches: Contemporary Neo-Paganism and Witchcraft in the United States*. Columbia: University of South Carolina Press, 1999.

Clifton, Chas S., and Harvey, Graham, eds. *The Paganism Reader*. New York: Routledge, 2004.

Hutton, Ronald. *The Triumph of the Moon: A History of Modern Pagan Witchcraft* (2nd edition). Oxford: Oxford University Press, 2016.

York, Michael. *Pagan Theology: Paganism as a World Religion*. New York: New York University Press, 2005.

2
Is Paganism a religion?

Suzanne Owen

The short answer to the question of whether Paganism is a religion is, it depends. Pagans have been subject to social prejudice, especially in media representations and public accusations associating Pagans with child abuse, devil worship, and immorality in general. Being recognized as a religion in some official capacity may offer Paganism some protections.

Many Pagans, however, object to the categorization of what they do as "religion," especially when religion is conceived of as having a church and creed, based on Protestant Christian assumptions. The term "religion," as it is currently understood, emerged within European Christian contexts at the time the authority of state was being distinguished from the authority of church, and "religion" was further relegated to the "private sphere," which acted both to shield it somewhat from state scrutiny and to prevent religious leaders from meddling in politics. In this sense, applying the term "religion" to what Hindus, Buddhists, and others do is always going to distort them when taking them out of culture, politics, and so on. Christianity, too, suffers a similar distortion through the conception of religion as something special, set apart from the rest of society, as it is in cases of law. Charity registration in England and Wales has a separate category for "religion," and "religion or belief" is recognized as a characteristic in the United Kingdom's Equality Act and in the EU Charter of Fundamental Rights.

When the Druid Network (TDN) registered as a charity for the advancement of religion, many other Druids, including some of TDN's members, thought this meant that TDN had "joined the establishment," and others were adamant that Druidry was not a religion. Before this, and also afterward, the Pagan Federation (PF) tried several times to register as a religion but was rejected on each occasion, mainly for lacking cohesion, as each member was free to interpret the principles themselves, which for the charity commissioners was simply not characteristic of (a Protestant

Christian) religion. However, both TDN and PF were eventually admitted as members of the Inter Faith Network UK, after at first being rejected because admission might, they presumed, upset existing members.

Some Pagans campaigned to have everyone who identified as a Pagan (whether Wiccan, Druid, etc.) write "Pagan-Wiccan," "Pagan-Druid," and so on to have more accurate numbers of Pagans in the national censuses in the United Kingdom. For the first time, "Pagan" was listed as an option in the Scottish census in 2022; before, people had to write it in under "other." All this assumes, of course, that Paganism is a religion, whether or not various Pagans agree with this.

Emma Restall Orr, who founded TDN, stated that one of her reasons for applying for registration as a religion was so that Druidry could be taken more seriously. Whether or not that has proved to be the case, it has given Druids more of a voice in the United Kingdom. There are also Pagan chaplains for hospitals and prisons, and it makes it easier to have Paganism recognized in cases of bias, for example, in employment tribunals if it is considered a religion. Some groups in the United Kingdom have also produced education materials for schools, which would only be possible to include in a religious education class. Therefore, though the concept of religion is based on certain assumptions, it can work in Pagans' favor if they do play this game.

About the author

Suzanne Owen is an associate professor in the study of religion at Leeds Trinity University in the United Kingdom researching British Druidry and Indigeneity in Newfoundland.

Suggestions for further readings

In this book
See also chapters 3 (What is the difference between "Pagan," "pagan," "Paganism," and "neo-Paganism"?), 6 (How many Pagans are there?), and 9 (Is there anything common to all Pagan religions?).

Elsewhere
Crowley, Vivianne. "Standing Up to Be Counted: Understanding Pagan Responses to the 2011 British Censuses." *Religion* 44(3) (2014): 483–501.

Owen, Suzanne. "The Problem with Paganism in Charity Registration in England and Wales." *Implicit Religion* 21(3) (2018): 271–284.

Owen, Suzanne, and Teemu Taira. "The Category of 'Religion' in Public Classification: Charity Registration of the Druid Network in England and Wales." In *Religion as a Category of Governance and Sovereignty*, edited by T. Stack, N. Goldenberg, and T. Fitzgerald, 90–114. Leiden: Brill, 2015.

3
What is the difference between "Pagan," "pagan," "Paganism," and "neo-Paganism"?

Graham Harvey

People's choices about what to call themselves and their religions are rarely casual. Names are part of the building of communities of like-minded friends with shared values and practices. They can sum up vibrant and complex worldviews. At the same time, names can also be used to contrast oneself with others. Even as single words or short phrases, names are often eloquent about what people consider important to convey about themselves and their place in the world. Whatever we think about the choices and claims people make, it is helpful to reflect on how naming aids understanding. What is it that people want to communicate by naming themselves or their religion one way rather than another?

As you are reading this book, you are clearly interested in Paganism—or do I mean "neo-Paganism"? We are already struggling with names! What difference does it make to add or subtract "neo"? What do the capital letters indicate? How is "Paganism" different from "paganism"? Names cannot be defined only by the way they were used in the past—rather, they express contemporary concerns. So rather than starting with the ancient Latin word *pagus*, I'm going to focus on contemporary usage. This is justified because these name choices are not primarily about the past but about what is important to people now.

Let's start on common ground. Whatever differences there might be in the *names* "Pagan" and "neo-Pagan," the people to whom these labels are applied are not very different from one another. They celebrate similar seasonal festivals, conduct similar ceremonies (often in circles), venerate similar deities (or none), often consider "magic" effective, and seek ways to make life better for all living beings. Other entries in this book will answer questions about different kinds of Paganism or neo-Paganism. These will reveal the kind of diversity that is evident in all religions and societies. For now, it will be enough to say that honoring the larger-than-human world (or "nature") is what unites Pagans—or neo-Pagans!

Now I can make two other relatively uncontroversial statements. First, the term "neo-Paganism" was, until recently, more popular than the term "Paganism" among both scholars and practitioners in North America than it was elsewhere. Second, the term "neo-Paganism" recognized a distinction between the new movement and ancient "pagans." The lowercase "pagan" is used by scholars of classical Rome and Greece to contrast later cultures and religions. As "pagan" (Latin: *pagus*) was not a term for a specific religion in ancient Rome, it is not capitalized. It originally meant something like "people who live in defined communities" (like "parishes" in modern Britain). But it became useful to those who wanted to contrast older ways of life with (the then new) Christianity. They selected "pagan" because it suggested a contrast with the alleged universality of Christianity. It soon became the term for all religions other than Christianity—or other than monotheistic religions.

For some people, "neo-Paganism" recognizes this history and acknowledges differences between ancient and modern movements. But it is not always used neutrally. Rather, it can suggest that "paganism" was made obsolete by the rise of Christianity. However, in modern times, a relatively new association of "pagan" with rural peasantry took a dramatic twist. Rather than epitomizing foolishness or primitivism, "pagan" came to be linked with the positive celebration of "nature" and sensuality. This usage became popular among Romantic poets and others. It could be used with pride. In recent decades, the term "neo-Paganism" has decreased in popularity. This is possibly because Pagans and scholars became less concerned with stressing the newness of this Paganism—just as no one talks about "neo-Christians" or "neo-Buddhists." "Pagan" was enough to signal more confidence about traditions and practices centered on celebrating the earth and the senses.

In summary, using a capital letter for "Pagan" and "Paganism" indicates that this is the name with which people choose to identify themselves and their traditions. "Neo-Pagan" can mean the same thing but generally overemphasizes the novelty of this religious movement as if that were its defining characteristic. The lowercase "pagan" is often used to label ancient religions or cultures. Sometimes it labels Indigenous and other religions, but this is a hangover from an era when it seemed acceptable to view Christianity or perhaps other monotheisms as the only legitimate religions. Finally, when people refuse to capitalize the names that Pagans—or members of other religions—use for themselves, they are usually expressing dismissive or derogatory views of others.

About the author

Graham Harvey is emeritus professor of religious studies at the Open University, United Kingdom. His research largely concerns Indigenous religions and the "new animism." His participative research among Pagans has resulted in publications including *Listening People, Speaking Earth: Contemporary Paganism* and *Researching Paganisms* (coedited with Jenny Blain and Douglas Ezzy).

Suggestions for further readings

In this book
See also chapters 5 (What is the relationship between ancient and contemporary Paganism?) and 60 (Why do some polytheists reject the term "Pagan"?).

Elsewhere
Adler, Margo. *Drawing Down the Moon* (revised edition). London: Penguin, 1997.

Strmiska, Michael F. "Comparative Perspectives." In *Modern Paganism in World Cultures: Comparative Perspectives*, edited by Michael F. Strmiska, 4–10. Santa Barbara, CA: ABC-CLIO, 2005.

4
How did modern Paganism begin?

Sabina Magliocco

As a new religious movement, modern Paganism, as we understand it today, did not exist before the twentieth century. Yet the ways of knowing and practices that led to its development have traceable roots in the pre-Christian spiritual practices of Mediterranean cultures. The earliest written records of ideas and customs that are part of modern Paganism are in texts from the second and third centuries CE known as the Greek and Demotic magical papyri, the Chaldean oracles, and the Corpus Hermeticum. Together, this set of documents preserves most of what we know today about religion and magic in classical antiquity. Their cosmology describes an animated universe filled with divine forces embodied in natural, human, and animal forms, as well as complex rites used to communicate with and control these forces. In these texts, we can find the notion that the four Aristotelian elements—air, fire, water, and earth—are the building blocks of the universe; their correspondence to the four cardinal compass points (east, south, west, and north); belief in the existence of multiple deities as well as other spirits; the idea of correspondences between deities and aspects of the natural world, such as planets, herbs, minerals, colors, days of the week, and hours of the day; the magical principle of sympathy, such that all phenomena are connected and interrelated; the use of amulets, spells, invocations, and special tools to control the forces of the universe; and cults in which members underwent initiations involving religious ecstasy and the revelation of divine mysteries. These ideas were so pervasive in late antiquity that they were part of the oral traditions of numerous pre-Christian religions and cults. They form the building blocks of modern Pagan practices.

A later set of ideas that also influenced the development of modern Paganism can be found in the writings of the Neoplatonists, a group of late-classical philosophers who expanded Plato's metaphysical concepts.

The main teaching of the Neoplatonists was the essential oneness of the universe. This idea had a great influence on the development of Western mysticism, from early Christianity to the Renaissance magi to the Romantic revival of the early nineteenth century, from which it entered modern Paganism.

While Christianity denounced these ways of knowing, it could not completely obliterate them. They were preserved as part of vernacular or everyday magic, which gave them a Christian veneer, as well as by the Byzantine and Islamic courts, the heirs to the learning of classical antiquity. They came to constitute a body of hidden or "occult" knowledge that, like a substrate of magma, has lain just below the surface of Western culture for 1,500 years, bursting forth during certain historical periods in a flowering of interest in esoteric themes, artworks, expressions of the imagination, and social reform movements. With the Crusades, bits of this knowledge system began to reenter Western Europe. The Italian Renaissance reintroduced Greek and Roman deities and mythology to European art and literature; magic became a path to enlightenment and self-development reflecting the period's emphasis on humanism. The development of the printing press made magical books available to a larger number of readers, contributing to the diffusion of esoteric knowledge.

Yet while scholarly knowledge of ancient magic was increasing, folk magic, which had preserved some of the elements of the Western magical heritage through oral tradition, came under fire from both Catholic and Protestant authorities. The witch persecutions construed the practice of magic and nonmainstream ways of knowing as devil worship, punishing the accused with imprisonment and death. Seasonal traditions associated with Christian holidays, which were expressions of identity and spirituality for ordinary people, came to be understood as "pagan" and idolatrous by Protestant reformers, who banned them. It was not safe for the Western magical tradition to come out of the closet until after the Scientific Revolution and the Enlightenment had stigmatized belief in witchcraft and magic and made the dominant worldview one of disenchantment.

The Romantic movement of the early nineteenth century began as a rebellion against the disenchantment of the world embraced by the Enlightenment. During this period, increasing urbanization and industrialization led artists, writers, and poets to idealize the rural past and associate it with a better way of life that embodied harmony with nature and spiritual authenticity. These artists also idolized the cultures of ancient Europe, creating art and literature inspired by Greek, Roman, Egyptian, Norse, and Celtic myths. These creative works encouraged a rebirth of interest in pre-Christian religions: the first neo-Druid orders arose in England during the early 1800s, while in France, the occultist Eliphas Levi reimagined ancient Egyptian magic. At the same time, the emerging scholarly disciplines of folklore studies and anthropology promulgated the idea that the customs of European peasants preserved ancient pagan customs that were similar to those of colonized peoples in Africa, Asia, and the Americas. In light of this new perspective on the past, the witchcraft persecutions were reinterpreted as a misunderstanding of a pre-Christian fertility religion that had worshipped a "Horned God" and an earth "Mother Goddess." Witches were simply preserving the vestiges of an ancient pagan religion. The stage was set for the birth of a new religious movement: modern Paganism.

About the author

Sabina Magliocco is professor of anthropology and chair of the Program in Religion at the University of British Columbia in Vancouver.

Suggestions for further readings

In this book

See also chapters 5 (What is the relationship between ancient and contemporary Paganism?), 9 (Is there anything common to all Pagan religions?), and 15 (What is the relationship between Theosophy and Paganism?).

Elsewhere

Hutton, Ronald. *Blood and Mistletoe: The History of the Druids in Britain.* New Haven, CT: Yale University Press, 2009.

Hutton, Ronald. *The Triumph of the Moon: A History of Modern Pagan Witchcraft.* Oxford: Oxford University Press, 1999.

Hanegraaff, Wouter. *Hermetic Spirituality and the Historical Imagination: Altered States of Knowledge in Late Antiquity.* Cambridge: Cambridge University Press, 2022.

5
What is the relationship between ancient and contemporary Paganism?

Caroline Tully

Ancient paganism and contemporary Paganism are quite different but do have some similarities. Ancient paganism refers to the pre-Christian religions of civilizations such as the Egyptians, Greeks, Romans, Celts, and Norse as understood through the academic study of ancient literature and material culture. These religions were not called "paganism," which was a Roman designation for unsophisticated rural peoples and later came to be used by Christians to describe non-Christians. In the ancient world, religion in state-level societies, like those of the Mediterranean and Near East, was a response to the understanding that the world was full of gods, and ritual was the technology used to influence those gods. Classified into hierarchies of power, the most important deities (often in family groups) were situated at the top, with their own elaborate temples and priestly personnel, and worshipped in state-run ceremonies, while various less-powerful gods, nymphs, and heroes were venerated in simpler domestic and rural shrines. One of the central characteristics of ancient Greek, Roman, and Norse religions was animal sacrifice in which a meat meal was shared between gods and humans. In Greek and Roman ritual, the gods received the bones of the animals wrapped in fat and were envisaged as enjoying the fragrant odor as they burned, while human participants received the meat. Religious festivals were often the only time nonelite people got to consume meat from large, expensive animals.

Animal sacrifice exemplifies the transactional nature of ancient Greek and Roman religions: I give so that you may give. Providing sacrifice to a deity, or votive offerings, such as figurines, garments, or jewelry, was intended to secure their favor. In classical and Hellenistic Greece and in Rome, there were also "mystery religions" in which participants underwent initiation into secret aspects of the cult of certain deities in order to be guaranteed a better afterlife. Most mystery religions were open to both women and men, except for Mithraism, which only admitted men. Magic was not part of ancient Greek and Roman religion and was considered a private and nefarious activity that did not occur (openly) within temples, in contrast to ancient Egypt, where magic was part of formal state-run temple practice.

Contemporary Paganism can be divided into Pagan reconstructionism and neo-Paganism. Pagan reconstructionism is the attempt to practice ancient religions in a historically correct manner. Practitioners refer to the textual and archaeological evidence of ancient religions as their source of information on how to interact with ancient deities in ritual. Pagan reconstructionists are often "hard polytheists" who believe in the literal reality of the deities. One of the most successful forms of Pagan reconstructionism, Norse Paganism, termed "Heathenry" by its followers, often includes animal sacrifice as part of the historically correct practice of the religion. In contrast, neo-Pagan ritual is based on a twentieth-century Wiccan format, which is in turn derived from a late nineteenth-century British ceremonial magic model (that included some aspects of ancient Egyptian religion). While neo-Pagans eschew animal sacrifice, they regularly incorporate magic into their rituals, conduct their ceremonies within a magical circle, and generally understand their Pagan ritual as synonymous with "magic."

Contemporary Paganism incorporates a few features of ancient paganism; for example, the Wiccan second-degree initiation ritual is loosely based on the Mesopotamian myth of the "Descent of Inanna," and the Wiccan third-degree initiation ritual (itself based on early twentieth-century magician Aleister Crowley's "Gnostic Mass") has echoes of both Hindu Tantra and the Mesopotamian "Sacred Marriage" ritual. Other ancient aspects have been filtered through centuries of Christian reception of ancient paganism, such as the pairing of the Roman goddess Diana with Herodias (the chief female villain in the biblical New Testament) and late nineteenth- / early twentieth-century archaeological and anthropological publications such as James G. Frazer's *The Golden Bough* (1890), which contributed the concept of a divine heterosexual pair to neo-Pagan theology.

Rather than focus on a pantheon consisting of a family, Pagans tend to be duotheists, conceiving of deity as a "great Mother Goddess" and a "dying and rising God," understandings of which range from literal belief to "soft polytheism," where the gods are seen as metaphors for natural forces or psychological archetypes. Wicca sees itself as a mystery religion, with the term "mystery" understood in two ways: (1) as a synonym for the ineffable and (2) in regard to "women's mysteries" and "men's mysteries," concepts that derive from the anthropological study of rites of passage rather than ancient Greek and Roman mystery cults. Contemporary Paganism can therefore be considered to be inspired by but only very loosely based on ancient pagan religions.

About the author

Caroline Tully is an archaeologist at the University of Melbourne, Australia. Her research interests include religion and ritual in the Aegean Bronze Age, reception of the ancient world, and contemporary Paganisms. She is the author of *The Cultic Life of Trees in the Prehistoric Aegean, Levant, Egypt and Cyprus* (Peeters 2018) and many academic and popular articles.

Suggestions for further readings

In this book
See also chapters 3 (What is the difference between "Pagan," "pagan," "Paganism," and "neo-Paganism"?), 4 (How did modern Paganism begin?), and 49 (Do Pagans practice sacrifice?).

Elsewhere
Campbell, Drew. *Old Stones New Temples: Ancient Greek Paganism Reborn*. Bloomington, IN: Xlibris, 2000.

Davy, Barbara. "Reconstructing the Procession of Nerthus: A Contemporary Heathen Ritual Offering of Sacrifice." *Pomegranate: The International Journal of Pagan Studies* 24(1) (2023): 96–122.

Hutton, Ronald. *The Triumph of the Moon: A History of Modern Pagan Witchcraft*. Oxford: Oxford University Press, 1999.

Tully, Caroline. "The Artifice of Daidalos: Modern Minoica as Religious Focus in Contemporary Paganism." In *New Antiquities: Transformations of Ancient Religion in the New Age and Beyond*, edited by Dylan Burns and Almut-Barbara Renger, 76–102. Sheffield: Equinox Publishing Ltd., 2019.

6
How many Pagans are there?

Vivianne Crowley

Worldwide, hundreds of millions of people practice Indigenous religions that could be classified as Pagan, often combined with Christian, Muslim, Hindu, Buddhist, or other religious practices. Many would not, however, choose to identify with the label "Pagan." Looking specifically at Western countries, Pagans are a small but growing part of the religious landscape, but the individualized nature of contemporary Paganism makes it difficult to estimate numbers. The main sources of data are national censuses, surveys of social trends, and research analyzing data drawn from these sources.

In the United Kingdom, the addition of an optional question on religion to the England and Wales, Scotland, and Northern Ireland 2001 censuses was the first opportunity to obtain a breakdown of religious affiliation. Excluding "none" and the spoof "Jedi Knights," at around 42,000 adherents, Paganism emerged behind the six world religions as the seventh largest religious category, but numbers were well below Ronald Hutton's 1999 estimate of 125,000 Pagans in Britain.

The discrepancy is unsurprising, given that the religion question was voluntary and there was no "tick box" for the category "Pagan." Pagans had to take the initiative and write in their religion if they wanted to record it. Another inhibiting factor is that UK censuses are completed by households rather than by individuals. Prejudice against Pagans has meant that not all adherents are willing to share their religious affiliation with family or housemates. Added complications are that Paganism attracts people who are individualistic, mistrustful of authority and data collection, and resistant to labeling.

In the 2011 UK censuses, some 60,000 people wrote "Pagan" on their census forms, and a further 25,000 wrote in a particular kind of Paganism. This reflected increased numbers plus Pagans' greater confidence in being open about their beliefs. Extrapolating from earlier data and underlying trends resulted in an estimate of around 180,000–240,000 Pagans in Britain in 2011, around 0.3 percent of the population. Directly comparable census data are not available for the United States, which has a similar timeline to Britain in the development of contemporary Paganism, but the latest large-scale survey data available (from the Pew Research Center in 2014) gave a similar estimate of around one million people, or 0.3 percent of the US population, identifying as some form of Pagan. The third iteration of the optional religion question for the England and Wales 2021 census resulted in a figure of some 107,000 Pagans. Unlike England and Wales, the Scottish census in 2022 offered for the first time "Pagan" as a tick box category rather than a write-in option. This resulted in just over nineteen thousand Pagans, a fourfold increase since the 2011 census, making Paganism Scotland's fourth largest religion.

The predominant forms of Paganism vary according to countries' religious and cultural histories. In the United States and United Kingdom, Wicca and other forms of Pagan witchcraft have been the largest groupings, but the 2021 England and Wales census data show a growing number of people identifying with shamanism. In Iceland, by contrast, Ásatrú (Norse Paganism) has been recognized as a religion since 1973. In 2023, 1.5 percent of the population identified as Heathen or Ásatrú, rising from 0.03 percent in 1990.

Despite the greater availability of census data, it is becoming increasingly difficult to estimate Pagan numbers because not all practitioners categorize their spiritual practice as a religion. In Britain, for example, spiritual and cultural Paganism is an increasing part of everyday life, with the media routinely covering large Pagan seasonal celebratory gatherings at historic venues such as Stonehenge, advice on how to celebrate Pagan seasonal festivals appearing in popular media and women's magazines, and narratives about the Pagan origins of traditional customs and practices featuring in ostensibly secular events such as the National Trust's seasonal wassailing celebrations. As a result, while the numbers of people who readily identify with Paganism as a religion are rising slowly, the numbers of those who engage in Pagan practices are rising much more rapidly.

About the author

Vivianne Crowley is a lecturer in psychology of religion at Nottingham Trent University, United Kingdom. Her research interests include contemporary Paganism, religious experience, and women religious leaders.

Suggestions for further readings

In this book
See also chapters 2 (Is Paganism a religion?) and 7 (Are most Pagans solitary practitioners?).

Elsewhere
Crowley, Vivianne. "Standing up to Be Counted: Understanding Pagan Responses to the 2011 British Censuses." *Religion* 44(3) (2014): 483–501.

Crowley, Vivianne. "The Changing Face of Contemporary Paganism in Britain." In *Visioning New and Minority Religions: Projecting the Future*, edited by Eugene V. Gallagher, 87–99. New York: Routledge, 2017.

Hutton, Ronald. *The Triumph of the Moon: A History of Modern Pagan Witchcraft*. New York: Oxford University Press, 1999.

7
Are most Pagans solitary practitioners?

Helen A. Berger

Most contemporary Pagans, regardless of their spiritual path, are now solitary practitioners. This was not always true. When I began my research on Paganism in 1986, it was normative for Pagans to be in groups, such as covens for Wiccans and Witches or groves for Druids. When I did my original survey with Andras Arthen in 1990–1991 (which served as the basis for my second book, *Voices from the Pagan Census*), just over half of the respondents were solitary. Twenty-five years later, when I conducted a second survey with James Lewis (which informed my fourth book, *Solitary Pagans*), the percentage of solitaries jumped to about three-quarters of my respondents. Although my research focused primarily on the United States, as the responses were more robust for this country, I received data from around the world in my second survey. Internationally, solitary practice is the primary form of practice for Pagans worldwide. In England, as in the United States, about three-quarters of practitioners are solitaries.

There are a number of reasons that solitary practice has increased steadily since I began my research. The first and most important is that information is available outside of one-on-one or group training. Initially, traditions like Wicca were learned only in small groups. People entered a coven and were trained by the elders of the coven. They were sworn to secrecy that they only share the knowledge they had gained with others in a coven or other group of those who were being initiated or seeking initiation.

This changed with the publication of books that shared most, if not all, occult or secret information that was available. Scott Cunningham, who wrote books such as *Wicca for the Solitary Practitioner*, was one of the most important writers; his works were part of the early wave of publications and were very popular. There were others as well, such as Silver

Raven Wolf, who geared her books to teenagers. With the advent and spread of the internet, information became shared on web pages as well as in books. Today, in addition to books and websites, there are TikTok Witches who post short video clips about their practice and influencers whose popular blogs are followed by hundreds of thousands of people, in some instances.

This has had several effects. All the data available have shown a steady increase in the number of contemporary Pagans throughout the world. As it has become easier to become a Pagan, more people have self-identified as Pagans. There is a growing number of teenagers who self-define as Pagans, particularly as Witches. This is both because there are books and websites geared to the young and because there have been positive images of Witches in the media. As Melissa Harrington indicated in her essay "The Perennial Teen Witch" (in *The New Generation Witches*, edited by Hannah Johnston and Peg Aloi), when *The Craft* and *Sabrina the Teenage Witch* first came out in the 1990s, the Pagan Federation in the United Kingdom received an increase in interest from people who wanted to learn more about Witchcraft.

Douglas Ezzy and I found in our book *Teenage Witches* that while increased interest resulted in increasing numbers, not all who expressed interest joined. Among those who initially explored it, only a small percentage stayed. We discovered that often, three or four teenage girls would join together to explore Witchcraft, and only one would stay. The others would lose interest rather quickly. And there were undoubtedly some groups in which none remained as Witches. So while the media helped stimulate interest, these programs did not necessarily turn teens into Witches.

One other effect of more people learning about Paganism online or through books is that there has been an increased number of Pagans who self-define as eclectic Pagans or Witches. They have formed their own practice, normally by combining aspects of Wicca with some other forms of Paganism and their own inspiration. My data indicates that the young are more likely to be solitary and eclectic than older Pagans.

Although most Pagans are solitaries, they are not isolated. Almost every solitary in my sample was connected to other Pagans. They texted, phoned, emailed, or met for spiritual and personal get-togethers. They also interacted on the internet on a regular basis. Since the spread of COVID and fears of infection, more interactions of all sorts have been done on the internet. Although I do not have data to confirm it, my guess is that the number of solitary practitioners has only grown, and with it, there has been a growth in eclectic practice since early 2020.

About the author

Helen A. Berger is a visiting scholar at the Center for the Study of World Religions at Harvard Divinity School and professor emerita of sociology at West Chester University. She has published four books as author or co-author and edited one volume on contemporary Paganism. Her first book, *A Community of Witches*, was one of the earliest to study the development of contemporary Paganism in the United States. Her most recent book, *Solitary Pagans*, is currently the only substantial research on the most common form of practice—practicing alone.

Suggestions for further readings

In this book
See also chapters 6 (How many Pagans are there?), 9 (Is there anything common to all Pagan religions?), 18 (What is the difference between an eclectic and a traditional Pagan or witch?), and 63 (Why is witchcraft popular among teenagers?).

Elsewhere
Berger, Helen A. *Solitary Pagans: Contemporary Witches, Wiccans, and Others Who Practice Alone.* Columbia: University of South Carolina Press, 2019.

Johnston, Hannah E., and Aloi, P., eds. *The New Generation Witches: Teenage Witchcraft in Contemporary Culture.* Bodmin, Cornwell: Ashgate Press, 2007.

Miller, Chris. "How Modern Witches Enchant TikTok: Intersections of Digital, Consumer, and Material Culture(s) on #Witchtok." *Religion* 13(2) (2022): 118–140.

8
What is a Pagan worldview?

Graham Harvey

"Worldview" refers to a way of seeing, experiencing, and understanding the world. It is an increasingly popular way of speaking about the ways in which groups (from nations to families) tend to share or encourage assumptions about the nature of the world and of people's place within it. "Worldviews" enable comparisons between different kinds of communities, not all of which are "religious." When it is used in reference to religions, it invites attention to actual life rather than primarily to official teachings.

One way of finding out about a community's worldview is to consider how people use common or distinctive terms. But this requires care: if someone says "sunrise," they probably do not think that the sun really *rises* each morning. Even though "sunrise" expresses our lived experience (or what our senses rather than our rational minds tell us), it is now used more poetically than scientifically. In addition to being expressed through shared words, worldviews can be revealed by actions that people deem appropriate or inappropriate, ordinary or remarkable. So how people dress, greet others, or eat together can tell us a lot about how they understand the world, themselves, and others.

To understand what a "Pagan worldview" might be, we might ask if there is one thing that all Pagans say, do, or think. Or is there one thing that *only* Pagans say, do, or think? In both cases, the answer is "no." Pagans do not all do the same things or see the world the same way. That's one explanation for why there are so many different ways to be Pagan. Also, the things Pagans do are not entirely unique to them. People in other religions (or nonreligious people) can say, do, and think the same things as Pagans.

So is it possible to answer the bigger question—"What is a Pagan worldview?"—without just saying, "It's complicated"? Because Pagans do seem to recognize one another and make distinctions between themselves and others, there must be some words and activities that reveal Pagans' common ground or shared interests. Even if these are not *uniquely* Pagan words or activities, they suggest a flavor or style that says, "This is a Pagan worldview."

Just as a "Christian worldview" might be revealed by people talking a lot about "Jesus," perhaps Pagans express their worldview by talking a lot about "nature." These are keywords in each worldview, but they are never simple. Christians differ about who Jesus is. Pagans differ about how to celebrate whatever "nature" means. Does "nature" include humans and cities or just "wild" places? Is it a deity or a community of ordinary but respected living beings? Despite there being many possible answers, Pagans typically recognize one another because they celebrate seasonal festivals, often outdoors and often in places that they mark as sacred. While anyone can watch the sunrise or the moon changing through phases from new to full to old, anyone can enjoy woodlands, collect stones on a beach, or find ancient stone circles fascinating, Pagans can structure their lives around such activities.

One word for a worldview that celebrates such seemingly ordinary experiences and practices is "enchanted." The modern world is supposed to be disenchanted, predictable, operating by laws that operate universally. But Pagans (among others) speak a lot about "magic." This might refer to the wonder of encounters with beings that others only read about in folklore or fantasy fiction—elves or boggarts, for example. Or "magic" can mean practices in which people aim to change themselves or the world around them through ritual performance, meditation, or visualization or by lighting candles, reading tarot cards, casting runes, and creating sigils. Pagans might not agree on how (or even whether) magical rituals work, but they share an understanding that they have a place in Pagan worldviews alongside the experience of wonder.

All of this takes us a long way toward understanding what makes a worldview "Pagan." But for all the variety of Pagan traditions and practices, there is something quite literal that makes a worldview "Pagan," and that is the world, the Earth. The sense that this small planet is worth celebrating, is responsive to respectful approaches, and needs more ethical engagement is at the center of Pagan worldviews. This is not to say that all Pagans are frontline eco-activists, though many are. It is not to assert that Pagans want to "save" the Earth or be saved by it/her/him, but a range of ceremonial and everyday acts reveal an enchanted view of the world at the heart of Paganism.

About the author

Graham Harvey is emeritus professor of religious studies at the Open University, United Kingdom. His research largely concerns Indigenous religions and the "new animism." His participative research among Pagans has resulted in publications including *Listening People, Speaking Earth: Contemporary Paganism* and *Researching Paganisms* (coedited with Jenny Blain and Douglas Ezzy).

Suggestions for further readings

In this book
See also chapters 1 (What is Paganism?), 10 (Is Paganism a nature religion?), 11 (How do Pagans view nature and the environment?), and 35 (What are pagan ethics?).

Elsewhere
Curry, Patrick. *Enchantment: Wonder in Modern Life*. Edinburgh: Floris Books, 2020.

Taves, Ann. "From Religious Studies to Worldview Studies." *Futures* 50(1) (2020): 137–147.

9
Is there anything common to all Pagan religions?

Jennifer Uzzell

The first important thing to note when considering this question is that not all, or even most Pagans consider their path to be a religion. Many Pagans consciously distance themselves from the word "religion" because, for them, the term is associated with hierarchical authority, dogma, and being told what to believe. Many refer to Paganism as their spiritual path or tradition, or just as a "way of life." Having said this, many modern scholars are using new definitions of religion. For example, in his book *Sex, Death and Witchcraft*, Douglas Ezzy suggests that religion is best understood as a set of tools that allow a person to lead a life endowed with meaning, and that its chief components are community, story or mythology, and ritual. If we use this definition, it is hard to see Pagan traditions as anything other than religion. Perhaps it is better to refer to Paganisms as religious traditions rather than as religions.

Furthermore, Paganisms do not behave in the way that religions are generally expected to. While some of the initiatory traditions, such as Wicca, do have priests and priestesses, there is no hierarchy of authority, no sacred or divinely revealed scripture, and usually no place of worship. There is a great deal of diversity between different Pagan traditions but also within them. It is a common joke that if you have five Pagans in a room, you will have at least seven different opinions on any given issue. Whatever it is that Pagans have in common, it is certainly not beliefs. Even within an individual tradition such as Wicca, Witchcraft, Druidry, or Heathenry, there will be a wide variety of ideas about deity, life after death, or ethics.

Paganism has been described as "orthopraxy" rather than "orthodoxy"; Pagans are far more likely to be united by what they do rather than by what they believe. For example, most Pagan traditions follow the Eightfold Wheel of the Year, a cycle of eight seasonal festivals designed by Gerald Gardner and Ross Nichols in the middle of the twentieth century, although it is based on ancient Celtic festivals. This provides Pagans with a way of connecting with the changing seasons and with the natural world as well as providing an opportunity for celebration every six weeks or so. Another common practice that many share is the casting of a circle in which to conduct ceremonies. The four directions are symbolically linked to the elements, together forming a representation of the cosmos. The guardians of the North and earth, the East and air, the South and fire, and the West and water are invited to be present and to aid the ritual. The idea of the sacred circle is to provide a space "between the worlds" and outside of time in which it is possible to connect with the world beyond the human. However, while most Pagans will take part in the casting of a sacred circle, not all will understand or experience it in the same way. It should also be noted that while these practices unite most Pagans, they are not universal. For example, Heathens (followers of Viking or Anglo-Saxon gods and traditions) follow a separate calendar and use different rituals.

It is perhaps best to think of Paganisms as a family of related religious traditions that have some common family traits, although as individuals, they are very different. Rather than a common set of beliefs, Pagans tend to share a way of orientating themselves toward the world: a worldview. Many Pagans experience the world as living and active and seek to connect with it in a relational and reciprocal way. There are key ideas that recur frequently within Paganisms, and while not every Pagan will accept every one of them, almost all will embrace one or more—leading to a set of ideas and attitudes that are generally indicative of a Pagan worldview. Central to this is a reverence for nature and a feeling that it is possible to connect with the divine, however it is understood, directly through the natural world. Another central concept is that each individual is ultimately responsible for their own spiritual journey and ethical decisions. One idea that is very near to being universal is the drawing of inspiration and a sense of identity from an idea or imagining of a pre-Christian past. In *Celebrating Planet Earth* (edited by Denise Cush), Graham Harvey suggests that if there is a single word that is foundational to the Pagan worldview, it is "re-enchantment": the desire to fill the world with magic and a sense of wonder and to reverse the feeling of alienation that for many has arisen from a Western, industrialized society.

About the author

Jennifer Uzzell (PhD, Durham University) is the education and youth manager for the Pagan Federation and senior examiner in religious studies at both GCSE and A level with a major awarding body and was head of religious education at a number of schools for many years.

Suggestions for further readings

In this book

See also chapters 2 (Is Paganism a religion?), 8 (What is a Pagan worldview?), 13 (Do all Pagans follow the same festivals?), and 16 (Can a Pagan follow more than one path or tradition?).

Elsewhere

Beckett, J. *The Path of Paganism: An Experience Based Guide to Modern Pagan Practice.* Woodbury, MN: Llewellyn, 2017.

Cush, Denise, ed. *Celebrating Planet Earth, a Pagan/Christian Conversation: First Steps in Interfaith Dialogue.* Charlotte, NC: John Hunt, 2015.

Ezzy, Douglas. *Sex, Death and Witchcraft: A Contemporary Pagan Festival.* London: Bloomsbury Academic, 2014.

10
Is Paganism a nature religion?

Ethan Doyle White

Many modern Pagans present either their particular tradition or modern Paganism as a whole as a "nature religion." The use of this term implies an intrinsic link between Pagan religions and the natural world, alluding to many Pagans' belief that the earth is sacred or that the deities they venerate personify or manifest as different forces of nature. Some Pagans even propose that a nature-centric perspective is a defining feature of modern Paganism, although this is probably misleading.

Conceptual linkages between the natural world and the idea of "paganism" long predate the emergence of modern Pagan religion. Many Christians argued that the error of the pagans—meaning those who did not venerate the God of Abraham—was that they worshipped God's creation rather than God himself. This Christian theological idea has contributed to the notion that pagans venerate features and forces of nature, an assumption that oversimplifies the complicated beliefs about divinity present in many non-Abrahamic religions.

While these ideas perhaps informed modern Paganism from its early days, modern Pagans only began regularly presenting their traditions as a "nature religion" or "earth religion" in the 1970s. Although initially noticeable largely in the United States, this rhetoric soon spread to countries like Britain and came to inform academic analysis; "Nature Religion Today" was the title of a pioneering scholarly conference on modern Paganism held in England in 1996.

The reasons behind the growing popularity of this designation are probably multifaceted. One reason likely stems from the growing influence of environmentalism in Western societies. In a world where ecological issues are ever more pressing, being seen as a "nature religion" would lend modern Pagan traditions an image of social validity and relevance. As "nature religionists," modern Pagans could claim to have (spiritual) answers to the international environmental crisis—even if, as environmental activists sometimes complained, most Pagans displayed little active commitment to the environmentalist cause.

A second reason for the popularity of this new terminology might be its public relations value. Rhetorically, the term "nature/earth religion" bore far less pejorative baggage than the term "Pagan," which would conjure mental images of ancient barbarity and blood sacrifice for many Westerners. In this sense, the embrace of "nature/earth religion" would bear similarities to the way that in the 1960s, the word "Wicca" came to be favored over the loaded term "witchcraft" by adherents of that particular Pagan religion.

Another suggestion, made by the historian Chas Clifton, is that American Pagans had embraced this term because they could not claim to be continuing religious traditions that were Indigenous to the land on which they lived. In Europe, conversely, Pagans often claim to be reviving ancient religions of the land (or, in a more ethnic-nationalist fashion, ancient religions of the people) and thus have less need to socially legitimate themselves through the "nature religion" label—even if, as in cases like Britain, many European Pagans clearly have embraced this new rhetoric.

A fourth reason may be that for modern Pagans, presenting their traditions as "nature religions" allows for links to be built (at least on a conceptual level) with other traditions that might be categorized in the same way. This would include a broad range of typically polytheistic non-Abrahamic religions, such as those of East and South Asia, of Africa and its diaspora, and of Native American communities. Many Pagans have been keen to emphasize links with these other non-Abrahamic religions, both because they genuinely feel a sense of spiritual kinship with them but also because they would like to be seen as part of a huge and ancient global family of related traditions rather than as followers of socially marginal new religions restricted largely to Europe and European-descended communities. Whether the rhetoric of "nature religions" will ever produce a widely held sense of unity among non-Abrahamic religions remains to be seen. Suggesting that this may be possible is the fact that in early twenty-first century Japan, advocates of Shinto are increasingly framing their tradition as a nature religion, again probably a response to growing environmentalist sensibilities.

It is important to note that, independently of its use by Pagans, the term "nature religion" has also been proposed as a scholarly term for academic analysis. This understanding of "nature religion" was devised by Catherine Albanese, an American professor of religious studies, who applied it to a broad range of North American worldviews, such as those of the Transcendentalists, in her 1990 book *Nature Religion in America*. It was only after devising this term that Albanese discovered that it had already been used by Pagans for several decades.

About the author

Ethan Doyle White has a PhD in medieval history and archaeology from University College London and has written extensively on modern Paganism and related forms of esotericism. His publications include *Wicca: History, Belief, and Community in Modern Pagan Witchcraft* (Sussex Academic Press, 2016), *Pagans: The Visual Culture of Pagan Myths, Legends and Rituals* (Thames and Hudson, 2023), and *The New Witches of the West: Tradition, Liberation, and Power* (Cambridge University Press, 2024).

Suggestions for further readings

In this book
See also chapters 11 (How do Pagans view nature and the environment?), 12 (Do Pagans have sacred sites?), and 54 (Can Paganism be applied to non-European religions, such as Shinto?).

Elsewhere
Clifton, Chas S. *Her Hidden Children: The Rise of Wicca and Paganism in America*. Lanham, MD: AltaMira, 2006.

Clifton, Chas S. "Earth Day and Afterwards: American Paganism's Appropriation of 'Nature Religion.'" In *Handbook of Contemporary Paganism*, edited by James R. Lewis and Murphy Pizza, 109–118. Leiden: Brill, 2009.

11
How do Pagans view nature and the environment?

Chas S. Clifton

Today's Pagan religions are often described as "nature religions" or "Earth religions." This usage appeared in the 1970s, during the rise of the environmental movement, and it largely replaced the idea that Wicca, in particular, was a surviving pre-Christian "fertility religion." The term "nature religion" was popularized first in the United States, but it found a ready reception in nations such as Britain and Australia because of the shared Western tradition of Romanticism. It remains useful because examining it leads to some of the key differences between contemporary Pagan religions and monotheistic traditions.

"Nature religion" is rooted in the literary culture of the Romantic period, beginning in the late eighteenth century. During that artistic and literary period, both the spiritual freedom of the individual and the value of the natural world were exalted. Mountain ranges such as the Alps, formerly viewed as terrible places that were a hazard to travelers, were now seen as "sublime" and spiritually uplifting. Writers began to explore the language of polytheism. The English poet Percy Bysshe Shelley (1792–1822) invoked a "sacred goddess, Mother Earth / Thou from whose immortal bosom / Gods and men and beasts have birth." In America, Philip Freneau's (1752–1832) poem "On the Religion Nature" suggested "that power of nature, ever blessed, 'bestowed religion with the rest.'" In other words, nature could tell the secrets of religion to any seeker, and there was no need for doctrines of sin, final judgments, and so forth.

Pagans were among the first religious groups to embrace an environmental ethic. The 1974 Council of American Witches (a one-time event) made Wicca's environmental credentials a priority, writing in its statement of principles, "We recognize that our intelligence gives us a unique responsibility toward our environment. We seek to live in harmony with Nature, in ecological balance offering fulfilment to life and consciousness within an evolutionary concept" (Wigington 2024). More recently, a book about the Reclaiming witchcraft tradition and its environmental tenets listed demonstrations and other actions that Reclaiming witches participated in or led, a list stretching from 1976 to 2019.

But what is nature/Nature? Most contemporary Pagans—like most people in industrialized countries—live in urban areas. Many speak of leaving the city to attend a festival held in a park or forest as "reconnecting with nature." Would not the idea of following a "nature religion" while living disconnected from it bring tension to one's life? Undoubtedly that is true, but a more complex understanding of the word "nature" can help resolve this.

The word "nature" derives from the Latin word for "born" (*natus*) and from older Proto-Indo-European words connected to the idea of birth. So in a simplistic sense, it means "all that is," or the "material world." This reading is comfortable for those who then say that "New York City is part of the material world; therefore, it too is 'natural.'" Yet that is not what the person leaving the city on a camping trip would think. They would see nature as "wild," and that word's history links to "feral," to "fierce," and to the Latin *silva*, meaning forest or grove. Within the idea of nature religion, wildness is important too, for it means everything that is larger than we are and everything that is outside our human egos' control.

For contemporary Pagans, then, "living in harmony with nature" means establishing relationships with areas of life and experience that are outside the ego. These "horizontal" or less-hierarchal relationships often outnumber and are more important than "vertical" relationships with an omnipotent deity who is "up there." They are especially crucial when we consider the body as nature and also at the level of "Gaian" nature, which is today the "natural world" as we commonly think of it: plants, animals, waters, and our atmosphere. (To the ancient Greeks, "Gaia" was both a goddess personifying the Earth and the Earth itself.) They also figure into the third type of nature discussed here: "cosmic" nature. In all three spheres, nature, not revelations of some prophet or messiah, is the source of sacred value, replacing scriptures and ecclesiastical authorities.

Start with the individual's mind and body. Much as our bodies are not under ego control in most respects (Do you tell yourself to breathe more when you run?), neither is the mind, as any psychoanalyst would say. Dreams are just one example of mental activity not controlled by the ego, as are psychic sensitivities, hunches, forebodings, and out-of-body experiences. Rather than be alarmed by these mental events, Pagans generally seek to learn from them through divination (by tarot cards, rune stones, and other methods) and dreaming, constantly opening themselves to information that, while nonrational, is still valid.

Many Pagans view bodily autonomy as resistance to "priest or scripture, man or law," as one song lyric puts it. At the same time, bodies, not physical structures, construct sacred space through costume and movement. Bodies connect practitioners with divine energies in multiple ways. "The Gods move through us in sacred sexual ecstasy," one Wiccan priestess wrote in the 1990s (Asher 1992, 186), and in some Wiccan groups, ritual sexual intercourse is enacted in some ceremonies. (More commonly, the divine union of their chief god and goddess is enacted symbolically with ritual tools.) In addition, practitioners themselves may "carry" or "aspect" the gods, a practice with deep historical roots in different parts of the world. In such cases, the person's ego is, so to speak, set aside, while a different consciousness—divine or, in some cases, ancestral—speaks and moves the body for a period of time before departing. It is common for Pagans to see the source of magical and spiritual power as outside the rational, thinking part of the mind, coming instead from emotions, intuition, and the unconscious.

At the Gaian or planetary level, Pagans seek harmony between themselves and nature, realizing that life in industrial societies makes finding such harmony a difficult quest. Some speak of feeling Earth's traumas to the point of suffering physical illnesses. Research from the 2000s suggested that American Pagans were slightly more environmentally active than the general population, with the caveat that a higher educational level among Pagans could be significant. Pagans frequently do connect rituals with environmental goals, and Pagan altars and households often display items from the natural world (such as animal bones, stones, tree branches, fossils, and feathers) in a totemic way—an acknowledgment that one's own skull and a deer skull found in the forest are all part of the same natural system.

Finally, the notion of living within natural cycles leads us to the sphere of "cosmic nature," where the human unconscious is subsumed into the World Soul or planetary unconscious, affecting everyone and, on a deep level, available to everyone. One personal expression of this idea is astrology, which sees each human being as living with a cosmic "clock" that creates the currents of their life, although it is up to the individual to navigate them.

About the author

Chas S. Clifton edits *The Pomegranate: The International Journal of Pagan Studies* and serves as coeditor of Equinox Publishing Ltd.'s Contemporary and Historical Paganism book series.

Suggestions for further readings

In this book
See also chapters 4 (How did modern Paganism begin?) and 10 (Is Paganism a nature religion?).

Elsewhere
Albanese, Catherine. *Nature Religion in America: From the Algonkian Indians to the New Age*. Chicago: University of Chicago Press, 1990.

Asher, Rhiannon. "When Sex Is a Sacrament." In *Living between Two Worlds*, edited by Chas S. Clifton, 165–187. St. Paul, MN: Llewellyn, 1992.

Clifton, Chas S. *Her Hidden Children: The Rise of Wicca and Paganism in America*. Lanham, MD: AltaMira, 2006.

Moon, Irisanya. *Honoring the Wild: Reclaiming Witchcraft and Environmental Activism*. Alresford, Hampshire: Moon Books, 2023.

Pike, Sarah. *Earthly Bodies, Magical Selves: Contemporary Pagans and the Search for Community*. Berkeley: University of California Press, 2001.

Shelley, Percy Bysshe. "Song of Proserpine While Gathering Flowers on the Plain of Enna." In *The Complete Poetical Works of Percy Bysshe Shelley*, edited by Thomas A. Hutchinson, 606. London: Humphrey Milford, Oxford University Press, 1914.

Wigington, Patti. "The American Council of Witches." Learn Religions, June 25, 2024. https://learnreligions.com/american-council-of-witches-2562880.

12
Do Pagans have sacred sites?

Ethan Doyle White

Many modern Pagans regard certain locations as special and will often frame these as "sacred sites," reflecting a terminological borrowing from Indigenous rights activism. These sites are usually those where pre-Christian (and often prehistoric) communities erected structures for some ceremonial or ritual purpose, as testified by either historical or archaeological evidence. In Greece, for example, this can mean the ruins of a classical temple, while in Britain, a modern Pagan sacred site will often be either an Early Neolithic chambered tomb or one of the stone circles erected in the Late Neolithic and Bronze Ages.

The reasons why these sites are chosen owe much to Pagans' own self-perception of their relationship with the past. Modern Pagans typically identify strongly with Europe's pre-Christian religions and often regard those who followed them as their "ancestors." In most cases, this means "ancestral" in the sense of sharing a landscape, a similar spiritual approach, or the same deities, although some ethnic-nationalist Pagans also emphasize a perceived genetic ancestry from particular pre-Christian populations. Using these prehistoric sites as places for contemporary ritual thus allows modern Pagans to evoke a connection with these ancestors as well as a perception of continuity from the past to the present. This, in turn, can have a legitimating effect for what are, in essence, new religions.

Given that modern Pagan communities almost always have white majorities, the situation regarding sacred sites is more complicated outside Europe. In North America and Australia, for instance, modern Pagans have performed rituals at prehistoric sites, but concerns about cultural appropriation increasingly overshadow such activities. While modern Pagans often feel a sense of spiritual affiliation with the traditional religions of Indigenous peoples in Australia and the Americas, these Indigenous communities have often been wary about white people adopting elements of their religious heritage.

A common notion among Pagans is that their sacred sites are home to preternatural entities, often referred to as "spirits of the place." These are sometimes identified with supernatural species from the folklore of various European societies, such as dryads, *landvættir*, or fairies. These entities may be greeted in ritual and provided with offerings as part of an animistic framework. Another recurring idea among many Pagans is that their sacred sites are loci for "earth energies" and may sit along ley lines that channel such energies through the landscape. For those Pagans who believe in these etheric forces, ritual may be employed to manipulate such energies for a specific purpose. Ideas regarding earth energies and ley lines have been inherited largely from the Earth Mysteries movement that emerged in Britain during the 1960s, although they fall well outside mainstream archaeological interpretations of prehistoric sites.

While many modern Pagans perform rituals at sacred sites that are within their own home regions, some have also embarked on pilgrimages to locations that are further afield. The many Neolithic and Bronze Age sites around Avebury and Stonehenge in Wiltshire, England, are popular not only with tourists interested in archaeology but also with many Pagans. Similarly, the Neolithic site at Çatalhöyük in Turkey has attracted tour groups involved in the Goddess movement—visitors who are often motivated by (disputed) claims that the site was once a hub of an ancient goddess-worshipping, matriarchal society.

Modern Pagan attitudes toward their sacred sites have sometimes generated conflict with archaeologists and heritage managers. Pagan ceremonial activity at these sites will often include the lighting of fires, the deposition (and sometimes burial) of offerings, as well as general footfall, all factors contributing to erosion at archaeologically sensitive locations. Many heritage managers (and many Pagans, too, it should be noted) have expressed concern about "ritual litter" left at these sites, and sometimes the different interest groups have worked constructively to mitigate any damage.

On the other hand, many Pagans express concern about the destruction caused by archaeological investigation. In the famous case of Seahenge, a Bronze Age timber circle excavated in Norfolk, England, in 1999, several Pagans employed direct action tactics in an unsuccessful attempt to prevent archaeological excavation. Another area of contention surrounds the retention (and display) of excavated human remains from pre-Christian periods of Europe's past. Again drawing on the language of Indigenous rights activism, some modern Pagans have urged the reburial of these remains as a way of showing respect for the dead. Most archaeologists and certain other Pagans have opposed these calls, believing that doing so would undermine scientific inquiry.

About the author

Ethan Doyle White has a PhD in medieval history and archaeology from University College London and has written extensively on modern Paganism and related forms of esotericism. His publications include *Wicca: History, Belief, and Community in Modern Pagan Witchcraft* (Sussex Academic Press, 2016), *Pagans: The Visual Culture of Pagan Myths, Legends and Rituals* (Thames and Hudson, 2023), and *The New Witches of the West: Tradition, Liberation, and Power* (Cambridge University Press, 2024).

Suggestions for further readings

In this book
See also chapters 34 (Do Pagans worship Ancestors?), 36 (How do Pagans interact with deities and spirits?), and 56 (How much of Paganism is based on cultural appropriation?).

Elsewhere
Blain, Jenny, and Robert J. Wallis. *Sacred Sites, Contested Rites/Rights: Contemporary Pagan Engagements with the Past*. Eastbourne: Sussex Academic, 2007.

Rountree, Kathryn. "Archaeologists and Goddess Feminists at Çatalhöyük: An Experiment in Multivocality." *Journal of Feminist Studies in Religion* 23(2) (2007): 7–26.

13
Do all Pagans follow the same festivals?

Douglas Ezzy

There are three main factors that shape which festivals a Pagan might follow: tradition, location, and community. While many Pagans do celebrate the same festivals, there is also a great deal of variation. There are dates during the year when Pagans are very likely to celebrate a festival of some sort—the solstices, for example. However, exactly what they do on this date is likely to vary a great deal. Pagans tend to be very individualistic and creative, which means there is ongoing ritual adaptation and a large degree of diversity in practice.

First, each of the various Pagan traditions has a set of festivals that is common to people in that tradition. For example, Wiccans follow the Wheel of the Year—a set of eight festivals that marks the solstices, equinoxes, and cross-quarter days (that are approximately in between the solstices and equinoxes). In contrast, while some Heathens also celebrate these eight festivals, other Heathens see them as a recent invention and follow three ancient festivals: "Winternights, Yule and Sigrblot" (Harvey 2017, 58). Even though the rituals might be different, the Heathen festival of Yule is on the same date as the Wiccan festival of Yule in the Wheel of the Year.

Second, Pagans often attune their festivals to the seasons of their local environment. This is most graphically represented by the solstices. The date of the winter solstice (the shortest day) in the Northern Hemisphere is the same date as the summer solstice (the longest day) in the Southern Hemisphere. In Australia, most Pagans adapt the festivals to what is happening in the seasons where they are living. They turn the Northern Hemisphere festivals around, celebrating the rituals of the summer solstice in December and the winter solstice in June. Although, this is not always the case: when Paganism first started being practiced in Australia, some people celebrated the festivals following the dates set by a Northern Hemisphere calendar.

Some Pagans have taken this further, seeking a deeper sense of relationship with their local environment. They might, for example, celebrate Beltane (a festival of spring) or Samhain (a festival of entry into winter) at times marked by events in their local environment—such as the blooming of a particular flower that marks spring or the arrival of the first snow as a marker of the coming winter. They might also celebrate other events in their environment as key to the changing seasons with their own rituals.

Finally, some Pagans choose to celebrate festivals that are common to Pagan communities that are important to them. They may choose to do this even though these communities might be following a tradition and set of rituals that the individual Pagan does not follow themselves. For example, in regional locations, or where there are small numbers of Pagans, a Heathen might join in a Wiccan celebration of Samhain, even though the Samhain ritual used is not what she personally follows. Similarly, some Pagans in England choose to celebrate the summer solstice at Stonehenge. The year I was there, there were 60,000 people, and the stones were filled with people. The event was more about being with other people at the time of the solstice rather than performing specific rituals, which was difficult given the huge number of people.

In summary, no, Pagans do not all celebrate the same festivals. However, there is a similar set of considerations that shape their choice of dates of festivals, often linked to the cycles of the moon and the sun. The specific rituals that are performed reflect the overlapping influence of tradition, nature, and community. This means that within the diversity, there is considerable similarity in the traditions and festivals that Pagans follow.

About the author

Douglas Ezzy, PhD, is professor of sociology at the University of Tasmania, Australia. He is lead investigator of the Australian Research Council Discovery project "Religious Freedom, LGBT+ Employees, and the Right to Discriminate." He is a coinvestigator on the Canadian "Nonreligion in a Complex Future" project led by Professor Lori Beaman. His books include *LGBT Christians* (2017, with Bronwyn Fielder), *Sex, Death and Witchcraft* (2014), and *Teenage Witches* (2007, with Helen Berger).

Suggestions for further readings

In this book
See also chapters 9 (Is there anything common to all Pagan religions?) and 12 (Do Pagans have sacred sites?).

Elsewhere

Brett, Julie. *Pagan Portals—Australian Druidry: Connecting with the Sacred Landscape*. Winchester UK: Moon Books, 2017.

Ezzy, Douglas. "Cosmopolitan Witchcraft: Reinventing the Wheel of the Year in Australian Paganism." In *Cosmopolitanism, Nationalism, and Modern Paganism*, edited by K. Rountree, 201–219. New York: Berghahn, 2017.

Harvey, Graham. *Listening People, Speaking Earth: Contemporary Paganism*. London: Hurst, 2017.

Harvey, Graham. *Animism: Respecting the Living World*. New York: Columbia University Press, 2005.

Hutton, Ronald. *The Triumph of the Moon: A History of Modern Pagan Witchcraft*. Oxford: Oxford University Press, 2001.

14
Do Pagans have a holy book like the Bible?

Denise Cush

Pagan religions are not "religions of the book" in the same way as Judaism, Christianity, and Islam. There is no sacred text seen as divinely revealed by God or accepted as authoritative for all Pagans. Readers may come across Pagan publications describing themselves as a "Bible," such as the well-known *Witches' Bible* by Janet and Stewart Farrar (a compilation of two earlier books), but this is more in the sense of a comprehensive handbook than implying a divinely revealed scripture.

Various categories of writing or other texts are, however, important for Pagans. Many of today's leading Pagans are prolific authors, and many Pagans first came to their tradition through reading, often reporting that someone had put into words what they had always believed, thought, or felt to be true. These books may be written by founders or contemporary leaders of particular Pagan groups. They may be historical sources describing ancient pagan beliefs and practices—such as Roman, Greek, Egyptian, Celtic, or Norse—whether actually dating back to ancient pagan authors or filtered through much later, often Christian, compilers. Heathens have access to the Icelandic Eddas, and Druids make use of stories from the Welsh *Mabinogion*, a favorite being the story of the bard Taliesen gaining poetic inspiration and magical powers from ingesting three drops from Ceridwen's cauldron.

As well as ancient myth and legend, some Pagan stories and practices may come from relatively recent literature, such as Leland's *Aradia* or Robert Graves's *The White Goddess* or even novels (see chapter 66 in this volume).

Beyond books, important "texts" can be found in other media. Archaeology can provide material evidence of ancient pagan practices, and much has been made of, for example, the prevalence of goddess figurines in the earliest cultures. Film, TV, and internet sources such as websites, blogs, social media, and online courses are all increasingly important. Some young Pagans may favor "pop culture Paganism," where characters, story lines, and motifs from popular culture in diverse media may provide the material for personal ritual, mythology, identity, and meaning-making. Whatever the sources used, they can provide a common vocabulary and shared references, which helps build a sense of Pagan community.

Mention should be made of the Wiccan idea of a *Book of Shadows*. According to Ronald Hutton (1999, 226), Gerald Gardner, the founder of Wicca, gave this name to his "collection of rituals which represented the sacred text of his witch religion." This collection was continually added to and revised by Gardner, his younger colleague Doreen Valiente, and other members of his group. Valiente's revision of the "Charge of the Goddess" is so frequently reproduced in Wiccan sources today that it could be said to have become something of a sacred text in itself. The Gardnerian Book of Shadows also forms the basis of the Farrars' publication mentioned above. The idea of a *Book of Shadows* is now also often used for a particular group's inherited shared handbook and/or an individual witch's journal.

However, the main source of authority in contemporary Paganism tends to be personal experience, whether individual or communal, including the transformative experiences of ritual. Druid bards may refer to *awen*, the creative force flowing through the natural world, which can inspire poetry and song. So although "revelation" in the form of a sacred text delivered to a prophet is not found in Paganism, the divine may be intuited from observing and interacting with the natural world and the beings and energies that dwell within it. In conclusion, it can be argued that there is actually one sacred text that unites most Pagan religions—not a literal book but the "Book of Nature."

About the author

Denise Cush is professor emerita in religion and education at Bath Spa University. She has published on Buddhist, Hindu, Christian, and Pagan traditions as well as pluralist religious education. From childhood, she has loved books about witches or magic and myths and legends from all traditions.

Suggestions for further reading

In this book
See also chapters 66 (How do Pagans use fiction and film?) and 67 (Is Paganism make-believe?).

Elsewhere

Cush, Denise. "Contemporary Paganism in the UK." *Discovering Sacred Texts*. The British Library, 2019.

Farrar, Janet, and Farrar, Stewart. *A Witches' Bible: The Complete Witches' Handbook*. Custer, WA: Phoenix, 1996.

Hutton, Ronald. *The Triumph of the Moon: A History of Modern Pagan Witchcraft*. Oxford: Oxford University Press, 1999.

15
What is the relationship between Theosophy and Paganism?

Yves Mühlematter

The relationship between Paganism and Theosophy is a multifaceted and intriguing one, warranting a more comprehensive exploration than a mere summary can provide. First, it is crucial to differentiate between Theosophy with a capital "T" and Christian theosophy, associated with the ideas of Jakob Böhme (1575–1624). The focus here is on Theosophy as propagated by the Theosophical Society, founded in 1875 in New York City by prominent figures such as Helena Petrovna Blavatsky (1831–1891) and Henry Steel Olcott (1832–1907). Helena Blavatsky, a noted medium before the society's inception, claimed to have received initiations from "the Masters" in the occult wisdom religion. Her seminal works *Isis Unveiled* (1877) and *The Secret Doctrine* (1888) laid the foundation for what is now known as "modern" Theosophy.

A core tenet of Theosophy is the belief in an ultimate "Truth" or highest religion, often referred to as philosophia perennis. This concept has a historical lineage, with roots attributed to thinkers like Giovanni Pico della Mirandola (1463–1494). Blavatsky asserted that this wisdom religion was preserved by Theosophical Masters, who occasionally imparted their knowledge to chosen disciples. These Masters were perceived as evolutionarily superior beings, and their teachings were considered to be scattered throughout various religions and philosophies. Consequently, the Theosophical Society encompassed a vast array of ideas from diverse sources, including numerous religious, philosophical, and scientific traditions. In this inclusive approach, Theosophy also exhibited a significant interest in "pagan religions." The definition of "paganism" can vary, but if we understand it as traditions suppressed during Europe's Christianization and later rediscovered during the Renaissance, then Theosophy indeed incorporated these ideas, particularly in the forms of Neoplatonism and folk religions. Moreover, if "paganism" is understood as referring to religions that were labeled as such by Christian missionaries all over the world, Theosophy again displayed a keen interest in them. However, when we examine the works of some of the best-known figures of Theosophy—such as Blavatsky, Olcott, Alfred Percy Sinnett (1840–1921), and Annie Besant (1847–1933)—it becomes apparent that ideas from spiritualism, Christianity, and most significantly, Buddhism and Hinduism played more prominent roles. The Theosophical Society, despite its cohesive name, was far from monolithic. It consisted of diverse branches and divisions, with its representatives holding a wide range of positions. As a result, the figures mentioned above should be considered significant in the context of Theosophy but not necessarily representative of it in its entirety. The local branches and lodges within the society often exhibited significant variations and, at times, even advocated opposing ideas. At the very least, they differed from one another in their interpretations of Theosophy. Notably, the concept of "pagan" ideas appeared to strike a chord in regions where rich folk religious traditions thrived. For instance, in Ireland, these ideas found greater resonance. Conversely, Adyar Theosophy, closely linked to the society's initial headquarters situated in Adyar, India, forged robust ties with Indian religions. This connection was further strengthened by the presence of numerous Indian members within the Theosophical Society, who made substantial contributions to the evolution of Theosophical concepts.

As for the contemporary relationship between "Paganism" and the Theosophical Society, research on this topic is scant, making it challenging to provide a definitive assessment. Initial analyses, however, indicate notable thematic parallels. Theosophy places significant emphasis on the quest for esoteric wisdom and arcane knowledge, viewing them as pathways to profound occult insights. This perspective inherently posits the existence of an unadulterated "truth" and transcendent, immaterial dimensions. Additionally, the concept of the expansion of consciousness, equated with initiation in Theosophical thought, holds paramount significance. This expansion, as posited by Theosophy, ultimately culminates in the recognition of unity or monism, a philosophical stance that underscores the interconnectedness of all existence. Such notions find strong echoes within neo-Pagan paradigms. Given these overlapping themes, it is plausible to suggest that certain principles of contemporary Paganism either derive directly from Theosophical teachings or, at the very least, have appropriated Theosophical concepts, whether directly or indirectly.

It is undeniable that the Theosophical Society held a pivotal position as one of the most influential "esoteric" organizations of the nineteenth century, with enduring impacts that continue to ripple through various spiritual and philosophical movements, including Paganism. However, this connection remains underexplored and calls for further investigation to shed light on its nuanced dimensions. In summary, the connection between Paganism and Theosophy forms a complex and intricate network of ideas and influences. This intricate web is molded by historical, geographical, and philosophical elements, offering an ongoing opportunity for scholarly investigation and analysis.

About the author

Yves Mühlematter is a postdoctoral researcher at the University of Zurich, with a PhD in religious studies from the University of Freiburg. His research expertise covers a wide range of subjects, including the interplay between educational concepts and utopian-dystopian visions of the future, historical interconnections, religious studies, and a particular specialization in the Theosophical Society, notably focusing on Annie Besant. His outstanding work in this field earned him the ESSWE thesis prize in 2022.

Suggestions for further readings

In this book
See also chapters 4 (How did modern Paganism begin?) and 5 (What is the relationship between ancient and contemporary Paganism?).

Elsewhere
Godwin, Joscelyn. *The Theosophical Enlightenment*. SUNY Series in Western Esoteric Traditions. Albany: State University of New York Press, 1994.

Hanegraaff, Wouter J. *Western Esotericism: A Guide for the Perplexed*. London: Bloomsbury Academic, 2013.

Mühlematter, Yves. *Accelerating Human Evolution by Theosophical Initiation: Annie Besant's Pedagogy and the Creation of Benares Hindu University*. Okkulte Moderne 6. Boston: De Gruyter Oldenbourg, 2023.

Pagan religions

16
Can a Pagan follow more than one path or tradition?

Caroline Tully

Within contemporary Paganism, the terms "path" and "tradition" refer to different types or denominations of Paganism. Individual Pagans use the term "path" to describe their own particular "brand" of Paganism. When a Pagan speaks of their "path," this can indicate a specific set of practices—for example, the path of a "green witch" would focus on plants, particularly herbalism; a "shamanic Pagan" path may center on ecstatic practices such as trance and communication with spirits; and a "Hellenic Pagan" path designates a worshipper of the ancient Greek gods. Pagan paths can have a practical focus, where what one does (such as healing, for example) is the main theme of the path, or a focus on ethnic identity, as in the case of Stregheria or Italian American witchcraft. One of the popular "paths" evident on social media sites such as Instagram is the "poison path," which involves studying poisonous plants that are often psychoactive in small doses. "Path" can also mean the overall journey of discovery, study, and practice of Paganism. The concept of "paths" within Paganism is the way that individual practitioners describe their study focus, beliefs, practice, and identity.

The term "tradition" is often capitalized to show that it is an official descriptive classifier of a specific Pagan religion, such as Wicca. "Tradition" tends to be used primarily within British Traditional Wicca to describe types of Wicca and can be considered a synonym for "history," "lineage," or "authority." Initially, there was only one type of Wicca—that which was founded by Gerald B. Gardner in the late 1940s, now known as Gardnerian Wicca. As Wicca increased in popularity, it became necessary to define the different variations based on the identities of their founders and the kinds of modifications they introduced: these types are termed "traditions." Early rivals to British Traditional Wicca called themselves "traditional witches" and claimed to predate the founding of Wicca, although they were obviously based on it. It is common for Wiccan third-degree initiates to leave their parent coven (termed "hiving-off") and start their own group. In the United States, these are often deliberately modified and designated as new "traditions." Wicca has now faceted into a broad range of activities, all classified under the path (not tradition) of "witchcraft"—a word that now spans a wide range of practices but generally designates the working of magic.

A Pagan can usually follow more than one path or tradition according to their individual interests and the time they have available to pursue them. This is because Paganism generally does not require a participant to leave or repudiate any previous religion they may have belonged to or adhere solely to one path or tradition. This has been the case since the 1960s, when Gardnerian Wiccan high priestess Doreen Valiente joined Robert Cochrane's traditional witchcraft group, the Clan of Tubal Cain. In the 1990s, prominent Alexandrian Wiccans Janet and Stewart Farrar joined the Church of All Worlds, an American Pagan religion based on Robert Heinlein's science fiction novel *Stranger in a Strange Land*. It is not unusual for Pagan practitioners to be members of more than one path or tradition; cross-membership is evident between Wicca, ceremonial magic orders such as the Ordo Templi Orientis or Golden Dawn, Druid orders, and Heathen kindred.

On the other hand, some Pagans consider it a virtue to focus on only one path or tradition. Some American Wiccans have been very disparaging in online fora, such as the Yahoo group "Amber and Jet," about people who belong to "unofficial" or "unrecognized" traditions, designating such practitioners "eclectic" and even "icklectic" to show their disapproval of such apparently incorrect practices. Within this discourse, the term "eclectic" signified disorderly, chaotic, unauthorized practice. In more recent years, however, the term has acquired much more neutral connotations and is used as a self-designation by those whose Pagan interests span a range of paths and traditions. The majority of Pagans are solitary practitioners who may only participate in group activities at particular times of the year or for specific events (Berger 2019). The term "path" is more appropriate to describe individual practitioners undergoing a personal exploratory journey, whereas "tradition" is more specific to group practice, where the practitioner has been formally accepted into the group and taught its beliefs and practices, which they are generally expected to reproduce correctly.

About the author

Caroline Tully is an archaeologist at the University of Melbourne, Australia. Her research interests include religion and ritual in the Aegean

Bronze Age, reception of the ancient world, and contemporary Paganisms. She is the author of *The Cultic Life of Trees in the Prehistoric Aegean, Levant, Egypt and Cyprus* (Peeters 2018) and many academic and popular articles.

Suggestions for further readings

In this book
See also chapters 9 (Is there anything common to all Pagan religions?), 18 (What is the difference between an eclectic and a traditional Pagan or witch?), and 53 (Can a Christian also be a Pagan?).

Elsewhere
Berger, Helen A. *Solitary Pagans: Contemporary Witches, Wiccans, and Others Who Practice Alone*. Colombia: University of South Carolina Press, 2019.

Harvey, Graham, and Hardman, Charlotte, eds. *Pagan Pathways*. London: Thorsons, 1996.

Hobsbawm, Eric, and Ranger, Terrence. *The Invention of Tradition*. Cambridge: Cambridge University Press, 2012.

Hutton, Ronald. *The Triumph of the Moon: A History of Modern Pagan Witchcraft*. Oxford: Oxford University Press, 1999.

17
What is the difference between hard and soft polytheism?

Jefferson Calico

Paganism is a diverse religious movement that includes many ideas about the numinous world of Gods, spirits, and other-than-human beings. The terms "hard" and "soft" polytheism reflect efforts to categorize two contrasting ways that contemporary Pagans conceptualize the Gods.

Take the Gods Aegir, Neptune, Poseidon, and Lir. Are these each distinctive and different Gods of the sea, or do they represent a singular Sea God who was experienced and expressed differently in various cultural groups? What about the deities Frigg, Hera, Juno, and Isis? Are these each ontologically real beings who act as divine mothers in their own cultures and spheres, or do they represent the energy of one Mother Goddess experienced and expressed within different cultural settings? Or as some Pagans might suggest, are these figures archetypes within the mind and not externally real beings at all? These questions and how we go about answering them are the crux of the debate between hard and soft polytheism.

Hard polytheists understand and relate to each God as a disparate and ontologically real being with a distinctive personality, cultural context, and history. They emphasize the integrity of the mythic cycles and characteristics that distinguish each deity from the others. This view represents the most straightforward and literal reading of the stories of the Gods. Critics might interpret hard polytheism as an insufficiently nuanced account of the divine.

Soft polytheists understand and experience the deities as cultural manifestations of a deeper numinous reality, aspects of a great God and Goddess who may appear in many shapes, guises, and mythic variants. They take account of the similarities and the patterns that exist among the multicultural panoply of Gods. This position reflects Platonic and Neoplatonic teaching of the forms and the One and the philosophy of perennialism that arose from these schools. Critics might argue that soft polytheism undervalues the historical and cultural integrity of these divine entities.

The debate over hard and soft polytheism has been shaped by three important conditions. First, Pagan polytheism exists in a contemporary intellectual context shaped by more than a century of anthropology, history of religions, and comparative mythology. These disciplines have changed our perspective on religion and made modern people keenly aware of the diversity of deities worldwide and of the similarities that exist among them. Hard polytheism responds to this plethora of Gods by taking a pluralist approach that conserves, maintains, and defends these divine identities as sacred knowledge from the past. In contrast, soft polytheism takes a harmonizing approach that celebrates the rich array of different cultural forms while ultimately reconciling them into the greater divine reality of a numinous Goddess and God.

Second, this debate originated in the internecine politics of the contemporary Pagan movement. In the mid-1990s, hard polytheists—particularly practitioners of Asatru—sought to carve out their own identity distinct from the Wiccan-dominated Pagan scene. In this jostling for positionality, the hard and soft theological perspectives were used to differentiate Asatru from Wicca and to establish clear ideological boundaries between these two movements. Using theological differences to serve political and sociological ends is quite common in the history of religions and explains why the debate has taken such an antagonistic tone at times.

Third, it would be reductionist to consider the two positions mutually exclusive. A serious exposure to living polytheist traditions will show that they are rich and complex systems of meaning-making, ritual and practice, geography, infrastructure, and material culture. Robust polytheisms accommodate multiple perspectives about the divine with an accompanying diversity of religious practices. Hinduism makes room for the philosophical monism of Advaita Vedanta with practices of meditation and mysticism, tantric Shaktism with its conceptions of sacred energy released through kundalini yoga, and bhakti devotionalism with its multiplicity of temples, pilgrimages, and pujas. Durga, Kali, and Lakshmi are all experienced as real, different, and distinct entities while also being considered manifestations of the Mahadevi. The religious worlds of ancient Greece and Rome gave rise to complex, nonlinear, and nonsystematic ways of experiencing and conceptualizing the sacred. The stories and cults of the Gods existed side-by-side with Platonic conceptions of a world of forms in which the many Gods reflected the greater reality of the One or the Good. Approaches like *interpretatio Romana* demonstrate that these ancient Pagans held complex views of divine ontology. In the end, these two contemporary positions are starting points for deeper theological explorations within Paganism and the development of robust polytheist religious cultures.

About the author

Jefferson Calico is a teacher, writer, and religious studies scholar working in the Appalachian region of the upper South. His book *Being Viking: Heathenism in Contemporary America* was published by Equinox Publishing Ltd. in 2018.

Suggestions for further readings

In this book
See also chapters 30 (How do Pagans conceive of gods?) and 36 (How do Pagans interact with deities and spirits?).

Elsewhere
Calico, Jefferson F. "Hard Polytheism in a Soft World." In *Being Viking: Heathenism in Contemporary America*, 264–306. Sheffield: Equinox Publishing Ltd., 2018.

Doyle White, Ethan. "Wiccan Theology." In *Wicca: History, Belief, and Community in Modern Pagan Witchcraft*, 86–96. Brighton: Sussex Academic, 2016.

Puca, Angela. "Gods in Paganism—Hard vs Soft Polytheism." Angela's Symposium. April 17, 2022. YouTube video, 17:55. https://youtu.be/5a-OrUkaRYI?si=pd8Kedio2PNCBk2W.

Keltoi, Ocean. "Hard Polytheism vs. Soft Polytheism." September 2, 2021. YouTube video, 20:01. https://youtu.be/7LSd3iLCUtU.

18
What is the difference between an eclectic and a traditional Pagan or witch?

Angela Puca

Paganism is a diverse and fluid spiritual phenomenon encompassing a variety of belief systems, practices, and traditions. Within this broad umbrella, individual practitioners often define their paths and approaches differently, leading to distinctions such as "eclectic" and "traditional" Pagans or witches.

Traditional Paganism and witchcraft refer to spiritual paths that are rooted in established systems and historical practices, often emphasizing adherence to specific doctrines, rituals, and customs. Traditional Pagans and witches generally follow a particular tradition, such as Gardnerian Wicca, Alexandrian Wicca, or Asatru, which have well-defined structures and teachings derived from the writings of their founders or historical sources. These traditions often have a hierarchical organization, with initiatory lineages and clear distinctions between various levels of experience and authority.

Traditional Pagans and witches often place great value on maintaining the integrity and continuity of their specific tradition, as they believe that these practices have been passed down through generations and hold sacred wisdom. They may participate in closed initiatory groups known as covens, groves, or kindreds, which are led by experienced elders who oversee the spiritual development of their members and ensure that the teachings of the tradition are preserved and transmitted accurately.

In contrast, eclectic Pagans and witches embrace a more individualistic and flexible approach to spirituality, drawing on a variety of sources, beliefs, and practices to create a personalized spiritual path. Rather than adhering to a single tradition or doctrine, eclectic practitioners may incorporate elements from various Pagan traditions as well as non-Pagan belief systems such as Eastern philosophies, shamanism, or even monotheistic religions. Eclectic Pagans and witches prioritize personal experience, intuition, and creativity in their spiritual practices, often adapting or modifying rituals and beliefs to suit their individual needs and preferences.

Eclectic practitioners may participate in open, nonhierarchical groups or circles or choose to practice solo as solitary witches or Pagans. They may engage in a wide range of spiritual practices, such as meditation, divination, energy work, or spellcasting, depending on their personal interests and beliefs. While some eclectic Pagans and witches may still identify with a specific tradition or label, such as Wicca or Druidry, they often do so in a more fluid and adaptable manner, acknowledging the influence of multiple spiritual sources and the ongoing process of spiritual growth and exploration.

Both traditional and eclectic Pagans and witches contribute to the vibrant tapestry of the modern Pagan movement. The diversity in belief systems and practices fosters a sense of inclusivity and allows for a wide range of spiritual expressions. Ultimately, the choice between a traditional or eclectic path depends on the individual's preferences, values, and spiritual goals.

Traditional Pagans and witches may find a sense of stability, guidance, and connection to history by adhering to established traditions and practices. They may appreciate the structure and accountability provided by hierarchical organizations, as well as the opportunity to learn from experienced elders and participate in a shared spiritual lineage. Traditional paths can offer a strong foundation for spiritual growth alongside a sense of continuity and belonging within a specific community.

On the other hand, eclectic Pagans and witches may be drawn to the freedom, creativity, and personal autonomy afforded by a more flexible spiritual approach. They may value the opportunity to explore a variety of spiritual influences and practices, integrating diverse elements into a unique and evolving path. Eclectic paths can foster self-discovery, empowerment, and a broader understanding of spiritual perspectives and experiences.

It is important to note that the distinction between traditional and eclectic Pagans and witches is not always clear-cut, as many practitioners incorporate elements of both approaches in their spiritual journeys. Some may begin as eclectic practitioners and later join a traditional group or vice versa, while others may choose to blend aspects of various traditions within their own personalized framework. This fluidity and adaptability are hallmarks of the modern Pagan movement, reflecting the resilience and vitality of these spiritual paths in an ever-changing world.

About the author

Angela Puca, PhD (2021), is an independent religious studies scholar and university lecturer. She is bridging the gap between academia and the general public with her social media project Angela's Symposium, where she disseminates peer-reviewed research to a wide audience engagingly. She's the author of the forthcoming *Italian Witchcraft and Shamanism*, to be published by Brill, and coeditor of *Pagan Religions in Five Minutes* for Equinox Publishing Ltd.

Suggestions for further readings

In this book
See also chapters 7 (Are most Pagans solitary practitioners?), 19 (Are all witches Pagan?), and 21 (What is the difference between Wicca and witchcraft?).

Elsewhere
Berger, Helen A. *A Community of Witches: Contemporary Neo-Paganism and Witchcraft in the United States*. Columbia: University of South Carolina Press, 1999.

Hardman, Charlotte, and Harvey, Graham. *Pagan Pathways: A Complete Guide to the Ancient Earth Traditions*. London: Thorsons, 2001.

Magliocco, Sabina. *Witching Culture: Folklore and Neo-Paganism in America*. Philadelphia: University of Pennsylvania Press, 2004.

19
Are all witches Pagan?

Mary Hamner

Whether or not we consider witches to be Pagan depends entirely on what frameworks we have in place for defining Paganism. If we think of Paganism as a contemporary religious movement that emphasizes nature-based spirituality and healing, which has been a common definition in academic spaces, then the answer is a simple *no*. If we think Paganism is a revivalist movement invested in rediscovering and reclaiming pre-Christian religion and folk practice, then the answer is, at best, *sometimes* or *maybe*. If we think Paganism is a convenient umbrella term that includes many kinds of occultism, magical practice, alternative healing modalities, and folk tradition, then possibly, we get as close as we can to *yes*. At this point, however, our definition is so broad as to be mostly useless!

It is always difficult to make sweeping, definitive statements about any religious category, and this is especially true in witchcraft and contemporary Paganism due to the decentralized, individualized nature of these traditions (indeed, if "traditions" is even the most appropriate term). Witchcraft and Paganism both potentially include a staggering variety of belief systems, magical practices, organizational structures, communities, and regional flavors, and these may or may not overlap. It takes little effort to find examples of practitioners that defy any neat definition we might concoct. To further complicate this problem of categorization, the use of both of these terms has shifted as new waves of practitioners, authors, content creators, and teachers have developed within Pagan and witchcraft communities.

In earlier decades, it was common for both practitioners and scholars to assert that contemporary witchcraft (which includes Wicca as well as many other traditions) belonged under the larger umbrella term of Paganism, or sometimes "neo-Paganism." Paganism, as we have seen, is a broad term that includes a number of possible definitions. It has variously been described as including any and all "earth-based" religions, as a term interchangeable with polytheism, as specifically a contemporary movement born out of the twentieth-century occult revival in England, or as a tradition developing alongside the American New Age. More recently, Paganism has popularly become less of a catchall and more highly specified by practitioners pursuing individual cultural traditions (for example, Celtic, Norse, Italian, or Slavic religions, which may use different descriptors entirely). These practitioners may also eschew the term "Pagan" in an attempt to distance themselves from the contemporary Pagan movement, preferring to identify as only polytheists or, sometimes, "devotional polytheists."

Today, a rising number of witches assert that their practices and beliefs are not religious at all but instead fall under the banner of secularism. For them, witchcraft is a practice—a collection of folkways, practical techniques, and magical perspectives—and not a spiritual or religious tradition in and of itself. Individual witches may belong to religious groups and may incorporate religion into their witchcraft, but this is a personal choice and not a reflection on witchcraft as a whole. Pagan religions commonly serve as the foundation for many of these practitioners, but they are just as likely to look to Catholicism, Judaism, Buddhism, and a wide variety of other traditions, often with ancestral or familial significance to the individual witch. In this way, witchcraft may serve to augment religious practice. For many, however, it is exclusively a magical system—a toolkit available to anyone, religious or not, who desires to learn to use it.

Pagans and witches often occupy the same spaces, both online and off. They are likely to attend the same festivals, consume much of the same media, and share a lexicon. At the individual level, practitioners may identify as both, and some may at times conflate the two categories. However, distinctions exist, and these have become more significant and striking as different kinds of practitioners—especially practitioners of color and queer practitioners—become more vocal and these movements develop across various mediums. Where possible, it is always wise to ask individuals what they mean by their terms and what distinctions they draw for themselves.

About the author

Mary Hamner is at the University of North Carolina at Chapel Hill specializing in religion and culture. Her research interests include religion and social media, ethnography, secularism, and contemporary witchcraft. She publishes about Wicca and witchcraft and maintains a social media presence under the name Thorn Mooney.

Suggestions for further readings

In this book
See also chapters 18 (What is the difference between an eclectic and a traditional Pagan or witch?), 20 (Can anyone be called a "witch"?), and 21 (What is the difference between Wicca and witchcraft?).

Elsewhere
Grossman, Pam. *Waking the Witch: Reflections on Women, Magic, and Power.* New York: Gallery Books, 2019.

Pike, Sarah M. *New Age and Neopagan Religions in America.* New York: Columbia University Press, 2004.

Monteagut, Lorraine. *Brujas: The Magic and Power of Witches of Color.* Chicago: Chicago Review Press, 2021.

20
Can anyone be called a "witch"?

Francesca Po

There are three primary ways individuals might be called a "witch": (1) with derogatory intent, (2) as a formal practitioner of Wicca, and (3) broadly relating to Pagan, Indigenous, or esoteric aesthetics or practice. The use of "witch" is inseparable from issues of power and oppression, which makes it potentially problematic if used without careful consideration.

The original use of the label "witch" was with derogatory intent by those in power to accuse individuals—usually women, Indigenous people, and ethnic minorities—of causing harm to others by way of evil practices. Christians were notoriously known to use it in this way since the Early Middle Ages in the practice of "witch-hunting." Throughout time and history, this has revealed itself to be an oppressive—if not violent—practice, used to perpetuate problematic power dynamics against women and minorities. This derogatory use continues to persist today within different religions, primarily in developing nations and less so, though still present, in developed nations.

Wicca, as a formal religion with traces in the nineteenth century, was introduced to the public in the 1950s by Gerald Gardner. In the previous century, there were many forms of esotericism that emerged among the educated middle to upper class, particularly upper-class women, combining European Pagan and Indigenous philosophy and practice with the popular esoteric ideas of the time. Furthermore, throughout Europe, the formal practice of witch-hunting had nearly been eliminated. Practitioners of Wicca embrace the term "witch" and find it empowering to appropriate a commonly used derogatory term in this new context.

Since the 1960s, the term "witch" has been used more broadly, relating to Pagan, Indigenous, or esoteric aesthetics or practice, in developed nations. It may be used to identify someone from the outside, or it may be an intentional label one might use for oneself. A "witch" might be a practitioner of Pagan, Indigenous, or esoteric spirituality but might also simply enjoy the aesthetic associated with witches or witchcraft throughout history in an exclusively secular way through fashion, decoration, or entertainment. More recently, the term "witchy" is being used as a descriptive term to refer to this broader use of "witch."

As already stated, the use of "witch" is inseparable from issues of power and oppression, which makes it potentially problematic if used without careful consideration. The following guidelines are given by individuals who identify as witches, ranging from Wiccans to unaffiliated practitioners.

Firstly, being a witch and practicing witchcraft continue to be punishable by death in many parts of the world. Those who can safely identify as a "witch" are in an extremely privileged place to be able to do so. Witches, therefore, have a responsibility to recognize this privilege and represent witchcraft in ways that advocate for the oppressed, as well as not perpetuate negative stereotypes about witches.

Secondly, considering many of the practices of witchcraft, or "the Craft," derive from Pagan and Indigenous traditions, it is important for a witch to know and understand the background and history of one's practices and that one has proper permission to use these practices. Again, recognizing a position of privilege, appropriating the practices of historically oppressed people without permission can be considered a contemporary form of colonialism.

That being said, in general, the use of the term "witch" as a personal identity is tolerated by the practitioner community:

> Wicca came long after that term ["witch"], and there are people who practice witchcraft who have nothing to do with Wicca. It's open and it's available to whoever wants it. We don't own it. We might've made it popular again, but we can't take it. . . . It's for everybody. (Lisa Grace, personal communication)

About the author

Francesca Po, DPhil (University of Oxford), is a scholar of religion and nonreligion with research interests in religious change, alternative spirituality, and contemporary witchcraft. She is a member of the Board of Directors at the Metta Center for Nonviolence, is an executive leader in spiritual formation for the Salesians of Don Bosco, served in the US Peace Corps in Kazakhstan, and is the author-editor of *Religion and Peace* (2022) and *The Study of Ministry* (2019).

Special thanks to Alison Eve Cudby, Lisa Grace, and Zachariah Griffin.

Suggestions for further readings

In this book
See also chapters 18 (What is the difference between an eclectic and a traditional Pagan or witch?), 19 (Are all witches Pagan?), 21 (What is the difference between Wicca and witchcraft?), and 55 (Can witch doctors and Africana spiritual traditions be regarded as Pagan?).

Elsewhere
Grossman, Pam. *Waking the Witch: Reflections on Women, Magic, and Power.* New York: Gallery Books, 2019.

Hutton, Ronald. *The Witch: A History of Fear, from Ancient Times to the Present.* New Haven, CT: Yale University Press, 2017.

Po, Francesca. "'Witchy' Activism: Self-religion in Global Peace Movements." In *The Wiley Blackwell Companion to Religion and Peace*, edited by Jolyon Mitchell, Suzanna R. Miller, Francesca Po, and Martyn Percy, 242–254. Hoboken, NJ: Wiley Blackwell, 2022.

Sabin, Thea. *Wicca for Beginners: Fundamentals of Philosophy and Practice.* Woodbury, MN: Llewellyn Worldwide, 2013.

21
What is the difference between Wicca and witchcraft?

Mary Hamner

One of the perennial difficulties in witchcraft communities collectively is the differentiation between various strains of magical practice. Practitioners may use a number of terms to describe their traditions and beliefs, and often those terms are personal and vary by generation, region, and even which social media platforms or texts the individual witch occupies or consumes. Traditions and communities often overlap, and it is common for witches to belong in multiple spaces, claiming various descriptors, even where they appear to contradict. Furthermore, practitioners are likely to describe their witchcraft differently depending on context or circumstance, choosing terms based on their conversation partners and whatever agenda may be at hand. For the casual observer, new scholar, or religious seeker, this regularly leads to the assumption that terms are interchangeable. Nowhere is this more apparent than in the confusion that often surrounds the use of the term "Wicca."

Wicca has come to be the name of a modern witchcraft tradition developed in the mid-twentieth century in England and subsequently popularized in various iterations throughout the United States and elsewhere in the world. Its earliest proponent was a British civil servant and amateur anthropologist named Gerald Gardner, who publicly claimed to have been initiated into a surviving witch cult in England's New Forest. Influenced by the popular theories of Margaret Murray, Charles Leland, and others, Gardner believed that witchcraft was a pre-Christian survival of an Indigenous European religion. Driven underground during centuries of intense Christian persecution, Gardner and his contemporaries asserted that witches had maintained their traditions and beliefs through the practice of intense secrecy, organizing themselves into small groups called covens and passing their wisdom through initiatory rites or within families. Those beliefs and traditions included the worship of a moon goddess and a horned god of death and resurrection, the observance of seasonal rites centered on fertility and a belief in reincarnation, and the practice of magic. Gardner published several books about the witch cult, most notably *Witchcraft Today* (1954) and *The Meaning of Witchcraft* (1959), which he claimed to have been permitted to do by his coven in order to keep the tradition from dying out. By all accounts a charismatic individual, Gardner attracted a great deal of interest and initiated many others into the movement, most notably Doreen Valiente, who would go on to produce her own books and a great deal of ritual liturgy and poetry that would come to be seen as canonical by contemporary witches of many varieties.

Much of the confusion surrounding the distinction between Wicca and witchcraft is the result of the absence of the term "Wicca" in early Wiccan texts and among early Wiccans. Gardner primarily referred to his tradition as "witchcraft," "the witch cult," "the old religion," and "the wica." Well into the late twentieth century, the word "Wicca" was popularly understood by practitioners (if less clearly so by linguists) to mean "wise" or "wise one" or to literally translate as "witch." This led to the terms appearing interchangeably in popular publishing, especially in the latter quarter of the twentieth century. During the era of the Satanic Panic in the United States, many practitioners, regardless of tradition, described themselves as Wiccan as a way of mitigating the public fear surrounding the words "witch" and "witchcraft." As witchcraft and occultism have entered the mainstream in recent years through television, publishing, and social media, much of that fear has dissipated. Witches describing other traditions—some with very different origins, practices, and beliefs—have come to the fore, many for the first time. Though practitioners of other witchcraft traditions existed and operated alongside and preceding Gardner's popularity, much of this nuance has been obscured.

For the purposes of simply navigating contemporary witchcraft spaces, Wicca is a *type* of witchcraft made up of a variety of traditions all tracing to Gerald Gardner—whether directly through an initiatory lineage or through the practices and beliefs publicly shared by Gardner and his successors in their published works. Wiccan witches may additionally identify as members of specific traditions (Gardnerian, Alexandrian, Blue Star, and others) and may simply refer to themselves as "witches" or use "Wicca" and "witchcraft" interchangeably where the distinction is not prescient (for example, among others of the same tradition). Practitioners of non-Wiccan forms of witchcraft are also likely to use additional descriptors (green witch, traditional witch, secular witch, folk witch, and more) but may similarly prefer to simply call themselves "witches" without further characterization.

About the author

Mary Hamner is at the University of North Carolina at Chapel Hill specializing in religion and culture. Her research interests include religion and social media, ethnography, secularism, and contemporary witchcraft. She publishes about Wicca and witchcraft and maintains a social media presence under the name Thorn Mooney.

Suggestions for further readings

In this book

See also chapters 18 (What is the difference between an eclectic and a traditional Pagan or witch?), 19 (Are all witches Pagan?), and 20 (Can anyone be called a "witch"?).

Elsewhere

Hutton, Ronald. *The Triumph of the Moon: A History of Modern Pagan Witchcraft* (2nd edition). New York: Oxford University Press, 2019.

Doyle White, Ethan. *Wicca: History, Belief, and Community in Modern Pagan Witchcraft*. Brighton: Sussex Academic, 2019.

22
What is Heathenry?

Jefferson Calico

Heathenry is a contemporary Pagan religion based on and inspired by the pre-Christian religions of ancient and medieval Norse and Germanic societies. Like other forms of Paganism, it is past oriented, polytheistic, nature based, and ancestor venerating and incorporates magical practices. However, Heathenry has developed a distinct textual tradition that distinguishes it from other Paganisms. Heathens use a corpus of historical works sometimes referred to as "the Lore" that make up the primary sources from which Heathenry reconstructs its religious culture. These works include the *Poetic Edda*, containing mythological poems in Old Norse; the mythological stories and poetic themes compiled in the *Prose Edda*; and the hero and family stories contained in the Norse and Icelandic sagas, among others.

Heathens make use of these sources to describe a symbolically rich and meaning-laden world that inspires and animates Heathen religious thought and practice. This world consists of several families or clans of Gods: the Aesir, the Vanir, the elemental or chthonic Jotuns and Rokkr, and a host of other beings such as light and dark elves and spirits of nature and place. Heathens relate to these beings and form religious communities through two primary rituals: a rite of sacrifice called *blót* and a rite of fellowship known as *sumbel*, which connect Gods, ancestors, and living practitioners into a sacred community. The Heathen cosmology is a porous and interconnected ecology of nine realms or homes envisioned as a great world tree, Yggdrasil. Heathens use distinctive metaphysical concepts like *ørlög* and *wyrd* to describe the dynamic ways that the past influences and shapes the present. Humans wield supernatural power through the oracular and transformative Norse magic called *seiðr*, rune magic, and many other forms of folk magic described in the Lore and borrowed from other sources. The ways that individuals and groups put these pieces together map out the various branches and divisions within Heathenry.

Like other Paganisms, Heathenry incorporates influential tributaries from contemporary cultural history, such as Wicca and witchcraft and popular culture. Unfortunately, other tributaries include the nineteenth-century *völkisch* Germanic nationalist movement and the mid-twentieth-century Nazi legacy of racism and anti-Semitism. This accounts for the ongoing struggle with white supremacy, white power ideology and militancy, and racist rhetoric and violence within the Heathen movement. Racism remains entrenched in various groups in Heathenry, although this should not be considered definitive of the entire movement. Inclusive Heathenry espouses an antiracist approach and encourages diversity in Heathen religious culture.

Calling oneself a Heathen is an act of reclamation and defiance. For most of its history, the term has carried a range of meanings associated with the ugly side of Christian colonial dominion. As early as the fourth century CE, the term appeared in Gothic language translations of the Bible, referring to those outside of the Christian faith. As Christianity assumed a culturally hegemonic position in the Western world, the term quickly took on derogatory and imprecatory uses, implying savagery, immorality, and godlessness. During the Viking Age and the period of conversion in northern Europe, "Heathen" was used specifically to denigrate those who maintained the Norse Pagan customs in opposition to Christianity. In the nineteenth and twentieth centuries, it became a term of radical othering, employed broadly and aggressively to dehumanize the supposed enemies of Christian civilization such as Muslims and Native Americans and to legitimate their conversion, oppression, and genocidal elimination.

While Heathenry or Heathenism have become the preferred terms referring to contemporary Norse Paganism, there are a variety of others. "Asatru," or "faith of the Aesir," was prominent in the beginning of the movement in the early 1970s and is still used widely among Norse Pagans. Because Asatru is associated with Icelandic forms of Norse Paganism, some practitioners consider it too culturally specific to adequately express the full diversity of Heathen practice. In the American context, "Asatru" is a term claimed by folkish groups, leading inclusive and antiracist practitioners to prefer the "Heathen" moniker. At times, "Heathenry" is used to distinguish the movement from closely related Pagan approaches like Norse-influenced Wicca, Anglo-Saxon-based Theodism, or Northern Tradition Paganism. Other practitioners might use terms that imply a particular cultural or ideological approach to their practice, such as Manx, Urglaawe, Danish Forn Siðr, Odinism, or folkish. And others might adopt terms that express controversial or minoritized Heathen identities such as Vanatru, Lokean, or Rökkatru. These different terms indicate the diverse approaches and contested identities that exist within the Heathen world of Norse Paganism.

About the author

Jefferson Calico is a teacher, writer, and religious studies scholar working in the Appalachian region of the upper South. His book *Being Viking: Heathenism in Contemporary America* was published by Equinox Publishing Ltd. in 2018.

Suggestions for further readings

In this book
See also chapters 17 (What is the difference between hard and soft polytheism?), 49 (Do Pagans practice sacrifice?), and 57 (Do Pagans have particular political views?).

Elsewhere
Blain, Jenny, and Robert Wallis. "Heathenry." In *The Handbook of Contemporary Paganism*, edited by J. Lewis and M. Pizza, 413–432. Leiden: Brill, 2009.

Calico, Jefferson F. *Being Viking: Heathenism in Contemporary America*. Sheffield: Equinox Publishing Ltd., 2018.

Harvey, Graham. *Contemporary Paganism: Religions of the Earth from Druids and Witches to Heathens and Ecofeminists*. New York: New York University Press, 2011.

Rood, Joshua. "Heathen: Linguistic Origins and Early Context." *Óðrærir* 2 (2012): 6–16. https://www.academia.edu/3483117/Heathen_The_Linguistic_Origins_and_Early_Context.

von Schnurbein, Stefanie. *Norse Revival: Transformations of Germanic Neopaganism*. Leiden: Brill, 2016.

Snook, Jennifer. *American Heathens: The Politics of Identity in a Pagan Religious Movement*. Philadelphia: Temple University Press, 2015.

23
What is the difference between Druidism and Druidry?

Jennifer Uzzell

Druids compose one of the largest Pagan groups in the modern world; however, Druidry is complex and diverse, even when compared to other Paganisms. Not all Druids are Pagan, for example, and many combine Druidry (as a set of spiritual practices and a way of looking at and approaching the world) with other religious traditions such as Christianity, Buddhism, and Wicca. This makes talking about Druids in a meaningful way as a homogenous group notoriously difficult. Even the language used can cause as much confusion as clarity. Druidism is a term that was more widely used in the past by the emerging Druid groups at the turn of the twentieth century. It is very rarely used by "spiritual" Druids today, and the majority of books about Druidry do not mention the term at all. In his introduction to his 2007 book *The Druids*, Ronald Hutton explains that he has chosen to use the term Druidry because Druidism, to him, is associated with "formal religious systems," whereas the more recent "Druidry" is a much looser term.

Druidry itself is a fluid concept. Broadly speaking, there are three distinct strands of people in Britain calling themselves "Druids," all of whom emerged during the period from the late eighteenth century to the early twentieth century and all drawing their inspiration and identity to some extent from the ancient Druids, who seem to have been the priestly class of the Iron Age "Celtic" peoples. As very little is known of the original Druids, and even less is certain, this means that people can cast them into the image that best suits their own ideas and purposes, be those cultural, political, aesthetic, or spiritual. The three separate but related strands could be termed fraternal, cultural, and spiritual or religious. All draw language, rituals, and imagery from the writings of the Welsh scholar Iolo Morganwg, who was active in the late eighteenth century and whose writings in *The Bardas* were an attempt to reconstruct what he believed to have been the beliefs of the ancient Druids, preserved through the Welsh bardic tradition. While most of what is in *The Bardas* is now known to be Morganwg's own invention, it has been foundational to Druidry as it exists today, at least in the United Kingdom. The fraternal Druid groups modeled themselves on Free Masonry and specifically rejected any discussion of politics or religion. They drew much of their symbolism and ritual from the writings of Morganwg. Best known of the fraternal orders was the Ancient Order of Druids, of which Winston Churchill was a member. The second branch of Druid traditions is concerned primarily with "Celtic" cultural heritage, language, and identity and with the bardic arts, particularly poetry. The Gorsedd of the Bards of Wales, which is instrumental in the National Eisteddfod in Wales, is one such group, and it is into this group that Queen Elizabeth II was initiated in 1946. The third group is the spiritual Druids, for whom Druidry is a spiritual or religious tradition. This group first emerged in an organized way toward the end of the nineteenth century and into the beginning of the twentieth, when a group called the Universal Bond first associated themselves with Druidry and met at Stonehenge to celebrate the summer solstice. This early form of spiritual Druidry had its roots in the occultism of the Golden Dawn as well as in the writings of Morganwg. It was a clearly defined set of practices and philosophies to which all members were expected to conform, and as such, "Druidism" fit well as a description of a religious system.

Since the days of the Universal Bond, spiritual Druidry has developed in a variety of different ways. There are many Druid orders in the United Kingdom and across the world. In the United Kingdom, the biggest and best-known orders are the OBOD (Order of Bards, Ovates, and Druids), the BDO (British Druid Order), TDN (the Druid Network), and in America, ADO (Ár nDraíocht Féin). Each has a slightly different approach to Druidry, although many Druids belong to more than one order. There are also solitary Druids who are not affiliated with any order. It is almost impossible to find a satisfactory definition for Druidry, as it comprises so many different beliefs and practices. Most Druids share a reverence for nature as a way to access the divine, include ancestors in their religious practice, and are concerned with *awen*, or creative inspiration, which is often expressed in poetry, music, and storytelling. However, there is no universally defining set of beliefs or practices that unite all Druids, and this is one reason why the term "Druidism," with connotations of a unified and coherent religious tradition, has been largely replaced by the much less rigid and fluid term "Druidry."

About the author

Jennifer Uzzell (PhD, Durham University) is the education and youth manager for the Pagan Federation and senior examiner in religious studies at both GCSE and A level with a major awarding body and was head of religious education at a number of schools for many years.

Suggestions for further readings

In this book
See also chapters 4 (How did modern Paganism begin?) and 24 (Is Druidry the Indigenous religion of Europe?).

Elsewhere
Hutton, Ronald. *Blood and Mistletoe: The History of the Druids in Britain.* New Haven, CT: Yale University Press, 2009.

Shallcrass, Philip. *Druidry: A Practical and Inspirational Guide.* Devizes: Pretanic, 2023.

Billington, Penny. *The Path of Druidry: Waking the Ancient Green Way.* Woodbury, MN: Llewellyn, 2011.

24
Is Druidry the Indigenous religion of Europe?

Suzanne Owen

Julius Caesar (100–44 BCE) wrote, "It is believed that the training for Druids was discovered in Britain and from there it was transferred to Gaul. And now those who wish to learn the matter carefully depart for Britain for the sake of learning" (quoted in Koch 2003, 21–22). Pliny the Elder (23–79 CE) also placed them in Britain and Gaul and described Druids wearing white cloaks and cutting mistletoe, while Strabo (63 BCE–ca. 24 CE) identified the three "grades" observed in modern Druidry: "the Bards, the *Vates* and the Druids." At the time of the Romans, Druids served a priestly function, though much else claimed about them must be treated with caution, as no writing by an ancient Druid has survived, if it ever existed. However, Caesar's belief that Druidry originated in Britain has helped support recent views that Druidry (in Britain and western Europe, at least) is a "native spirituality."

There are a few reasons why Druidry might be regarded as an Indigenous "religion," at least in parts of Europe, though with some caveats. Druids today in general do not claim their practice is a continuation of ancient Druidry, though Druid fraternities of the seventeenth and eighteenth centuries did consider themselves "revivals." Nor do they claim to be "Indigenous" according to any ethnic or cultural criteria. It would also be a stretch to describe Druidry as "kinship based" or even an oral tradition, which is how some scholars in religious studies have defined Indigenous religion.

However, as a tradition engaging with the land, Druidry is the closest western Europeans have to what many admire in Native American and other Indigenous religious traditions. Indeed, it had led Dakota scholar Vine Deloria Jr., in *God Is Red*, to encourage European Americans to look to "Druidism" rather than Native American spirituality, referring to Britain and parts of Europe as "Druid lands." In its application for charity registration in England and Wales, the Druid Network stated that

"Druidry is based on the reverential, sacred and honourable relationship between people and the land" (quoted in Owen 2020, 79).

Much of what we call Druidry, though, has drawn heavily from the forged "ancient" Druid manuscripts of Iolo Morganwg (Edward Williams, 1747–1826), such as the "Druid's Prayer," along with whatever could be gleaned from primarily Welsh and Irish sources, such as the thirteenth–fourteenth-century *Book of Taliesin*, written down centuries after the periods in which they purport to have been composed and with much of the context and meaning left uncertain. Though such sources offer scant material to work with, many contemporary Druids rather do what they imagine Indigenous people do—engage with the environment, learn local history and prehistory, observe seasonal changes, and respect the flora, fauna, and other beings that share the space. Some have revived ancient crafts—from mead making to metalwork—and pursue the "bardic arts" of poetry and music. While this resembles a form of Romanticism, it rarely strays into the nationalistic tones of the nineteenth-century Celtic revivalists.

As part of a globalizing tradition, Druids are encouraged to make connections with their own seasons and ecosystems. Druid teachings are available to all, with the correspondence course of the Order of Bards, Ovates, and Druids (OBOD) particularly successful throughout the world. There is no ethnic criterion for being a Druid, nor must it be practiced in a particular geographical location, and contemporary Druids are not members of a nondominant people or culture. For this reason, Druidry would not be considered an Indigenous religion. However, I once proposed a broad definition of Indigenous religion "as that which relates to the land, the people . . . and that which has gone before" (Owen 2013, 86), which could include Druidry, though it is important to stress that Druids themselves are not Indigenous people.

About the author

Suzanne Owen is an associate professor in the study of religion at Leeds Trinity University in the United Kingdom researching British Druidry and Indigeneity in Newfoundland.

Suggestions for further readings

In this book
See also chapters 23 (What is the difference between Druidism and Druidry?), 34 (Do Pagans worship Ancestors?), and 54 (Can Paganism be applied to non-European religions, such as Shinto?).

Elsewhere

Hutton, Ronald. *Blood and Mistletoe: The History of the Druids in Britain.* New Haven, CT: Yale University Press, 2009.

Koch, John T. *The Celtic Heroic Age: Literary Sources for Ancient Celtic Europe and Early Ireland and Wales* (4th revised edition). Aberystwyth: Celtic Studies Publications, 2003.

Owen, Suzanne. "Druidry as an Indigenous Religion." In *Critical Reflections on Indigenous Religions*, edited by James L. Cox, 81–92. Farnham: Ashgate, 2013.

Owen, Suzanne. "Is Druidry Indigenous? In the Politics of Pagan Indigeneity Discourse." In *Indigenizing Movements in Europe*, edited by Graham Harvey, 71–83. Sheffield: Equinox Publishing Ltd., 2020.

25
What are Technopagans?

Chris Miller

"May the astral plane be reborn in cyberspace." So writes Erik Davis in his 1995 *Wired* article that coined the term "Technopagan." This term bounced around Pagan circles in the 1990s and 2000s, then gained notoriety through the hit show *Buffy the Vampire Slayer*. But what does it actually mean? To put it briefly, Technopagans are Pagans who explore technology for professional, recreational, and religious purposes. This chapter will highlight several ways this term is understood and address whether/how Paganism and technology intertwine.

In his article titled "Technopagans," Erik Davis explored the overlap between two fringe communities in California: techies and Pagans. Encapsulating how Technopagans blend new and old, Davis describes an event called CyberSamhain, during which celebrants connected four computers to invoke the cardinal directions. For participants in this ritual, there was little difference between physically meeting in a forest and navigating this virtual landscape. Sure, participants are *aware* of sensory differences but consider these unimportant. More significant is how technology allows one to connect with nature or imagine new possibilities.

From seemingly primitive equipment in the 1990s to modern advances, many people dismiss the authenticity of technology. However, when it comes to religion, deciding which experiences are "real" is complicated. Consider rituals from other religions that take place in person. Participants perform actions—consuming Christ's blood, washing a deity—which observers might view differently (drinking wine, rubbing a statue). Technopagans highlight that all rituals require imagination. For instance, in traditional Pagan rituals, members "cast a circle" to mark that space as sacred. An observer sees people waving their arms, but participants can feel the energy shift. For Technopagans, rituals might involve sitting at a computer and typing directions, but participants know their actions have deeper meaning.

In addition to using technology in rituals, Technopaganism suggests that electronics are part of the "natural" world. While this too might seem nonsensical, it invites reflection on how Pagans understand nature. The dagger and chalice used in rituals, for instance, do not naturally occur in nature. They *contain* natural elements, but their production requires mining and processing raw materials. Nonetheless, these tools represent deeper, natural meanings—whether the womb and phallus or earth and fire. Following this logic, Technopagans appreciate the natural materials found in manufactured goods—like the aluminum in a computer or fossil fuels that provide electricity—and may also imagine figurative connections between nature and technology. A computer's motherboard, for instance, may resemble a spider's web or tree branches.

If electronics are connected to nature, Technopagans also have control over (or work *with*) technology. Obviously, anyone can "control" technology in the sense of turning on a computer. Sirona Knight and Patricia Telesco take control one step further in their *Cyber Spellbook* (2002). Outlining how Pagans can blend traditional Witchcraft with a hint of technology, the authors recommend making protection charms with AAA batteries or using an air conditioner and scent diffuser to enhance meditation. They also provide guidance on how to better engage with technology, such as advising which deity offers protection from computer viruses. Although calling themselves cyber Witches, these authors share the underlying outlook of Technopaganism: Paganism enables one to interact with energy throughout the universe, and technology—though made by humans—is still connected to the natural world.

It is appropriate to close with the most notorious source of the term: the hit teen drama *Buffy the Vampire Slayer*. Jennifer Calendar (played by Robia LaMorte) is a schoolteacher who also possesses supernatural powers. Appearing in a dozen episodes over the first two seasons, Jenny aids the protagonists by teaching them about magic and also the possibilities and pitfalls of technology. Jenny self-identifies as a Technopagan and embodies the themes already highlighted. She performs ancient spells and values nature but also belongs to a "cyber-coven" and uses the internet to perform magic. *Buffy*'s popularity likely encouraged others to call themselves Technopagans or simply embrace that one can be an "authentic" Pagan and use modern technology.

In the post-Y2K era, the term "Technopagan" has fallen out of fashion. However, one could argue that Technopagans still exist wherever Pagans integrate technology into their practices. In other words, though someone may not call themselves a Technopagan, they might still mirror the practices. Many Pagans belong to virtual covens and attend online rituals or use electronic music and videos to enhance in-person rituals. Pagans say that social media algorithms are "enchanted" when they deliver you the right content. So while labels may fade, the impact of Technopaganism seems clear: validating the relationship between magic, nature, and technology.

About the author

Chris Miller is a postdoctoral fellow with the Nonreligion in a Complex Future project, hosted at the University of Ottawa.

Suggestions for further readings

In this book

See also chapters 64 (Do Pagans avoid technology?) and 66 (How do Pagans use fiction and film?).

Elsewhere

Davis, Erik. "Technopagans: May the Astral Plane Be Reborn in Cyberspace." *Wired*, July 1, 1995. https://www.wired.com/1995/07/technopagans/.

Cowan, Douglas E. *Cyberhenge: Modern Pagans on the Internet*. New York: Routledge, 2005.

Evolvi, Giulia. "Materiality, Authority, and Digital Religion: The Case of a Neo-Pagan Forum." *Entangled Religions* 11(3) (2020): 1–15.

26
What was ancient Slavic "paganism"?

Giuseppe Maiello

The ancient religion of the Slavs is reported only from a very limited number of written sources. On the other hand, central and eastern European archaeology have brought to light numerous habitation locations that leave a lot of room for interpretation. These interpretations help us conceive a—if not exhaustive, at least sufficient—picture of the belief system of the Slavs. This is accompanied by numerous ethnographic surveys dating back predominantly to the nineteenth century, when the system of *dvoeverie*—that is, the very close proximity of pagan symbols and beliefs alongside those of Christianity—was still in force in the countryside of eastern Europe.

Other sciences, such as linguistics, paleobotany, paleogeography, zoology, and above all, ethnology, have been used to allow scholars to create an overall picture of Slavic paganism, or of the religion of the Slavs before their culture dissolved—slowly—into Western and Eastern Christian systems.

At the present stage of studies, there are two rather idiosyncratic conceptions of the substance of Slavic paganism. The first—more traditional—is based mainly on nineteenth-century linguistics and sees the religion of the Slavs as very similar to that of "all the other Indo-European peoples" (Niederle 1917, 19). It would therefore be a patriarchal religion with a male divinity at the head of the pantheon, who the Slavs called Perun. According to the Greek historian Procopius of Caesarea, the supreme god was "the creator of lightning, sole master of the universe, to whom livestock and birds of various types were sacrificed" (Procopius 1905, *Goth* 3.14.23–24). This model is also based on the fact that, according to historical sources, in 980 AD, Vladimir, the prince of Kyiv, eight years before converting to Christianity, had institutionalized a "Slavic pantheon." Accompanying Perun (albeit in a slightly subordinate position) are four other gods—Khors, Dazhbog, Stribog, and Simargl—and one goddess, Mokosh. In this system, the great West Slavic deities—Svantovit, Triglav, Radegast, Yarovit, Zhiva, and others—mentioned in various medieval Saxon sources may also be included.

The second conception is based predominantly on archaeological, paleozoological, and ethnographic sources, which show that traditional Slavic society was linked to the cult of Mother Earth—therefore of fertility, of the feminine, and of the respect for spirits of nature, not necessarily elevated to the rank of gods. According to this conception, the great divinities would have appeared only at a late time of Slavic paganism and in situations of clashes with Christian armies, led by their powerful God and by the apparatus of saints characteristic of both Western and Eastern Christianity.

As in any type of "paganism," also in the Slavic one, the external divinities were recognized. Indeed, some of the names of the deities appear to have origins outside the Old Slavic language: Khors evokes the Persian word *korshid* (sun god); Simargl summons the *simurg*, which is the benevolent Persian mythical bird with a dog's head; Svantovit evokes Saint Vitus, the patron saint of the Saxons, western neighbors of the Slavs of the Elbe.

Other examples can be found that have been the fruit of numerous discussions by philologists and historians of the religion of the Slavs. But the controversy would be sterile because it is a common fact in nonmonotheistic religions that the deities of others are often respected as their own, to the point of becoming themselves part of the local pantheon.

A separate discussion must be made for Veles, a divinity that appears from some medieval written sources and is also reported in songs and refrains collected by nineteenth-century ethnographers. There is reason to believe that Veles is the trickster of the ancient Slavs—that is, an ambivalent figure prone to both good and evil at the same time.

The trickster, a modern word of North American origin, is present not only in the African and American continent mythologies but also in European ones. Among the most famous deities recognized today as tricksters, we have Loki in Norse mythology or Hermes in Greek mythology. Although the Slavs also had their own trickster archetype, it was only rarely taken into consideration. Today, it can be said that this inconsistency in scientific research has also been resolved.

Tricksters, and some other pre-Christian deities, converged in popular literature but then took on negative connotations due to the stigmatizing intervention of Christian preachers. Also, in the case of central and eastern Europe, these preachers, not being able to get completely rid of the memory of the Slavic past of the new ethnic groups that came into being, accentuated the negative characteristics of the ancient deities until they became demonic beings to be defeated and eradicated.

About the author

Giuseppe Maiello is an associate professor and head of the Department of Social Sciences at the University of Finance and Administration in Prague, Czech Republic.

Suggestions for further readings

In this book
See also chapters 27 (What is Romuva in Lithuania?) and 59 (Are Pagans involved in the war in Ukraine?).

Elsewhere
Gasparini, Evel. "Slavic Religion." In *Encyclopaedia Britannica* (15th edition), 874–876. Chicago: Encyclopaedia Britannica, 1974.

Jakobson, Roman. "The Slavic God Velesъ and His Indoeuropean Cognates." In *Selected Writings: Contributions to Comparative Mythology: Studies in Linguistics and Philology*, edited by R. Jakobson, R. Stephen, 1972–1982. New York: De Gruyter Mouton, 1985.

Maiello, Giuseppe, and Danišová, Nikola. "Veles as a Slavic Mythological Trickster." In *New Researches on the Religion and Mythology of the Pagan Slavs 2*, edited by P. Lajoye and S. Zochios, 47–76. Lisieux: Lingva, 2023.

Niederle, Lubor. *Slavic Antiquities*. Vol. 2. Praha: Bursík & Kohout, 1917.

Pettazzoni Raffaele. "West Slav Paganism." In *Essays on the History of Religions*, 151–163. Leiden: Brill, 1967.

Procopius. *Procopii Caesariensis Opera Omnia*. Vol. 2, *De bellis libri*, 5–8. Leipzig: Teubner, 1905.

27
What is Romuva in Lithuania?

MildaAlišauskienė

The Ancient Baltic religious organization Romuva aims to reconstruct pre-Christian beliefs and practices in contemporary Lithuania, grounding this process in folklore and ethnographic research. As a representative of contemporary Paganism, Romuva aims at reconstructing the local—that is, Baltic, Lithuanian, pre-Christian beliefs and practices; in doing this, it relies on the local landscape, mythology, and social and political contexts. In 2017, Romuva stated that its faith was founded on the natural and prehistoric religion, which served as the basis for different manifestations of this religion throughout Lithuania's history, including communal practices and the official religion of the country. The roots of this faith's persistence can be found in the forefathers, who have retained the fundamentals of religion in their rituals, rites, songs, laments, and other aspects of traditional culture.

Romuva's first two organizations were registered in Lithuania in 1992, while the group considers 1967 the beginning of its activities. Historical research also referred to the tourist clubs and so-called travelers' clubs that began to form in the three Soviet Baltic republics in the early 1950s to showcase Lithuanian culture, study the nation's customs and traditions, and care for historical monuments. It was the convention for these tourist clubs to celebrate various Pagan festivals, particularly the Rasos (or summer solstice) festival, and perform rituals. The 1967 celebration of the Rasos paved the way for establishing the Romuva movement, according to ethnologist Jonas Trinkūnas and others who had participated.

Romuva beliefs are promoted as life nurturing when life includes biological entities as well as the sun, moon, earth, water, trees, stones, and so on. Romuva strives for harmonious coexistence between nature and human beings. They believe the world is eternal. Romuva is centered on the pantheon of gods and goddesses related to nature. Led by the god Dievas (or Praamžius or Sotvaras), the pantheon includes the goddesses Žemyna, Laima, and Gabija. Žemyna is Earth Mother; she is the goddess of Earth's fertility and the mother of the deceased. Laima is the goddess of birth and destiny and is worshipped during birth, naming, and marriage ceremonies. She is thought to accompany people throughout their lives. Gabija is the goddess of fire, and fire is associated with life and light.

Romuva organization consists of many communities called Romuvas, in Lithuania and beyond. In 2023, seventeen Romuvas were registered in the country, usually named after the location of the altar of fire of each community. Each Romuva community is led by a leader called a *vaidila*, who is appointed by the highest priest. Leaders of Romuvas gather in the highest governing body of Romuva—*krivūlė*, which elects the highest priest and decides about other organizational matters. In 2002, ethnologist Jonas Trinkūnas was elected and consecrated as the highest priest of Romuva—*krivis*. After he passed away in 2014, his wife, Inija, was elected as the highest priestess—*krivė*—for a term of three years and consequently reelected twice. In 2015, she was consecrated in Vilnius. Although the will to elect his wife as *krivė* was voiced by Jonas Trinkūnas, this election of a female leader has been met with ambiguous reactions from the members, particularly men, stressing that there was no sufficient evidence of female leadership in the past (Ališauskienė 2021, 2023).

Romuva is the largest and most recognizable among religious organizations that practice the ancient Baltic religion in Lithuania; its popularity has risen recently, and the group has a few thousand adherents. Romuva members, also known as Romuvans, come from different age groups, genders, and social statuses. Ethnic Lithuanians make up the majority of Romuvans, while a few foreigners residing in Lithuania and sympathetic to its ideals and traditions have also joined. In contrast to the other minority religions in Lithuania, social research data show that Romuva is well regarded by the common public.

Research into contemporary Paganism shows that its followers tend to create identities in opposition to the dominant religion in their societies, usually Christianity; however, at the same time, empirical evidence shows the mingling of Paganism and Christianity in many European countries. The *krivė* consecration ritual in 2015 illustrated the way Paganism and Christianity shared common sacred spaces and heritage in Lithuania, and sometimes this coexistence became a contestation that supported the identity of Pagan groups (Aleknaitė 2018).

Political views of contemporary Pagans have been discussed extensively by Michael Strmiska (2018), and he concluded that there was a diversity of political views among pagans in Europe falling into the spectrum from left wing to right wing. On the one hand, there is a strong desire for Paganism to act as a vehicle for maintaining and preserving European ethnic heritage; on the other hand, contemporary paganism is defined as a blend of European heritage and a willingness to embrace modern ethnic diversity, multiculturalism, and other spiritual traditions. Romuva fits the description of Strmiska, including competing political ideologies seeking to embrace ethnic and religious diversity and striving to preserve the Lithuanian language, culture, and tradition.

The first decade of Romuva legal activities was marked by unsuccessful attempts to be included in the list of traditional religions in Lithuania, including nine religions that existed in the country for at least three hundred years. In 2017, Romuva applied for state recognition, an intermediary status between registered and traditional religion, which might be granted after twenty-five years of registration by the parliament of the Republic of Lithuania. However, in 2019, Romuva was not granted state recognition and appealed to the European Court of Human Rights, which in 2021 ruled that the Republic of Lithuania has discriminated against the religious group, with expectations that Romuva would be granted state recognition.

About the author

Dr MildaAlišauskienė is a professor at the Department of Sociology at Vytautas Magnus University, Kaunas, Lithuania. She has published more than thirty social scientific research articles on religion in contemporary Lithuania and the Baltic States and contributed to collective monographs and studies on the social exclusion of minority religions and Lithuania's secularization process.

Suggestions for further readings

In this book
See also chapters 26 (What was ancient Slavic "paganism"?) and 28 (Is Romuva an official religion in Lithuania?).

Elsewhere
Aleknaitė, Eglė. "Participation of Contemporary Pagans in Heritage Politics in Lithuania." *Pomegranate: The International Journal of Pagan Studies* 20(1) (2018): 92–114.

Ališauskienė, Milda. "Women's Leadership in New Religions and the Question of Gender Equality in Post-Communist Lithuania." *Nova Religio: The Journal of Alternative and Emergent Religions* 24(4) (2021): 84–103.

Ališauskienė, Milda. "Sun the Mother and Moon the Father: Gender Roles and Family Practices in Romuva." *Nova Religio: The Journal of Alternative and Emergent Religions* 27(1) (2023): 79–98.

Pranskevičiūtė, Rasa. "Contemporary Paganism in Lithuanian Context: Principal Beliefs and Practices of Romuva." In *Modern Pagan and Native Faith Movements in Central and Eastern Europe*, edited by Kaarina Aitamurto and Scott Simpson, 77–93. Durham: Acumen, 2013.

Strmiska, Michael. "Pagan Politics in the 21st Century: 'Peace and Love' or 'Blood and Soil'?" *Pomegranate: The International Journal of Pagan Studies* 20(1) (2018): 5–44.

28
Is Romuva an official religion in Lithuania?

Rasa Pranskevičiūtė-Amoson

The Romuva movement is one of the main contemporary Pagan denominations in Lithuania, and it is an "official religion" in Lithuania. However, there are various ways of being an official religion in the country.

The first Romuva religious community was registered by the Ministry of Justice of the Republic of Lithuania on May 20, 1992. It then gained recognition as a "nontraditional" religion in 1995, when the Law on Religious Communities and Associations was passed in Lithuania in the same year. To understand Romuva's legal status and the relationship with the state, it is worth looking into the interrelation of law and religion in Lithuania.

The Constitution of the Republic of Lithuania stipulates equality of all people before the law. Freedom of religion, together with freedom of thought and conscience as well as freedom of religious practice, is embedded in the Constitution. The granting of privileges or discrimination on grounds of religion is forbidden. There is no state religion in Lithuania, as the state and the church are separate.

However, the Law on Religious Communities and Associations of the Republic of Lithuania embedded a differentiation of religious communities, as well as the model of cooperation between state and religious organizations. It divides religions into three groups: "traditional" religious groups supported by the state, "recognized" religious groups, and "other" religious groups, which must register with the government to gain legal status.

The first group includes nine traditional religious communities and associations that comprise a part of Lithuania's historical, spiritual, and social heritage and are extended by the state with special benefits. These groups are Roman Catholic, Greek Catholic, Evangelical Lutheran, Evangelical Reformed, Russian Orthodox, Old Believer, Judaist, Sunni Muslim, and Karaite. The second group of religious organizations is scheduled for state recognition if their teachings and practices do not conflict with law or public morals. Currently, four "recognized" nontraditional religious communities and associations have more limited benefits extended by the state: the Evangelical Baptist Union of Lithuania, Seventh-day Adventist Church, Pentecostal Evangelical Belief Christian Union, and New Apostolic Church of Lithuania. The third group—other religious communities and associations—must follow the requirements of the Law on Religious Communities and Associations of the Republic of Lithuania to register with the government to gain legal status. According to the Ministry of Justice, at the end of 2021, there were 1,127 traditional and two hundred nontraditional religious organizations (communities, associations, and centers) that were officially registered legal entities.

According to Lithuanian law, when a religion has been registered for twenty-five years, it can receive the status of being a religion recognized by the state as well as receive financial support from the state, provided it has good standing in the society. The decision on recognition is made by the Seimas (parliament). However, some cases appear as examples of why questions of human rights and equality before the law on a case-by-case basis should not be decided by the Seimas. Romuva applied for legal recognition in Lithuania in 2017, and as of this writing, the process is still ongoing. The Romuva case reveals difficulties faced by religious minorities seeking state recognition in Lithuania. The delay in the decision on Romuva is partly due to this case being reviewed by politicians with a Catholic perspective who are interested in advancing Christian religious communities over others.

On June 27, 2019, the Seimas did not grant the status of a state-recognized religion to Romuva, nor did it make any decision regarding Romuva, leaving the religious association in the stage of legal uncertainty. Subsequently, Romuva prepared a case for the European Court of Human Rights in 2019, which was won in 2021. In *Romuva v. Lithuania*, the court ruled in favor of the Old Baltic Faith community Romuva and said that the Seimas had violated Article 9 of the Convention for the Protection of Human Rights and Fundamental Freedoms: Freedom of Thought, Conscience, and Religion. Moreover, the Constitutional Court of Lithuania decided that the provision of the law under which religious associations may apply for state recognition following a period of twenty-five years from the date of their initial registration was not in conflict with the constitution.

The question of state recognition for Romuva came toward the end of 2021, when the project regarding granting such a status for Romuva was registered. On September 29, 2022, the Seimas again did not make a final decision regarding this issue. The draft resolution was returned to the initiators—the Committee for Human Rights—for improvement.

The resolution regarding the recognition of Romuva was reregistered in October 2022.

At the same time, amendments to the Law on Religious Communities and Associations, Article 6, were prepared and came into action in May 2023. These amendments were intended to change the legal situation of religious communities denied state recognition and remaining in a legal vacuum when no other decision on the community was being made. As a result of adopting these amendments, the Seimas would be obliged to adopt one or another resolution regarding the recognition of Romuva and, in case of disapproval, to indicate the reasons. However, on September 19, 2023, after not having approved the draft resolution to grant state recognition to Romuva and later refusing to consider an alternative draft resolution to confirm officially that it *does not* grant the recognition, the Seimas voted that the alternative project be developed. On January 15, 2024, Romuva appealed for the second time to the European Court of Human Rights, expressing concern about the failure of the Seimas to respond to the previous demands for clarifications from the European Court of Human Rights and for not granting recognition to the community. To date, the situation has not yet been resolved.

About the author

Rasa Pranskevičiūtė-Amoson is an associate professor in cultural studies and anthropology of religion at the Institute of Asian and Transcultural Studies, Vilnius University, Lithuania. She has published on (post-)Soviet religiosity and alternative religious movements and subcultures, including Romuva, and was the president of the Lithuanian Society for the Study of Religions (2018–2022).

Suggestions for further readings

In this book
See also chapters 2 (Is Paganism a religion?) and 27 (What is Romuva in Lithuania?).

Elsewhere
Pranskevičiūtė-Amoson, Rasa. "The Old Baltic Faith *Romuva* Movement and State Recognition." *International Journal for Religious Freedom* 17(1) (2024): 127–143. https://doi.org/10.59484/ORUH4320.

29
How has Paganism developed in Brazil?

Karina Oliveira Bezerra

In Brazil, adherents of contemporary Paganism have been known since the 1970s, but the practice of Pagan witchcraft in England started appearing in the Brazilian media as early as 1951. During the 1970s, a few books mentioning Wicca were published in Brazilian Portuguese, and the Brazilian version of the famous French magazine *Planète* was founded. It published articles about Wicca, Druidry, and shamanism. However, in the 1980s, we first see evidence of practitioners in Brazil. By the end of this decade, Pagan topics appeared on television, while a large and very important esoteric store, Alemdalenda, was founded. It was aligned with and connected to the primarily middle-class New Age movement, whose followers were those who could afford to go abroad or had access to foreign books as well as those few translated into Portuguese.

From the early 1990s, Brazilian Pagans flourished. They started showing their faces in public, trying to connect with others, writing books, and appearing on TV. By the end of the decade, the internet had made Pagan gatherings easier, and the turn of the millennium saw further popularization of Paganism. More recently, Brazilian Pagans have begun to search for legitimation and the authenticity of tradition, which has led to some disputes and criticism regarding modern influences on Paganism—even the term "Paganism" was questioned.

The first book about Wicca translated into Portuguese and released in Brazil was *Power of the Witch* by Laurie Cabot in 1990. Other book translations would follow, and in 1993, a Brazilian witch, Marcia Frazão, released her first book on what we classify as natural witchcraft, followed shortly by a book on Wicca. At this stage, people from the New Age circuit—with a practical knowledge of natural magic and reading on Wicca, as well as participation in foreign groups—showed themselves as witches. Mirella Faur, responsible for promoting the "tradition of the Goddess" in Brazil, for example, made pilgrimages to the United Kingdom and Ireland in 1991 and 1993 before she felt ready for public work. Both Alemdalenda, which held celebrations, and *Planète* magazine, which published readers' contacts so they could exchange letters with one another, facilitated communication among people interested in Wicca before the advent of the internet. The first known person initiated by a Wiccan tradition (Old Dianic) was Claudiney Prieto, who said that in 1993, when he was sixteen years old, he was introduced to Wicca through an Englishman at a cousin's wedding. In 1998, Claudiney and four other significant Wiccans held the first witchcraft meeting in São Paulo, Brazil, which led many others within the witchcraft circle who didn't want to go public to "attack" them. In 2001, together with Maversper Ceridwen and Gwyndha, Claudiney founded the Dianic Tradition of Brazil. After the boom of the early 2000s, it was only in 2015 that Gardnerian Wicca officially arrived in Brazil.

Druidry arrived in Brazil via France, not England, through what is called meso-Druidry, following the division created by Isaac Bonewits. In 1980, Savu Septimus undertook initiation at the International College of Celtodruidic Studies. Thus, he is recognized as the first promoter of this Druidic lineage in Brazil. At the end of the 1980s, a matriarchal Druidic order was founded. While meso-Druidry continued its activities, neo-Druidry emerged with book translations such as *Elements of the Druid Tradition* by Philip Carr-Gomm in 1994. Many of these Druids started off in Wicca and then turned to neo-Druidry, believing it to be more "Celtic." At the beginning of the millennium, Claudio Crow Quintino founded a publishing company specializing in this, as there was a lack of Celtic spirituality books. Due to this shortage, it was Marion Zimmer Bradley's novel *The Mists of Avalon* (1982) that awakened interest not only in Wicca but also in Celticism and Druidry. Claudio, who was later initiated into the British Druid Order, was the first Brazilian to write a book about Celtic religion. He also brought John Matthews and Emma Restall Orr to Brazil and represented the Druid Network in Brazil. From the early 2010s, the reconstructionist approach gained strength. Marcílio Nemetios, for example, was once involved in shamanism, Wicca, and later Druidry and active in the Pagan community. However, from the early 2010s he no longer identified himself as neo-Pagan or Druid and founded the Ibero-Celtic Assembly of Brazil in 2016.

Neo-shamanism was introduced in Brazil by a fifty-five-year-old woman, Carminha Levy, from a feminist perspective and without the use of ayahuasca, only using musical instruments. In 1981, she was initiated into shamanism in California by none other than Michael Harner, founder of core shamanism. Then, in 1990, she created and founded her own school of shamanism—Paz Geia Shamanic Research Institute—along with her own branch, matricial shamanism. This was an attempt to put Riane Eisler's Gylany system into practice, fused with Carminha's personal beliefs. In the same year, Leo Artese created the "Universal Shamanic Movement." Before this, Artese had been initiated in Umbanda and then, alongside shamanism, converted to Santo Daime, practicing both. Universal shamanism includes different belief systems adapted for contemporary life alongside the ritual use of so-called medicines, such as ayahuasca. In the 2000s, there was a search for more traditional ways, and thus the Sacred Fire of Itzachilatlan (a branch of the Native American Church) was founded in 2003 in Brazil by Haroldo Evangelista Vargas, while the "Way of the Warrior" was founded by Marcos Ninguém in the early 2010s, where traditional ceremonial designs from various Indigenous peoples, most of them from Peru, appear alongside the use of several medicines during the same night. By this time, an exchange among Brazilian Indigenous and neo-shamanic groups gained strength, which resulted in changes on both sides.

About the author

Karina Oliveira Bezerra is a historian with a PhD in religious studies.

Suggestions for further readings

In this book
See also chapters 4 (How did modern Paganism begin?) and 56 (How much of Paganism is based on cultural appropriation?).

Elsewhere
Bezerra, Karina Oliveira. "Paganismo no Brasil: A magia da realidade" PhD diss., Universidade Católica de Pernambuco, 2019.

Lewis, James R., and Murphy Pizza, eds. *Handbook of Contemporary Paganism*. Leiden: Brill, 2009.

Pagan beliefs and practices

30
How do Pagans conceive of gods?

Vivianne Crowley

The deities venerated by Pagans include gods and goddesses from pre-Christian pantheons, generalized deities such as "the Goddess," and broad concepts such as "the divine" as an impersonal life force. Pagans may also venerate quasi-divine nature spirits located in particular places or in natural phenomena such as trees, fire, water, air, and earth. Practitioners may be drawn to deities associated with their ethnic and family heritage, to deities formerly worshipped in the area in which they live, or to deities of a particular type of Paganism—for example, the Celtic deities of Druidry, the Norse deities of Heathenism, or the deities of ancient Egypt, who have wide-ranging international appeal. Some branches of Paganism are eclectic in their choice of deities. Wicca venerates the "Triple Goddess," the Horned God, and other goddesses and gods according to the individual practitioner's preferences. In recent decades, Pagans' choice of deities has been influenced by popular culture, including Pagan folk rock, gaming, and television. The television series *Vikings*, for example, led to an upsurge of interest in Norse deities among people who have no cultural connection to the pantheon.

Although contemporary Paganism represents a wide spectrum of beliefs, these beliefs have underlying themes that reflect social concerns. These have included sexual liberation, feminism, environmentalism, and individualism. The popularity of different deities has waxed and waned, therefore, throughout the Pagan revival and reflects changing social attitudes, as well as the growth of Paganism in different countries and cultures.

The late nineteenth and early twentieth centuries saw a focus on the Horned God, Pan, as a symbol of sexual liberation. Twentieth-century feminism encouraged a Pagan rebalancing of patriarchal monotheism by focusing on the divine feminine as goddesses or the Goddess. Concern about the degradation of the natural environment and, more recently, climate change has led to the veneration of nature as a manifestation of the divine and an animistic focus on nature spirits. The last decade has also seen a growth in popularity of androgynous, intersex, gender-fluid, and homosexual deities, such as the Greek god Antinous, reflecting contemporary concerns about inclusivity, sexual orientation, and gender identification.

Contemporary Paganism is highly individualized, and Pagans are unconstrained by the requirements of doctrinal orthodoxy in determining how they conceive of deity. For "hard" polytheists, individual deities have an objective reality beyond that of the human imagination. For "soft" polytheists, different deities are aspects of one divine mind. For some, the forms in which deities are worshipped are culturally and historically determined, but they represent an underlying reality that the human mind frames in ways that it best can understand. For others, the gods are the creative product of human imagination, but these archetypal forms have power and agency. For others, they are symbols of human aspirations and needs with no independent existence of their own.

Few Pagans apply theological labels to their beliefs, but in theological terms, contemporary Paganism includes polytheism, meaning belief in many gods; henotheism, meaning devotion to a particular deity among the many; pantheism, in which the divine is a conscious force immanent in the natural world but does not exist outside it; panentheism, in which the divine is immanent in but also preexists the natural world; animism, in which the natural world and features of it are alive and conscious; and agnosticism, meaning openness to the idea of divine beings without drawing conclusions on the matter. In recent years, some Pagans have begun to describe themselves as atheist, rejecting ideas of veneration or worship and viewing their Paganism as a philosophy, a spirituality, or an honoring of heritage and culture rather than as a religion. Pagans will often move freely between different theological viewpoints, and their beliefs may reflect one or more positions simultaneously.

The varying views of deity within contemporary Paganism reflect changes in attitudes toward religion in diverse multicultural globalized societies no longer dominated by a single religion claiming ultimate religious truth. In addition, they reflect a psychologizing of religion to emphasize the primacy of human states of consciousness rather than supernatural intervention as the source of religious experience. The focus on the inner, the private, and the symbolic means that for most Pagans, the experience of deity is validated not through the closeness of the experience to the templates provided by religious orthodoxy but by the extent to which it "feels" true and provides meaning.

About the author

Vivianne Crowley is a lecturer in psychology of religion at Nottingham Trent University, United Kingdom. Her research interests include contemporary Paganism, religious experience, and women religious leaders.

Suggestions for further readings

In this book
See also chapters 17 (What is the difference between hard and soft polytheism?), 33 (Are some Pagans atheist?), and 36 (How do Pagans interact with deities and spirits?).

Elsewhere
Kraemer, Christine Hoff. *Seeking the Mystery: An Introduction to Pagan Theologies*. Englewood, CO: Patheos, 2012.

York, Michael. *Pagan Theology: Paganism as a World Religion*. New York: New York University Press, 2003.

31
Is there salvation in paganism?

Michael York

"Salvation" refers to preservation or deliverance from destruction, difficulty, or evil. Within Christianity, it becomes the doctrine of redemption and the belief in rescue from damnation through faith in Jesus Christ (e.g., 2 Cor. 7:10). Paganism stresses a person's individual connection with the divine, placing emphasis on material, earthly concerns. Further, there is no conviction of sin as a reified intrinsic/extrinsic entity or conduct, and nor does it entertain the notion of an abode for eternal punishment.

Our word "salvation" derives from the Latin *salvare* (to save) and *salvus* (to be safe, whole, healthy, uninjured). Our words "solid," "solemn," "holo-," "sage," "salvo," "safe," and "save" are among the cognates deriving from the conjectured Indo-European root "sol-" or "solo-" (whole). Consequently, salvation within a pagan mindset is primarily a good, healthy, and secure life here on Earth rather than a heavenly beatitude that can only be attained at best through a kind of proxy surrogate (see York 2003).

The Platonic tradition of mysticism is significant for understanding the transcendental *soma sema* narrative of Christianity and the theistic/panentheistic assertions of various gnostic forms of paganism. By contrast, telluric pagan formations tend to dismiss any stress on otherworldly escapism and, like secular outlooks in general, see salvation in the present moment, in the here and now of earthly existence. Unlike Neoplatonic religiosity, earth- or nature-centered paganism does not consider the cosmo-human narrative to be about the attainment of redemption. Healing, yes, and restoration and preservation of natural harmony are pagan concerns but ones that seek to work with the corporeal and terrestrial rather than "escape" from these.

In his seminal *Conceptions of the Soul among Native North Americans* (1953), Akė Hultkrantz discerned soul-duality beliefs—namely, a life-soul/body-soul and a dream-soul/free-soul (e.g., the Lakota *woniya/nagi* and *nagila*), in which the former is what animates the body in life and hosts the development of egoic consciousness and the latter is what experiences dreams and trances to which the consciousness of the body transfers temporarily. Similar understandings are to be found worldwide—for example, the Egyptian *ka* and *ba*, the Greek *thymos* or *pneuma* and *psyche*, the Roman *genius/juno* and *animus/anima*, the Norse *hugr* and *hamr/fygja*, the English mind/spirit and soul, and so on. As Hultkrantz points out, these souls may be multiple. The plurality of the soul is often a universal feature—especially among those people who may be identified as "pagan."

Consequently, there are two basic possibilities for afterlife salvation in a pagan understanding. The body's soul either dies with the body or lives on in a shadowy existence (the fate of souls in the Greek Hades)—possibly for as long as it is remembered by family and descendants and ritually honored or remembered historically by the world at large. Another possibility is that the ego consciousness departs either just before death or at the time of death and unites permanently with the free soul to live in the otherworld (Elysium, Summerland, the Western Isles). Therefore, one possibility is for a departed free soul to become the guardian spirit to a newborn life soul—a conception that may be seen to relate to contemporary pagan acceptance of the dynamic of reincarnation.

Another possibility might be that the consciousness belonging to the body-soul merges, like a drop of rain falling into the ocean, into collective consciousness. Or we might view the afterlife salvation for the body/ego-soul as a reverse of evolution: from the biological state of animal consciousness toward a comatose condition—that is, a "regression" to a vegetative state of being. However, when the organism disintegrates and decomposes, there follows a bedrock existence of physical parts beyond the pleasure-pain dichotomy of consciousness to one of mineral bliss. Of course, regarding salvation, we cannot speak from personal empirical experience but almost only in terms of metaphors used by others. Perhaps Goethe in his *Maxims and Reflections* expresses a pagan position best when he declares that nature is all things. The present alone is perpetuity, and eternity—that is, endless salvation—is to be found only in the here and now.

Note: I employ lowercase paganism rather than uppercase Paganism because of my focus on the extensive generic earth-centered spirituality and its principally noninstitutional vernacular expression. For me, the generic includes but is not subsumed by Paganism in its efforts to achieve legal recognition and be recognized as a specifically identified proper noun organization. But I want also to stress the organic uniqueness of paganism in contrast to competitors like Hinduism, Buddhism, Christianity, Islam, Judaism, and the like.

About the author

Michael York, professor emeritus of cultural astronomy and astrology at Bath Spa University, England, has published *The Emerging Network* (1995), *The Divine versus the Asurian: An Interpretation of Indo-European Cult and Myth* (1995), and his *Paganism as a World Religion* series: *Pagan Theology* (2003), *Pagan Ethics* (2016), and *Pagan Mysticism* (2019).

Suggestions for further readings

In this book

See also chapters 35 (What are pagan ethics?) and 39 (Do Pagans believe in reincarnation or life after death?).

Elsewhere

Grene, Marjorie, ed. *Spinoza: A Collection of Critical Essays*. Garden City, NY: Anchor Books, 1973.

Hadot, Pierre. *N'oublie pas de vivre: Goethe et la tradition des exercises spirituels*. Paris: Éditions Albin Michel, 2008/2021.

Hultkrantz, Akė. *Conceptions of the Soul among Native North Americans: A Study in Religious Ethnology*. Stockholm: Ethnographical Museum of Sweden, 1953.

York, Michael. *Pagan Mysticism: Paganism as a World Religion*. Newcastle Upon Tyne: Cambridge Scholars, 2019.

York, Michael. *Pagan Theology: Paganism as a World Religion*. New York: New York University Press, 2003.

32
Can a person have Pagan beliefs without being Pagan?

Alessandro Testa

The survivalist paradigm that was in vogue in Victorian anthropology and folkloristics predicated that pre-Christian beliefs and practices may "survive" over time, like cultural relics, even though their bearers (peasantry and lower classes, for instance, so the argument went) were mostly unaware of the true origins of such beliefs and practices. That paradigm has long been surpassed, and anthropologists and historians today prefer debating in terms of cultural adaptation, reuse, refunctionalization, and reappropriation rather than "survival." There is, however, no denying that cultural traces of bygone times remain and that historical development can work in viscous and sometimes oblique or subterranean ways. Moreover, beliefs and practices from the past, such as pagan ones, may also be consciously revived *as such*, through forms of cultural bricolage, symbolic molding, and ritual creativity that seek to reconnect the pre-Christian times to the post-Christian ones.

After all, what a person thinks or believes is the product, like anything else, of a cultural stratification over time. No progress or change is possible that is not somewhat rooted in previous forms, for "ogni *phainómenon* è un *genómenon*" (every phenomenon is born out of its own seed), as historian of religions Raffaele Pettazzoni once wrote (1959, 10). Nothing escapes this iron rule. Our thoughts and deeds coexist with echoes of what our predecessors thought and did, and our own thoughts and deeds could not bloom and branch out without being a continuation of (or a reaction to) those of our predecessors.

These questions lie at the core of disciplines such as history and ethnology but also in the minds and practices of modern Pagans, for pre-Christian symbols, beliefs, and practices still living in us today are uncountable—although *religious* ones are certainly of a smaller quantity. Some of said beliefs are explicit: astrology, for example, is well-known to be pre-Christian and also non-Christian. In the past, this and other beliefs that are today considered (and often praised as) "Pagan" were considered "superstitious" or "backward" by both the clergy and educated people (with the notable exceptions of the esotericists) and were often associated with peasantry, simple-mindedness, lack of education, and unprivileged social backgrounds. Modern Pagans are everything but these things, in our times. But what about those who do not consider themselves Pagans (and who are, admittedly, the majority of the Western population)?

Astrology has been mentioned, but other examples could be named of beliefs that many non-Pagans may share with Pagans. Fear of ghosts or of the dead, which are well documented in practically all pre-Christian cultures, should have no place in either the Christian mindset or in an eminently scientific and materialistic one. And yet hardly anybody could think of spending a night in a graveyard without a shiver running down their spine. Western beliefs in good and bad luck, in fortunate coincidences, and in the idea of an animated nature also come more or less straight from pre-Christian times and religions, yet most of the people upholding or simply bearing such beliefs would hardly describe themselves as Pagans.

In my own ethnographic investigations in different European areas, I have very often come across a particular set of such beliefs, which I have named "popular Frazerism." This refers to the results of an operation of symbolic reuse and cultural bricolage of a popularized version of Frazer's theses on European agrarian festivities and folk rituals, particularly those concerning the notion of ritually fostered fertility, agrarian magic, and the supposed pagan origins of some popular European festivities—and, precisely, their being supposedly a "survival" of ancient rituals, at times thought to be of unfathomable antiquity. Examples of popular Frazerism often show a belief in ritual efficacy through superhuman agents or agency. People among whom I recorded this particular cultural complex mostly did not identify as Pagans at all. On the contrary, they were mostly Christians or even atheists; they were also generally unaware of the fact that their beliefs were elaborated by a Victorian scholar, going down the line of time and reaching them through an articulated but ethnographically recordable genealogy of cultural mediation, popularization, circulation, and transmission.

The interpenetration of pre-Christian (read: pagan) and Christian beliefs in historically recognizable forms of adaptation, reuse, incorporation, and syncretism is one of the great themes in the history and anthropology of religions. Several different strands of scholarship have developed ever since the survivalist approach (recalled in the opening of this text) was the conventional one. My concept of popular Frazerism—just like that of "southern Catholicism," theorized in the 1950s by Ernesto de Martino (2015), which tries to understand said coexistence and interpenetration in their philosophical and sociopsychological implications in Latin Catholic countries—is among the interpretative endeavors that have attempted to reconcile and understand the coexistence of past religious forms in a differently religious (and sometimes irreligious) present.

About the author

Alessandro Testa is associate professor at the Faculty of Social Sciences, Charles University, Prague. He specializes in the history of religions, social anthropology, and the ethnology of Europe. His latest publications include *Rituality and Social (Dis)Order* (2020), *Politics of Religion* (with Tobias Köllner, 2021), and *Ritualising Cultural Heritage and Re-Enchanting Rituals in Europe* (2023).

Suggestions for further readings

In this book
See also chapters 1 (What is Paganism?), 5 (What is the relationship between ancient and contemporary Paganism?), and 41 (Are astrology and the tarot part of Paganism?).

Elsewhere
de Martino, Ernesto. *Magic: A Theory from the South*. Chicago: HAU Books, 2015.

Pettazzoni, Raffaele. "Il metodo comparativo." *Numen* 6(1) (1959): 1–14.

Testa, Alessandro. "Fertility and the Carnival 2: Popular Frazerism and the Reconfiguration of Tradition in Europe Today." *Folklore* 128(2) (2017): 111–132.

33
Are some Pagans atheist?

Sarah Best

When people think of contemporary Paganism, they often envision a polytheistic belief system that incorporates one or more pantheons. However, the wide umbrella of Paganism comprises much more than just polytheism; adherents ascribe to a range of cosmologies and worldviews. Pagans today may also be pantheists, panentheists, animists, duotheists, agnostics, and yes—even *atheists*. While contemporary Paganism is inspired by the traditions of premodern polytheistic cultures, not all Pagans ascribe to a *literal* belief in gods or spirits. For some, deities, spirits, and other supernatural forces have no relevance whatsoever to their beliefs and practices. Others may practice a kind of "soft polytheism," working with deities as metaphors for elements of nature or archetypal representations of the psyche.

Not only do atheist Pagans exist, but they comprise a rapidly growing and increasingly heterogenous subgroup of contemporary Paganism. Which is to say, there are many ways of being an atheist Pagan today. Many ascribe to Naturalistic Paganism, a form of religious naturalism where nature is seen as being sacred *in and of itself*, without the need for deities and spirits. Honoring the natural world is a central component of most contemporary Pagan traditions, and practitioners often feel a deep sense of love for and kinship with the environment. Though Naturalistic Pagans experience this relationality through a materialist framework, the sense of awe and wonder felt in nature is nonetheless spiritually meaningful, despite lacking divine elements. There are also Humanistic Pagans who take a *human-centric*—rather than *deity-centric*—approach to religion and ethics. Like other religious humanists, Humanistic Pagans reject the need for gods or spiritual beings in defining what is good, instead emphasizing the necessity of human responsibility in our flourishing and well-being.

Atheopaganism is a distinct form of Pagan religion that draws from both Naturalistic and Humanistic Paganism. Founded by Mark Green (author of *Atheopaganism: An Earth-Honoring Path Rooted in Science*),

Atheopaganism is defined as a "rational religion" for people who value skepticism and empirical evidence. For Atheopagans, the sacred has nothing to do with divine beings but rather is rooted within our material world and all the love and beauty it encompasses.

If the idea of atheist Pagans still seems like an oxymoron, or if the notion of being a religious atheist remains confusing, it may be helpful here to unpack some central terms. "Atheism" derives from the Greek word *atheos*, which can be broken down into *a-*, indicating a negation of something, and *theos*, meaning "god" or "gods." As such, atheism is commonly understood as a lack of belief in God (or gods). Although "religion" is sometimes thought to be synonymous with a belief in divinity, it is important to note that this is a Western-centric (specifically, Christo-centric) and relatively modern way of understanding religion. As religious studies scholars have pointed out, it is only since the Protestant Reformation in the sixteenth and seventeenth centuries that religion became primarily associated with an inner belief in transcendence—prior to this, outward expressions of devotion were much more important to the understanding of religion. Indeed, many ancient pagan traditions were concerned not so much with *belief* in deities but rather with the *practices* involved in honoring the gods, such as rituals or offerings.

Atheist Pagans often engage in ritual practices that are similar to those of other Pagans, such as celebrating seasonal changes marked by the turning of the Wheel of the Year, participating in elaborate performances symbolizing inner transformation, or constructing meaningful altars in honor of nature, ancestors, and (metaphorical) deities. Some rituals are simpler; even one's daily hike or tending to the garden can be a means of mindfully and spiritually connecting with the earth. Some atheist Pagans even participate in forms of witchcraft, though often "magic" is attributed to psychological processes rather than energetic or divine forces operating in the world. In this sense, then, atheist Pagans can be considered Pagans because of what they *do* rather than what they *believe*.

Although there is no single accepted definition of religion, scholars have largely moved past the limited notion that religiosity requires a belief in transcendent beings or supernatural phenomena. Moreover, religions themselves are not static—they may undergo significant changes as they are adopted by different individuals and groups. In our current era of secular modernity, atheist Paganism offers a spiritual path for those who are drawn to certain elements of the religion (such as its rituals, communities, or nature-based values) without having to compromise a materialist or scientific worldview. As such, atheist Paganism blurs boundaries between categories like the sacred and the secular and religion and science, raising the question, Are such binary oppositions actually helpful for understanding what it means to be religious today?

About the author

Sarah Best is a doctoral candidate in religious studies at Wilfrid Laurier University in Ontario, Canada. She has an MRes in social anthropology from the University of St. Andrews and an MA in English and Digital Humanities. Her research focuses on the various intersections between religion, environmentalism, and science and technology in contemporary society.

Suggestions for further readings

In this book
See also chapters 2 (Is Paganism a religion?) and 30 (How do Pagans conceive of gods?).

Elsewhere
Alexander, Nathan G. "Rethinking Histories of Atheism, Unbelief, and Nonreligion: An Interdisciplinary Perspective." *Global Intellectual History* 6(1) (2021): 95–104.

Halstead, John, ed. *Godless Paganism: Voices of Non-Theistic Pagans*. North Carolina: Lulu, 2016.

Petersen, Jesper Aagaard. "Are Pagans and Satanists Really Atheists?" In *Atheism in Five Minutes*, edited by Teemu Taira, 71–74. Sheffield: Equinox Publishing Ltd., 2022.

Steinhart, Eric. "Atheists Giving Thanks to the Sun." *Philosophia* 49(3) (2020): 1219–1232.

34
Do Pagans worship Ancestors?

Jennifer Uzzell

In order to answer this question, it is necessary to first ask, "What does the term 'ancestors' mean to Pagans?" This is not as straightforward as may first appear. Most obviously, ancestors are those from whom a person is biologically descended and from whom they have inherited DNA. For many Pagans, this is the primary meaning of the term, and some trace their bloodlines through research as a way of learning about and honoring their ancestors. This can become problematic, and some right-wing and nationalist groups have hijacked the idea of blood ancestors in Paganism and Heathenry as a way of excluding people who do not have Celtic or Germanic ancestry. This has led to Pagan organizations such as the Pagan Federation, Asatru UK, BDO (the British Druid Order), and others rejecting any ideology that is linked to "purity of blood" in the strongest possible terms on their websites.

There are, however, other ways of understanding "Ancestors" within Paganism. In Druidry, in particular, it is common to speak in terms of Ancestors of blood, place, and tradition. Blood Ancestors, as we have seen, are those from whom a person inherits DNA; however, if this idea is traced far enough back, then "bloodlines" become merged and tangled. Many Pagans would point out that if we go far enough back, then an individual is related to everyone else through ancestry, and so "the Ancestors" include everyone who has ever lived.

Ancestors of place are those who lived and worked in the place where a Pagan currently finds themselves to be. These may or may not be related genetically, since populations move, but many feel it is important to establish relations with those who have walked the same land and whose bones may be laid in it. This may be particularly important to Pagans who are living away from the lands of their own blood ancestors, particularly where there has been a history of colonialism or persecution of Indigenous peoples. These Pagans may feel that it is important to establish a respectful relationship with the Ancestors of place and to attempt to make reparations for injustices done in the past.

Ancestors of tradition or spirit are those who have contributed to a person's value system or worldview or have been important teachers or mentors. They may or may not be connected to Paganism or Druidry but have helped shape the individual into the person they are today.

Ancestors have different significance to different Pagan traditions and are probably most important within Druidry and Heathenism. For many, the term "worship" or even "venerate" would be too strong. Opinions vary greatly on whether individual Ancestors exist as personalities that can be communicated with or are able to intervene on behalf of their descendants. For some, "the Ancestors" are understood not as individuals but as a homogenous collective of the wisdom and experience of those who have lived before, which can be accessed at need through meditation. Some do not believe in the survival of consciousness after death at all but rather feel a connection to the Ancestors because they feel that they are part of a continuity of experience and consciousness from the dim past into the remote future, and they wish to acknowledge this in ritual.

Many Heathens and Druids do include the Ancestors in their ritual and spiritual practice, although they might not use the word "worship" but would rather describe it as seeking to build a connection and relationship with the Ancestors in order to remember them with gratitude or seek their wisdom, support, and guidance. Many keep an altar with images of recent Ancestors, at which they might make offerings of candles, incense, food, or drink. Others might seek to make connections with the Ancestors through meditation or journeying or by visiting sites that were important to them, such as stone circles or barrows in the United Kingdom. Many invite the Ancestors to be present at the beginning of a ceremony and honor them during the ritual. Reverence and gratitude to the Ancestors are particularly expressed by Druids and other Pagans at the festival of Samhain (which takes place around the time of Halloween). At this time, the dead (particularly any who have died during the past year) are remembered and thanked. Some might set a place at the table for them or make offerings for them in their ceremonies.

About the author

Jennifer Uzzell (PhD, Durham University) is the education and youth manager for the Pagan Federation and senior examiner in religious studies at both GCSE and A level with a major awarding body and was head of religious education at a number of schools for many years.

Suggestions for further readings

In this book
See also chapters 12 (Do Pagans have sacred sites?) and 24 (Is Druidry the Indigenous religion of Europe?).

Elsewhere
Hughes, Kristopher. *As the Last Leaf Falls: A Pagan's Perspective on Death, Dying and Bereavement.* Woodbury, MN: Llewellyn, 2020.

Brown, Nimue. *Druidry and the Ancestors: Finding Our Place in Our Own History.* Lanham, MD: Moon Books, 2012.

White, Larissa. *World Druidry: A Globalizing Path of Nature Spirituality.* Belmont, CA: privately published, 2021.

35
What are pagan ethics?

Michael York

Pagan ethics resist any Christian monopoly on fusing the supernatural/preternatural/co-natural with ethical standards of right and wrong but rather merge the two with different understandings. Although most (if not all) religions, including paganism, formulate a conception of what is considered ethical behavior, ethics and moral responsibility are human phenomena alone, even when they are personified as gods and goddesses.

The pagan ethos has a universal appeal and relevance to persons who do not necessarily identify as pagan—its implicit ethics are important for us all in coming to terms with what we value in life while being respectful of each and every person's right to a meaningful and fulfilling life. If religion serves to identify the valuable and meaningful, ethics tells us how to engage with whatever we hold to be of worth and significance. One could assert that to be pagan is to be natural, to be natural is to be human, to be human is to be natural, and to be natural is to be pagan. Fundamentally, pagan morality as an ethics of respect and honor is universal, but perhaps what distinguishes pagan ethics from other understandings is that they are part of a spirituality that eschews the notion of absolutes. Upholding the value of freedom modifies any kind of extreme attachment where, within a pagan milieu, all is considered divine. The very plurality of paganism, as a spiritual reflection of the cosmos' paradox, allows no single moral code as universally applicable. Individual choice and communal selection become imperative, but a pagan emphasis is concentrated on such goals as freedom, honor, and pleasure while sharing with others those of health, comfort, productivity, and generosity.

There are two branches to ethical inquiry: (1) the development of a code or set of principles by which to live and (2) metaethics—that is, ethical theory that investigates either how people ought to behave or what is the good life. While classical thinkers tended to assume that if one knows what the good life is, he or she will automatically live accordingly, we know that this is not necessarily the case and that the two questions concerning the good life and correct behavior are not inevitably the same. In general, metaethics is not a primary concern for most pagans, who instead seek to locate the guiding norms of life as it is lived and directly experienced. To understand the terms "good," "evil," "right," and "wrong," some of the greatest philosophers (such as Plato and Aristotle) in the classical world have addressed these fundamental issues and have, in fact, been pagan thinkers.

Western pagan developments tend to include both the ecological biases of deep pagans and the Wiccan Rede, as well as the "and it shall harm none" high-choice ethics versus the "do what you will" best-choice ethics. Consequently, for both pagan and Christian alike, evil is understood as the antithesis of good or value. In essence, especially from a pagan perspective, evil is a relative term defined by what it excludes or negates. However, like value itself, evil can be either instrumental (a means to an end) or intrinsic (naturally inherent). For the most part, paganism does not hold that something can be evil in and of itself. It is more likely understood as something that is *done* rather than as something that *is*, in any ontological sense. In Western paganism, there is a particular reluctance to pass judgment on what is evil because doing so might infringe on another person's or group's freedom.

There is nothing intrinsic to paganism that precludes values being understood as natural, objective, absolute, intuitive, emotional, or relative. Pagans will interpret them in different ways. A problem arises because both the naturalists and intuitionists consider that value, the ethical good, and the ethical right are objective. The former sees these concepts as factors that can be empirically proven, while the latter sees them as actual essences that can only be known through intuitive reflection. More usual, though, is that the good, the right, and the valuable are typically understood as human proposals that stand for emotions (emotivism) or attitudes (relativism). It denies that ethical and axial terms and judgments stand for anything objective. The only way out of this philosophical quagmire is to adopt a pagan pluralistic approach that recognizes values and ethics as comprising a range of objective realities and intuited essences as well as subjective preferences and emotions.

Because of their orientation to the living world as a sacred primus inter pares, most pagans wish to engage in root-based conversation with nature, nature persons, human beings, and a deity or deities. Consequently, pagans tend to stress the importance of locality—the here and now. In general, pagan ethics interconnect with global and environmental considerations and within such frameworks as deep ecology (see Taylor 2009), animistic relationships (see Harvey 2011), and/or the pursuit of enchantment. In summary, pagans aspire to live in the best way possible, a way that is liberated from intimidation, fear, greed, myopia, and the counterproductive as much as is possible.

Note: See explanation on the use of lowercase paganism rather than uppercase Paganism in chapter 31 (Is there salvation in paganism?).

About the author

Michael York, professor emeritus of cultural astronomy and astrology at Bath Spa University, England, has published *The Emerging Network* (1995), *The Divine versus the Asurian: An Interpretation of Indo-European Cult and Myth* (1995), and his *Paganism as a World Religion* series: *Pagan Theology* (2003), *Pagan Ethics* (2016), and *Pagan Mysticism* (2019).

Suggestions for further readings

In this book
See also chapters 8 (What is a Pagan worldview?) and 9 (Is there anything common to all Pagan religions?).

Elsewhere
Casey, John. *Pagan Virtue: An Essay in Ethics*. Oxford: Clarendon, 1991.

Harvey, Graham. *Contemporary Paganism: Religions of the Earth from Druids and Witches to Heathens and Ecofeminists*. New York: New York University Press, 2011.

Rountree, Kathryn. *Cosmopolitanism, Nationalism, and Modern Paganism*. New York: Palgrave Macmillan, 2017.

Taylor, Bron. *Dark Green Religion: Nature Spirituality and the Planetary Future*. Berkeley: University of California Press, 2009.

York, Michael. *Pagan Ethics: Paganism as a World Religion*. London: Springer, 2016.

ID # 36
How do Pagans interact with deities and spirits?

Jenny Butler

The way in which Pagans interact with deities and spirits depends on how they subjectively understand what deities and spirits are. Some Pagans believe that deities and spirits are independently existing beings that have endured since ancient times or even a time before human beings existed. Others hold that they are representations of forces of nature. For some Pagans, Jungian psychology is influential, and they engage with mythology through the archetypes and symbols in the stories.

For those who understand deities and spirits as literally existing personages or forces, there are many ways and means of interacting with them. One way is through ritual, whether alone or in a group. In many forms of Paganism, including Wicca and Druidry, a circle is cast at the beginning of the ritual. To "cast" the circle means to mark it out on the ground or to visualize a circle of light or "energy" in which the ritual participants are enclosed. Many types of Paganism involve the calling of the quarters, where each direction is associated with an element and its associated magical quality—typically, earth in the north, air in the east, fire in the south, and water in the west, though there are different configurations of the elements and directions depending on the tradition of magical practice. In some traditions, spirits called elementals or Guardians of the Watchtowers are associated with each direction, and they are invited in when calling the quarters, either verbally or through thought or visualization—for example, gnomes for earth, sylphs for air, salamanders for fire, and undines for water. This interaction can thus be symbolic and simultaneously understood as an actual physical entry of these beings into the magical circle to participate in the ritual.

In a similar way, Pagans understand that deities can be symbolically or literally present during a ritual. In festivals that have a connection with a particular deity—for example, the festival of Lughnasadh with the god Lugh—that deity might be invoked in the ritual. Pagans sometimes make a distinction between "invocation," or calling in, and "evocation," or calling forth, where the former is viewed negatively as a demanding action, like a "summoning." There are different ways of understanding the practice of invocation. The Wiccan ritual of "Drawing Down the Moon" is sometimes described as an invocation because it is understood that the priestess is directly drawing or bringing down the force or energy of the goddess into herself. Pagan interaction with deities and spirits can be akin to spiritual mediumship or "trance possession," where the spiritual being is understood to go into the practitioner and speak and act through them. Sometimes divination is practiced by Pagans to get advice about the future or messages from the spiritual world through using a human being as a "channel" of communication.

Pagans also visit places connected with deities and spirits with the aim of interacting with them there through ritual or meditation. Some Pagans would visit trees or other places in the landscapes associated with fairies and leave offerings such as food, drink, or flowers. Pagans might visit the beach to leave offerings or do rituals for sea gods like Manannán Mc Lir or Poseidon or the forest to venerate the goddess Artemis. Some Pagans venerate deities from different pantheons and cultural traditions, whereas other Pagans hold strong views that one should venerate the deities of one's own land and culture. There are many debates about cultural appropriation within Paganism.

Related to the idea of deities and spirits being connected to land is the idea of appropriate language. Some Pagans claim that there is a "language of the land" and that language itself can be spiritual. For example, the Irish or Gaelic language in Ireland and Celtic languages in other regions like Breton in Brittany or Welsh in Wales might be important for Pagans to use when communicating with deities and spirits of that land. In Pagan culture, people are encouraged to be respectful to deities and spirits and to communicate with them courteously.

Another way that Pagans communicate with the spiritual world is through dreams and visions. Practitioners interpret the symbols in their dreams or visions as messages or signs from deities and spirits. Meditation and visualization are used for the same purpose. Creative activities like painting, sculpting, and making ritual items such as masks or wands are also ways to connect with deities and spirits. Some Pagans create artwork or altars in their homes that are a personal and unique way for them to interact with deities and spirits. For Druids, for instance, poetry might be important for devotional purposes. There are practitioners who work magically with one or more specific spiritual beings on a regular basis, which means they do rituals and perhaps leave offerings for that being and think about that deity or spirit often in their daily lives. Pagans might ask for healing or for help from deities in solving problems or getting on well in life.

About the author

Jenny Butler is a lecturer in the Study of Religions Department at University College Cork and a principal investigator at UCC's Environmental Research Institute. She researches in the areas of contemporary Paganism in Ireland and esotericism and Irish history.

Suggestions for further readings

In this book

See also chapters 17 (What is the difference between hard and soft polytheism?), 30 (How do Pagans conceive of gods?), and 56 (How much of Paganism is based on cultural appropriation?).

Elsewhere

Magliocco, Sabina. *Neo-Pagan Sacred Art and Altars: Making Things Whole*. Folk Art and Artists Series. Jackson: University Press of Mississippi, 2002.

Rountree, Kathryn. *Embracing the Witch and the Goddess: Feminist Ritual-Makers in New Zealand*. London: Routledge, 2003.

York, Michael. *Pagan Theology: Paganism as a World Religion*. New York: New York University Press, 2003.

37
What does a Pagan minister do?

Holli S. Emore

As a very new religious movement, Paganism in its many forms has only in recent years recognized the need for individuals trained in spiritual support, including what is typically called pastoral care or ministry. The subject has often been the subject of debate among Pagan practitioners, many of whom see the idea of ministry as an encroachment upon their newfound spirituality by the religion they have left behind. Over time, however, more Pagans have come to acknowledge a gap between the traditional training of a ritual leader and lore teacher and that of a person serving additional needs in the community. These may include a more robust foundation in practical ethics, an understanding of group dynamics and leadership, knowledge of substance abuse and recovery processes, family support, and more.

Because most Pagans are not part of an organized group, a mainstream Western model of ministry such as that found in churches, synagogues, masjids, and so on is unlikely to reach more than a modest number. Pagan groups are usually small and underresourced, even if they have a desire for a dedicated minister. Anyone seeking to serve the spiritual needs of Pagans must therefore be able to do so without the promise of financial support, let alone full employment.

For these reasons—difficulty reaching independent, "solitary" Pagans and the poor prospects of remuneration—a Pagan minister will often connect with others in a variety of ways that may or may not appear to be related. Some are authors, workshop presenters, and conference or festival speakers. Many have created podcasts, websites, video channels, and social media content to broadcast messaging or teaching. The COVID pandemic pushed both individuals and groups to adapt to virtual live meetings, widening the accessibility of ritual and teaching far beyond the previous limits of geography and transportation. In most, if not all, of these channels, a ministry-minded person is able to engage in a bi- or multidirectional interchange and, in so doing (and with permission), develop a contacts list for further activities and announcements.

One exception to this description is Pagans who are trained to enter the chaplaincy profession. A number of Pagans serve as professional chaplains in medical-health facilities, rehab clinics, or other venues. It is likely that in the near future, such Pagan professionals will also be employed by prisons and the military. Chaplaincy is distinct from other kinds of ministry because the chaplain must be able and willing to serve anyone with a need, regardless of their religious affiliation (or lack of affiliation). A minister is usually seen as an extension of the particular spiritual path with which they identify, whereas a chaplain's personal beliefs do not define their work.

Training for ministry is often confused with the idea of ordination. The former is education; the latter is a formal process of vetting and then ceremonially endorsing someone as received and recognized as clergy in a particular faith body. Initiatory traditions such as witchcraft or Druidry may convey priesthood on individuals who complete training in that tradition, but such training rarely includes the broader education needed by a Pagan minister, as previously described. Some Pagan organizations have developed their own curriculum that candidates for clergy (by whatever title the group may use) must complete before they can be endorsed.

What should someone expect if they turn to a Pagan for ministerial support? First, the minister should have a history of ethical behavior, including respect and compassion for others. A Pagan minister should be an excellent listener, someone comfortable with facilitating reasoned discussion of theology, personal situations, or sensitive topics. The minister should be able to maintain confidentiality while also understanding the times when mandatory reporting to appropriate authorities is required. No minister, Pagan or otherwise, should require sexual favors as part of their service to others.

A minister is seen as a leader; strong leadership is at its best when the leader is actively developing the potential of others, encouraging their strengths, and sharing responsibility. When a minister is challenged with a need for which they are not qualified or that poses a conflict of interest, the minister should be prepared to provide referrals: to therapy, recovery resources, medical support, legal assistance, and basic human needs. No one should expect a Pagan minister to have answers to all questions, provide solutions to every dilemma, or insist on an inflexible doctrine.

The 2018 Pagan Engagement and Spiritual Support Survey found that most survey participants felt the need for some kind of group affiliation. A majority also seek spiritual support from Pagan leaders. Strong training for Pagan ministers is essential to meeting this need. Recognition of the service that Pagan ministers can provide can strengthen and enhance Pagan communities in the years to come.

About the author

Holli S. Emore, MDiv, is the executive director for Cherry Hill Seminary and chair of Interfaith Partners of South Carolina and was the first regional lead for Disaster Spiritual Care for the American Red Cross in South Carolina. She is the founding priestess of Temple Osireion, which has developed its tradition based on ancient Egyptian religions.

Suggestions for further readings

In this book

See also chapters 7 (Are most Pagans solitary practitioners?), 35 (What are pagan ethics?), and 52 (Is there antipathy between Pagans and Christians?).

Elsewhere

Emore, Holli S. *Constellated Ministry: A Guide for Those Serving Today's Pagans*. Sheffield: Equinox Publishing Ltd., 2021.

38
What does the pentacle symbol mean to Pagans?

Angela Puca

Paganism encompasses a wide range of spiritual paths, beliefs, and practices, often characterized by polytheistic worldviews and reverence for nature. Central to many Pagan traditions are various symbols that hold significant meaning and convey important spiritual concepts. One of the most widely recognized symbols in Paganism is the pentacle.

The pentacle is a five-pointed star enclosed within a circle, often referred to as a pentagram when the circle is absent. Throughout history, the pentacle has been adopted by various cultures and religious traditions, including Pythagorean and Neoplatonic philosophy, medieval Christian mysticism, and modern Western esotericism.

Within the context of contemporary Paganism, the pentacle is most commonly associated with Wicca, but the symbol is also used by other Pagan traditions and is often seen as a general emblem of Pagan spirituality.

The five points of the pentacle represent the five elements: earth, air, fire, water, and spirit, which are fundamental to many Pagan belief systems. These elements are seen as the building blocks of the universe and are often associated with various gods, goddesses, and other spiritual beings. The circle that surrounds the star symbolizes the interconnectedness of these elements and the cyclical nature of life, emphasizing the importance of balance and harmony within the natural world and the individual's spiritual journey.

In addition to its elemental associations, the pentacle also carries various other meanings within Paganism. For example, some practitioners interpret the five points as representing the stages of human life (birth, adolescence, adulthood, old age, and death) or the five senses (sight, hearing, taste, touch, and smell). The pentacle can also symbolize the unity of the microcosm (the individual or human realm) and the macrocosm (the divine or cosmic realm), reflecting the belief in the interconnectedness of all aspects of existence.

The pentacle is often used in Pagan rituals and ceremonies, particularly in Wiccan practice. It may be inscribed on ritual tools, such as the altar or chalice, or worn as a pendant or ring for protection and spiritual guidance. During rituals, the pentacle may be employed to invoke the elements, consecrate sacred space, or direct energy for healing, divination, or other magical purposes.

It is important to note that the pentacle, despite its association with Paganism and Wicca, has sometimes been mistakenly linked to Satanism and other forms of dark magic. The inverted pentacle, which some Satanic groups have appropriated as a symbol of defiance against conventional religious authority, is largely to blame for this misconception. However, within the Pagan context, the pentacle is generally viewed as a positive and life-affirming symbol that represents harmony, balance, and spiritual growth.

In conclusion, the pentacle is a multifaceted and meaningful symbol within Paganism, particularly in Wicca and other Western esoteric traditions. Its five-pointed star represents the elements of earth, air, fire, water, and spirit, as well as various other associations, such as the stages of human life and the unity of the microcosm and macrocosm. The circle that encloses the star symbolizes interconnectedness, balance, and the cyclical nature of existence. The pentacle is often used in Pagan rituals for invoking elemental energies, consecrating sacred space, and directing magical intent.

Despite the occasional misperception linking the pentacle to Satanism and dark magic, the symbol is widely recognized within Paganism as an emblem of harmony, balance, and spiritual growth. As a powerful and enduring symbol within the Pagan tradition, the pentacle serves to remind practitioners of their deep connection to the natural world, the divine, and the infinite potential for transformation and self-discovery.

About the author

Angela Puca, PhD (2021), is an independent religious studies scholar and university lecturer. She is bridging the gap between academia and the general public with her social media project Angela's Symposium, where she disseminates peer-reviewed research to a wide audience engagingly. She's the author of the forthcoming *Italian Witchcraft and Shamanism*, to be published by Brill, and coeditor of *Pagan Religions in Five Minutes* for Equinox Publishing Ltd.

Suggestions for further readings

In this book
See also chapters 43 (Is there a difference between magic and magick?) and 50 (Are Satanism and Paganism the same?).

Elsewhere
Dyrendal, A., J. R. Lewis, and J. A. Petersen. *The Invention of Satanism.* Oxford University Press, 2015.

Hanegraaff, Wouter J. *Dictionary of Gnosis and Western Esotericism.* Brill, 2006.

Harvey, Graham. *Listening People, Speaking Earth: Contemporary Paganism.* Kent Town, S. Aust.: Wakefield, 1997.

39
Do Pagans believe in reincarnation or life after death?

Jennifer Uzzell

The Pagan traditions do not have scriptures in the sense that they are commonly understood; neither do they have a centralized priesthood or authority. There is no dogma or unified set of beliefs that followers of any Pagan tradition are required to follow. It is, therefore, hardly surprising that there is no consensus of opinion regarding the greatest mystery that humanity has grappled with: "What happens to us when we die?"

Not all Pagans believe that personal consciousness survives death in any form. Many whose worldview is animist reject any concept of a soul and believe that a person ceases to exist at death. However, they may argue that the person continues to live on in their children and in the memories and impact they made on family and friends. They may also live on in their art, music, or writings and so continue to affect the world as Ancestors. Many who do not believe in personal survival of life after death would nonetheless say that nothing is lost at death, since energy cannot be created or destroyed—the energy contained within a person must go somewhere when they die. This could be in the form either of being reused in the natural world or of merging into the universe. As some believe that the universe itself is conscious, in this case, the experience and wisdom of the person are absorbed into the whole. The physical elements of the body are recycled and so live on in the great cycle of life.

Of those who do believe that consciousness survives death, many do not know or even speculate on what form this might take. Common ideas are that the soul or spirit is on a journey through which it learns and evolves. A soul might choose to journey alone or with a "soul group" and may choose whether and when to reincarnate.

Reincarnation, in its simplest form, is the belief that the soul leaves the body upon death and enters another physical body to be born again into this world. This is the most common afterlife belief in modern Paganism, although it is by no means universal. Often it is believed that reincarnation will occur after a period of rest when the person considers what they have learnt and where they need to go next. This period of rest often takes place in "the Otherworld" or "the Summerlands." This should not be confused with Christian ideas of heaven. It is not a place of reward or punishment but rather a world much like this in many ways, in which various spiritual beings, including Ancestors, might be encountered. Many Pagans believe that the Otherworld can be visited by the living through meditation or shamanic journey.

For most Pagans who believe in reincarnation, its purpose is to acquire knowledge and understanding through many lifetimes until a soul is ready to "move on" by merging into the divine or into the universe, which is the source of all being. Some Pagans may refer to this as the Goddess, the Divine, or the Source.

For Heathens, followers of the Anglo-Saxon or Norse pantheon of gods, the *Prose* and *Poetic Edda*s (medieval Icelandic writings that tell the stories of the gods) sometimes assume a role similar to but not identical with scripture in the so-called Abrahamic religions. The *Edda*s speak of the valiant dead joining the gods in Valhalla or one of the other divine houses, and so many Heathens hope for this honor when they die. This is an uncommon perspective among Paganisms, in general, where the gods do not seem to feature greatly in afterlife beliefs.

Some Pagans reject the usual Western belief in a body/soul split, arguing that a person is made up not just of these two elements but of multiple "souls" that might have different destinations after death, with one part being reincarnated while another part goes on to join the Ancestors in the Otherworld or stays on earth to watch over descendants.

For Pagans who do believe in life after death, what unites them is not a particular set of beliefs or a shared understanding of what is meant by "the soul" but rather an expectation that death is part of a journey toward greater wisdom and understanding, in which personal choice plays a significant role. Speculation about life after death, however, is less important than how one lives in this life—with honor and integrity and as part of an interconnected web of relationships with people, animals, and spirits, regardless of whatever might come next.

About the author

Jennifer Uzzell (PhD, Durham University) is the education and youth manager for the Pagan Federation and senior examiner in religious studies at both GCSE and A level with a major awarding body and was head of religious education at a number of schools for many years.

Suggestions for further readings

In this book
See also chapters 31 (Is there salvation in paganism?) and 34 (Do Pagans worship Ancestors?).

Elsewhere
Hughes, Kristopher. *As the Last Leaf Falls: A Pagan's Perspective on Death, Dying and Bereavement*. Woodbury, MN: Llewellyn, 2020.

Starhawk and M. Macha NightMare. *The Pagan Book of Living and Dying*. San Francisco: Harper One, 2005.

La Fae, Phoenix. *What Is Remembered Lives*. Woodbury, MN: Llewellyn, 2019.

40
Do Pagans practice ritual sex?

Angela Puca

Ritual sex, also known as sacred sexuality or sex magick, has long been a subject of fascination and speculation within religious studies and popular culture. This topic has often been associated with Paganism, a diverse and complex religious phenomenon that encompasses a wide range of beliefs, practices, and traditions. To address the question of whether Pagans practice ritual sex, it is essential to first understand the nuances and complexities of Paganism and its various manifestations.

The concept of ritual sex in relation to contemporary Paganism is linked to ancient fertility cults and religious practices that aimed to promote fertility and abundance by symbolically uniting the masculine and feminine principles through sexual acts. Some scholars argue that these ancient practices have influenced the development of contemporary Paganism, particularly in the context of Western esoteric traditions such as Wicca and ceremonial magick. However, it is important to note that the historical evidence for the widespread practice of ritual sex in ancient Pagan societies is limited and often subject to debate.

In the contemporary Pagan context, the question of whether Pagans practice ritual sex is more nuanced and dependent on individual beliefs and practices. As previously noted, "Paganism" is an umbrella term that encompasses a wide variety of traditions and spiritual paths, each with its own unique approach to sexuality and sacredness. Consequently, it is difficult to make generalized statements about the role of ritual sex within Paganism as a whole.

That being said, it is important to recognize that some Pagan traditions do incorporate elements of sacred sexuality or sex magick into their beliefs and practices. One notable example is Wicca, where the Great Rite is a ritual that symbolically enacts the sexual union of the God and Goddess, often represented by a chalice and an athame (a ritual knife). While the Great Rite is typically performed symbolically, some Wiccan practitioners may choose to engage in actual sexual activity as part of the ritual, usually within the context of a committed and consensual relationship.

However, it is crucial to emphasize that the practice of ritual sex within Wicca and other Pagan traditions is generally a private and personal choice, not a mandatory or universally accepted aspect of the faith. Moreover, the majority of Pagan rituals and ceremonies do not involve sexual activity, focusing instead on other aspects of spirituality, such as reverence for nature, meditation, and personal growth.

In conclusion, the question of whether Pagans practice ritual sex is complex and multifaceted, reflecting the diversity and adaptability of Paganism as a religious phenomenon. While some Pagan traditions, such as Wicca, may incorporate elements of sacred sexuality or sex magick into their beliefs and practices, the extent to which these practices are embraced by individual practitioners varies widely. As a result, it is essential to approach this topic with nuance and sensitivity, recognizing that Paganism is a highly individualized and diverse spiritual path that cannot be reduced to simplistic stereotypes or generalizations.

About the author

Angela Puca, PhD (2021), is an independent religious studies scholar and university lecturer. She is bridging the gap between academia and the general public with her social media project Angela's Symposium, where she disseminates peer-reviewed research to a wide audience engagingly. She's the author of the forthcoming *Italian Witchcraft and Shamanism*, to be published by Brill, and coeditor of *Pagan Religions in Five Minutes* for Equinox Publishing Ltd.

Suggestions for further readings

In this book
See also chapters 11 (How do Pagans view nature and the environment?) and 43 (Is there a difference between magic and magick?).

Elsewhere
Hutton, Ronald. *The Pagan Religions of the Ancient British Isles: Their Nature and Legacy*. Hoboken, NJ: Blackwell, 2010.

Pearson, Joanne. *A Popular Dictionary of Paganism*. Abingdon: Routledge, 2002.

Purkiss, Diane. *The Witch in History: Early Modern and Twentieth-Century Representations*. Abingdon: Routledge, 1996.

41
Are astrology and the tarot part of Paganism?

Francesca Po

Astrology and the tarot are two separate practices that can be exclusive from one another and separate from formal Pagan affiliation. However, certain Pagan traditions may have their own formal astrological system and uses for astrology. Both practices can also complement Paganism in general and are often found within the Pagan milieu because of this.

There are three major systems of formal astrology used in the world today: (1) Western or Greco-Roman, used primarily in North America, Europe, Australia, and New Zealand; (2) Vedic, used primarily in South Asia; and (3) Chinese, used primarily in East Asia. There are also countless others from minority traditions. In general, while each system is used in its own particular way, with its own rules and procedures, astrology is a practice that has existed since the beginning of human civilization, where practitioners make observations of correlations between the arrangements of cosmic bodies (e.g., moon, sun, planets, asteroids, stars) and events on Earth.

In the West, while astrology has had an ambivalent relationship with the church since it came to power around the fourth century, it was a common practice among Christians and non-Christians alike until the Enlightenment, when it lost support from intellectuals. Since the Enlightenment, astrology has been marginalized and considered "Pagan" from the perspective of the scientific community and many major religious traditions, though it is not a necessary practice of all Pagans.

During the nineteenth century, astrology encountered a revival within spiritualist and esoteric movements, and in the 1930s, it gained even further popularity with the introduction of "sun astrology" or "horoscopes," as disseminated by print publications and media outlets. During the 1960s, its use was expanded alongside depth psychology and, in popular use, within the so-called New Age movement. Today, interest in astrology continues to rise. Between 2016 and 2017, YouTube videos on astrology experienced a 62 percent increase in views, Facebook posts on astrology experienced a 116 percent increase in views, and Twitter posts experienced a 600 percent increase in engagement. While astrology now enjoys a comfortable place in popular culture, it remains marginal, if not illegitimate, in the scientific community and some major religious traditions and continues to be recognized as a Pagan practice in this context.

It is notable that in South Asia, astrology comfortably coexists with science and religion—everyday people, highly educated professionals, and scientists consult astrology in their daily lives. In fact, it is so pervasive in South Asian culture that one would not start a business without consulting an astrologer. From this perspective, there is no common association between astrology and Paganism; this notion is primarily a Western one.

While there are countless tarot, oracle, and divination card decks on the market today, there is one deck that is most commonly associated with the practice: the Smith-Waite-Rider Tarot. While some scholars trace the origins of this deck as early as ninth-century China, and some practitioners argue its origins as early as antiquity, the general academic consensus is that the precursors of the Smith-Waite-Rider Tarot originated in the common deck of playing cards: it was a deck of illustrated cards used for entertainment by fifteenth-century European, particularly Italian, aristocracy. The imagery drew directly from both popular as well as official expressions of Roman Catholicism.

The first spiritual uses of the tarot can be traced to early eighteenth-century France, at which point it began to draw connections to symbolism from antiquity, immediately followed by its delegitimization by the church and its association with Paganism. As a result, it fell out of popularity, until a revival during the late nineteenth-century spiritualist and esoteric movements. It was then that the deck that we know today, complete with its artwork, interpretations, and use, became established: illustrated by Pamela Colman Smith, written and designed by Arthur Edward Waite (both members of the Hermetic Order of the Golden Dawn), and published by William Rider and Son in 1909. During the 1960s, the Smith-Waite-Rider Tarot deck gained popularity within the New Age movement, alongside the emergence of new tarot, oracle, and divination decks. Since the 1960s, the use of the tarot has been for either or both entertainment as well as spiritual purposes. Pagans may use the tarot as a complementary practice. However, considering its history, it has its own origins separate from any one Pagan tradition.

Both astrology and the tarot have their own unique uses and histories but have been associated with Paganism, minority traditions, and alternative spirituality because of their proscribed status from the perspective of the church.

About the author

Francesca Po, DPhil (University of Oxford), is a scholar of religion and nonreligion with research interests in religious change, alternative spirituality, and contemporary witchcraft. She is a member of the Board of Directors at the Metta Center for Nonviolence, is an executive leader in spiritual formation for the Salesians of Don Bosco, served in the US Peace Corps in Kazakhstan, and is the author-editor of *Religion and Peace* (2022) and *The Study of Ministry* (2019).

Suggestions for further readings

In this book
See also chapters 8 (What is a Pagan worldview?) and 32 (Can a person have Pagan beliefs without being Pagan?).

Elsewhere
Campion, Nicholas. *Astrology and Cosmology in the World's Religions*. New York: New York University Press, 2012.

Campion, Nicholas. *Astrology and Popular Religion in the Modern West: Prophecy, Cosmology, and the New Age Movement*. New York: Routledge, 2012.

Decker, Ronald, and Michael Dummett. *The History of the Occult Tarot*. London: Duckworth, 2002.

Farley, Helen. *A Cultural History of Tarot: From Entertainment to Esotericism*. London: I. B. Tauris, 2009.

Place, Robert. *The Tarot: History, Symbolism, and Divination*. New York: Penguin, 2005.

42
How do Pagans view magic?

Karina Oliveira Bezerra

In the way I approach it, the whole of reality is seen in contemporary Paganism as magic. Since its beginning and through its transformations, and notwithstanding its great diversity, contemporary Paganism also has magic as its glue.

Marcel Mauss contributed a way to think about magic—while exposing the exchanges between magic and religion—through the analysis of the place of speech, magical rites and their association with malefaction, the role of the agent, and the places of practices. His theory of magic shows it as an art of changing, inclined toward the concrete, embedded in and serving ordinary life, which seeks to know nature. In this sense, we could define Paganism as a magical religion. However, when we talk about magic and religion as separate, opposed concepts, we fall into a dualism created in Christian theology where religion is synonymous with Christianity, or with something "true," and magic is seen as demonic worship—that is, as a false religion. In Paganism these concepts are interconnected; there is no separation. The same can be said regarding science. Nonetheless, with the ambition to analyze all forms of culture under the "magic-religion-science" triad, the term "magic" serves as a dustbin, a controversial category of exclusion entirely dependent on normative distinctions between "true" and "false" religion, as well as between "true" and "false" science. The three terms were reified, perceived as sui generis universal categories to promote the hegemonic agendas (or as Paul Veyne would say, programs of truth) of the dominant parties in modern Western culture.

While acknowledging the stability of magical beliefs, Keith Thomas (1971), following the solidified thesis of disenchantment of the world among sociologists and historians, notes that these beliefs were now the object of disdain by educated people, unlike in the medieval and early modern periods, when they were taken seriously by the intelligentsia. What happened, though, according to Hanegraaff (2003), was a secularization of religion and magic, which allowed for the continuation of both to be practiced in a mechanistic world, where participation (a tendency of the mind that views experiences as facts that don't permit or require further explanation) is undermined by the instrumental causality (the tendency to explain events as a result of material causation). In previous historical periods, these two narratives coexisted without major problems, and for contemporary Pagans, this is also the case. The experience of a deeper unity with the surrounding world is represented in hierophany, achieved in rites and through magic, represented in myths, and observed in nature and in the human mind as well as culture, of which science is a part.

The importance of magic in Paganism is such that it encompasses reality itself. It is not just about doing spells. As a religion, Paganism sees reality beyond the physical. Even more so, it sees physical and corporeal reality as overvalued. In *The Magic of Reality*, biologist Richard Dawkins's criticism of religion as well as disregard of the supernatural in favor of physical reality (which is where magic would be found) can be seen as the secularized magical dimension. Paganism, then, can be viewed as a religion that dialogues with science. Dawkins explains in his book the "facts" of the real world—such as people, animals, night, day, seasons, sun, rainbows, and earthquakes—as understood through the methods of science. He shows that reality is magic in the sense that it is good to be alive. Since Paganism is an orthopraxic religion, what differentiates Pagans from other people who observe the sun is the honoring, the ritual that is performed for the star, not a supernatural idea about it or its physical reality. However, for Pagans, it is magic that creates life. As imagination and creativity are celebrated in Paganism, in the rite, imagination and reality are no longer opposed.

In Greek antiquity, philosophers criticized myths for depending on two truths, since they always mixed truth and falsity. The distinction between reality and fiction was not clear. However, their reasoning never denied the mythological, which was part of the Hellenic reality. In modernity, historical science is regarded as the "true" truth, while myth would be the "imaginary" truth. Yet modernity has also brought back poetic language in a Romantic way, shaping a new reality and giving birth to contemporary Paganism and other new movements. Secularized society and Romanticism produced changes that generated new religious movements (NRMs), the counterculture and New Age movements, and new esoterism or secularized esoterism. Paganism is an NRM with counterculture and New Age aspects. However, with the emergence of new codes for what can be viewed as truth—as traditions invented and fused with others—this reality has been changing.

Contemporary Paganism has given magic an ethical framework and, with that, a better reputation, along with democratized high magic and elevated popular magic. It simultaneously approaches and distances itself from occultism and the New Age by democratizing magic and ideally not profiting off it. Magic is viewed as an inexhaustible and renewable resource in Paganism. Pagans create and re-create their rites; there is no dogma as such. In each cycle, as with the seasons of nature, everything is renewed. Spring will always come, but it will always be different, and myths and rites are told and reinvented for each new generation through magic, in the creation of a new reality.

About the author
Karina Oliveira Bezerra is a historian with a PhD in religious studies.

Suggestions for further readings

In this book
See also chapters 8 (What is a Pagan worldview?) and 43 (Is there a difference between magic and magick?).

Elsewhere
Hanegraaff, Wouter J. *New Age Religion and Western Culture: Esotericism in the Mirror of Secular Thought*. New York: State University of New York Press, 1998.

Magliocco, Sabina. "New Age and Neopagan Magic." In *The Cambridge History of Magic and Witchcraft in the West: From Antiquity to the Present*, edited by D. Collins, SJ, 635–664. Cambridge: Cambridge University Press, 2015.

Puca, Angela. "Magic." In *Contested Concepts in the Study of Religion*, edited by A. Whitehead and G. D. Chryssides, 63–68. London: Bloomsbury, 2022.

43
Is there a difference between magic and magick?

Caroline Tully

The difference between "magic" and "magick" goes beyond a simple matter of spelling. The word "magic" derives from the ancient Greek μαγεία (*mageia*), which referred to the ritual activity of Persian priests, or *magoi*, and which was so different from Greek religion that the Greeks categorized it as "magic." Over subsequent centuries, there have been many definitions of "magic." As Wouter Hanegraaff says, "One will therefore receive very different answers depending on the historical period in question and the personal agendas of whoever is being asked" (2016, 403). Hanegraaff observes that magic has been defined as: "ancient wisdom," "worship of demons," "natural philosophy and science," "occult philosophy," "pseudo-science," "an enchanted worldview," and "psychology" (399). Although "magic" is understood differently within diverse historical and cultural contexts, in general, it can be described as the use of ritualized words and actions, usually outside the sanction of official religions, that attract supernatural beings to influence events.

Prominent British magician Samuel Liddell MacGregor Mathers (1854–1918) defined magic as "the Science of the Control of the Secret forces of Nature" (von Worms 1900, viii). His student Aleister Crowley (1875–1947) used the spelling "magick," which he defined as "the Science and Art of causing Change to occur in conformity with Will" (1929, xvi). John Symonds claimed that Crowley added the "k" to magick in order to signify the sexual nature of his brand of magic; the "k" stands for the Greek word κτεις (*kteis*, meaning "vulva"; lit. "comb") (1989, ix). However, Crowley's definition is inextricably linked to his concept of the True Will, which was developed from *Liber AL vel Legis* or *The Book of the Law*, an inspired text that he wrote in Egypt in 1904 while in a state of mystic trance. The central message of *The Book of the Law* and the religion of Thelema (the Greek θελημα, "will") that Crowley founded based on the book is, "Do what thou wilt shall be the whole of the Law. Love is the law, Love Under Will" (1975, 18–19, 25). Doing "what thou wilt" means discovering and enacting your true purpose on earth, which equals your True Will (Crowley 1929, xviii). The will is the self-motivated drive and the force exerted to perform your True Will. In Crowley's definition, magick is the exercise of willpower—not in the service of any impulsive whim or wish but through alignment with the individual's True Will. Change caused in accordance with your will is magick, while change that is in conflict with or irrelevant to your will is not. The magickal will can be applied through both ritual and nonritual means. Crowleyan magick can be performed in the traditional manner—that is, with the help of stronger or differently specialized supernatural beings such as gods, angels, spirits, or demons attracted or compelled through ritual—or it can be accomplished through effective physical acts that are not traditionally "magical" (Crowley 1929, xvii).

In the popular view, "magic" is a power that can be summoned instantaneously and that overrides physical reality; however, the idea that magic can dominate the natural world—that it is, in fact, an *overriding tool*—is not the case with Crowley's interpretation of magick. In his definition, you cannot impose your will onto something that is not part of your greater True Will, and the attempt to do so results in dissatisfaction and unhappiness (Crowley 1929, xix).

Crowley proposes that through the realization that you are part of (rather than separate from) the universe, you can successfully direct the forces within the universe in the pursuit of causing change in conformity with your will. He cautions, however, that a practitioner can only attract the forces that they are naturally suited to wield, again suggesting that magick cannot override nature. Crowley further defines magick as "the Science of understanding oneself and one's conditions. It is the Art of applying that understanding in action" (1929, xxiv).

Crowley's definition of magic has been modified in the work of subsequent magical theorists: Dion Fortune described magic as "the art of changing consciousness according to Will," Gerald Gardner explained magic as "attempting to cause the physically unusual," while for Anton LaVey, magic is "the change in situations or events in accordance with one's will, which would, using normally acceptable methods, be unchangeable" (Bogdan 2012, 11). While these authors dropped the "k," according to Bernd-Christian Otto, magick with a "k" is the predominant spelling in contemporary practitioner literature and signifies "the reality and efficacy of 'magic' despite living in modern secular or post-secular environments—in which this efficacy is usually denied by the dominant cultural and scientific discourses" (2023, n1).

About the author

Caroline Tully is an archaeologist at the University of Melbourne, Australia. Her research interests include religion and ritual in the Aegean Bronze Age, reception of the ancient world, and contemporary Paganisms. She is the author of *The Cultic Life of Trees in the Prehistoric Aegean, Levant, Egypt and Cyprus* (Peeters 2018) and many academic and popular articles.

Suggestions for further readings

In this book
See also chapters 38 (What does the pentacle symbol mean to Pagans?), 40 (Do Pagans practice ritual sex?), and 42 (How do Pagans view magic?).

Elsewhere
Asprem, Egil. "Magic Naturalized? Negotiating Science and Occult Experience in Aleister Crowley's Scientific Illuminism." *Aries: Journal for the Study of Western Esotericism* 8(2) (2008): 139–165.

Bogdan, Henrik. "Introduction: Modern Western Magic." *Aries: Journal for the Study of Western Esotericism* 12(1) (2012): 1–16.

Crowley, Aleister. *Magick in Theory and Practice*. Subscriber ed. Paris: Lecram, 1929.

Crowley, Aleister. *The Book of the Law*. Quebec: 93 Publishing, 1975.

Hanegraaff, Wouter. "Magic." In *The Cambridge Handbook of Western Mysticism and Esotericism*, edited by Glenn Alexander Magee, 393–404. Cambridge: Cambridge University Press, 2016.

Otto, Bernd-Christian. "Conjuring Planetary Spirits in the Twenty-First Century: Textual-Ritual Entanglements in Contemporary Magic(k)." *Entangled Religions* 14(3) (2023): n.p.

Otto, Bernd-Christian. "Historicising 'Western Learned Magic.'" *Aries: Journal for the Study of Western Esotericism* 16 (2016): 161–240.

Symonds, John. *The King of the Shadow Realm: Aleister Crowley; His Life and Magic*. London: Duckworth, 1989.

Tully, Caroline. "Walk like an Egyptian: Egypt as Authority in Aleister Crowley's Reception of *The Book of the Law*." *Pomegranate: The International Journal of Pagan Studies* 12(1) (2010): 20–47.

von Worms, Abraham. *The Book of the Sacred Magic of Abramelin the Mage*. Translated by S. L. MacGregor Mathers. London: John M. Watkins, 1900.

44
What is Chaos Magic?

Isis Mrugalla-Kalmbacher

Chaos Magic is a contemporary style of magic inspiring both emic and etic observers to describe it in superlatives. Scholar of religion Bernd-Christian Otto considered it "ultimately individualistic" due to its claimed liberalism and the spectacular combinations of "paradigms," meaning belief systems (2019, 759). In the view of actors in the magic scene I interviewed, it is the "most punk rock version of contemporary magic," referring to its attitude toward authority. Finally, the artist and occultist Austin Osman Spare's popular narrative and nonattachment technique of "neither-neither" (which describes a state of mind where reality options are considered to be both true and untrue at the same time) made historian Dave Evans declare Chaos Magic to be indescribable in the scholarly sense (Evans 2007, 351).

Despite Evans's pessimistic assessment, scholars have continually been trying to describe Chaos Magic (see, for example, Woodman 2003). Following this lead, I will outline some basic characteristics of both the idea within popular religion and the practice within Pagan networks.

As an idea in popular religion, the term "Chaos Magic" first appeared in *Liber Null and Psychonaut* by James Peter Carroll, if only belatedly in the second edition (1981). The name links this kind of magic with the mathematical and physical chaos theory, although in the discourse, Chaos Magic rather covers philosophical ideas about chaos. The British cliques revolving around Carroll (the London Stoke Newington Sorcerers) and his companion Ray Sherwin (Yorkshire Circle of the Weird, later Circle of Chaos) are most frequently referred to as the origin of Chaos Magic. However, in this formative era, most of the fluid elements of Chaos Magic—like "Paradigm Shift," techniques of ecstasy, and occult silliness—were not *invented* but newly *combined*. Chaos Magic has its roots in the nineteenth-century occult revival, the 1950s chaos movement and Discordianism, the 1960s psychedelic movement, the 70s punk rock movement, and the shamanism hype introduced by Mircea Eliade's popular book on shamanism, as well as the so-called New Age movement.

The early British Chaos Magicians (like many contemporary actors) were masters of eclecticism, with a mélange of then popular ideas, including the psychoanalytical reinvention of "sigilization" and the ZOS KIA system by Spare as well as core concepts of Daoism, Eliade's presentation of "shamanism," and James Gleick's presentation of chaos theory. Other bits and pieces were collected from Gnosticism, Thelema, mathematical information technology and coding, quantum physics, and further European and Asian philosophy. This list cannot ever be completed, since Chaos Magic intentionally lacks any authority and is, as a literary idea, an ongoing open-source project.

Many practitioners call Chaos Magic not a magical system but rather a "bare-bones" mechanism or "metatechnique" rejecting any fixed truth. Based on Carroll's writing, Chaos Magicians are expected to question all dogmata—both spiritual and nonspiritual truths. Belief (or in Chaos jargon, "paradigm") should only be used as a tool during a ritual and discarded (or "shifted") afterward. Shifting between paradigms should prevent the Chaos Magician from following any preset spiritual path and, instead, develop their own style of magic, stay mentally flexible, and make use of the randomness of the (chaotic) universe.

The aim of a (Chaos) magical act is widely understood as the realization (or "manifestation") of the magician's will. This is broadly viewed as the result of a placebo effect. To succeed and manifest a will, the magician must convince themselves that the pursued goal is perfectly logical and realistic or even already achieved. Here, the "psychic censor" becomes crucial. The concept was derived from the Austrian psychoanalyst Sigmund Freud. Chaos Magicians often visualize it as a filter that restricts human perception to the "consensus reality," filtering out all impossible (magical) options. Magic, on the other hand, is considered to manifest itself when a (magical) thought or perception surpasses the practitioner's censor and enters the subconscious mind (or "quantum mind"). Hence for magical success, the restrictive and hindering censor must be switched off, persuaded, or drowned. This is considered to be possible by using belief systems as tools and entering altered states of mind, like trance or ecstasy (in Chaos jargon, "gnosis").

Often, the technique called "Paradigm Shift" gets related to Ray Sherwin's writings on "Result Magic," where a heavy focus lies on the successful outcome of magical practice. This earned Chaos Magic the reputation of being "hardcore" pragmatic. Result Magic leads some practitioners to consider Chaos Magic to be a scientific operation.

In practice, Chaos Magic can be viewed as a Pagan network itself and a (fluid and changing) style of magic. It is performed *not only* for

Result Magic but also for any other purpose, like celebrations, community strengthening, gaining insights, exploration, self-development, and so on. Against its narrative, ethnographic research shows that practical Chaos Magic is not random but the outcome of shared work and experience exchanged within closely knit online and offline networks. It usually combines certain aesthetics, identities, popular belief systems, and explanations of magic.

The largest official Chaos Magic group is the discrete society Illuminates of Thanateros (IOT), which was founded in the early 1980s as a British-German cooperation. This magical order, also called "the Pact," operates internationally, with most of its participants living in German-speaking Europe and Great Britain and with further official branches in the Americas.

During the last fifty years, the style of Chaos Magic has reflected the political and social causes of each generation. In the first wave (1970–1980s), Chaos Magic was "blacker than black," following the hype of the left-hand path and punk rock and focusing on liberation. With the second wave (1990s), it lost its former stiffness and used popular culture ("occulture"), including science fiction lore, in ritual work. The third wave (2000s), increasingly adapted to urban and digital realities, was described as "postmodern magic." The current fourth wave is sometimes called the internet wave, for it became established and diversified online. Today, questions about (new ways of) survival in the given social and climatic context seem to be most relevant. Nevertheless, traits of all waves can still be found within the network, since generations overlap and pass on elements of their practice.

About the author

Isis Mrugalla-Kalmbacher is a junior researcher of studies of religion at the University of Tübingen in Germany. She researches contemporary practices of occultism and group magic in Europe.

Suggestions for further readings

In this book
See also chapters 66 (How do Pagans use fiction and film?) and 67 (Is Paganism make-believe?).

Elsewhere
Evans, Dave. *The History of British Magic after Crowley*. Harpenden: Hidden, 2007.

Otto, Bernd-Christian. "The Illuminates of Thanateros and the Institutionalisation of Religious Individualisation." In *Religious Individualisation: Historical Dimensions and Comparative Perspectives*, edited by Martin Fuchs, Antje Linkenbach, Martin Mulsow, Bernd-Christian Otto, Rahul Bjørn Parson, and Jörg Rüpke, 759–796. Berlin: De Gruyter, 2019.

Woodman, Justin. "Modernity, Selfhood, and the Demonic: Anthropological Perspectives on 'Chaos Magick' in the United Kingdom." PhD diss., University of London, 2003.

45
Do Pagans use the internet for their religion?

Franz Winter

At first sight, a modern Pagan movement with its claim to provide intimate contact with nature and a focus on an allegedly ancient, pre-Christian wisdom would not be the first natural candidate when it comes to the use of one of the latest inventions in the history of humankind: the internet. A closer look at the interrelation between religions and the internet, though, soon shows that this firsthand assumption is simply not true. On the contrary, Pagan movements seem to have an intense interest in the internet, and many modern movements take advantage of the new medium on various levels. This is not just a contemporary phenomenon but goes back to the early days of the internet: even before the establishment of the World Wide Web, Pagans were already active in its forerunners, such as the so-called Usenet with its often rather complex and sometimes confusing newsgroups. Nowadays, many Pagan movements use the internet actively not only for self-presentation, but they offer online rituals and actively engage with their members within the multifaceted possibilities of the new medium. The obvious importance of the new medium and the active engagement even led to the emergence of the designation "Technopagans" for those fully delving into the new medium.

Historically, this intimate connection is closely related to the origin of the internet itself. The emergence (or sometimes reestablishment) of many presently active Pagan movements took place in specific cultural contexts in the second half of the twentieth century, commonly referred to as countercultural movements (predominantly in the United States but also beyond). And this aligns with the religious context that became relevant in the early days of the internet: the initial references to religion and religious topics are mostly to alternative, nonmainstream contexts, such as esoteric or occult writers and their publications. All that began to float freely in the digital sphere as soon as it was accessible. Mainstream religions were rather hesitant and sometimes waited quite a time to jump on the bandwagon of the new medium, which left the new space open and largely free for others. In addition, there was a strong tendency to declare the new virtual sphere a yet unexplored but higher, even sacred world. Michael Benedikt (1992, 1), an early theoretician of the World Wide Web, pointed to the limitlessness of "a new universe, a parallel universe created and sustained by the world's computers and communication lines," and introduced a religious vision of the evolving "cyberspace" (as it was then called) that is open to anyone.

On the formal level, another characteristic of the Pagan movements is important: they simply do not have a relevant history of religious buildings specified for ritual purposes. In fact, the most commonly used mode to meet and practice rituals among Pagans would be in a "coven," which can be located anywhere and does not need any specific architecture or the like. Therefore, the introduction of "cybercovens" into the newly created virtual sphere was just a small step. Lisa McSherry, foundress and "high priestess" of the cybercoven "JaguarMoon" (https://www.jaguarmoon.org/), who is one of the pioneering figures in regard to the use of the internet for Pagan purposes but also an early theoretician, characterized the "cyberspace" as "a technological doorway to the astral plane" that provides the unique opportunity to "literally stand in a place between the worlds, one with heightened potential to be as sacred as any circle cast upon the ground" (McSherry 2002, 5). Therefore, the use of the internet is closely connected to the common organizational structure. Pagan movements tend to be loosely structured, and participation is floating. The possibilities of the internet provide unique opportunities to connect across vast distances and even might be of help to provide a feeling of connection in a higher realm.

The free use of the internet, though, also brings some problems. One major issue is the contested arena of authenticity, which is extremely important and closely related to the self-understanding and self-perception of Pagan movements as restorations of ancient traditions. The internet makes this even more complicated, as anyone could pose his claims on a website without any responsibility to prove them. Consequently, the variety of Pagan movements on the internet is immense and multifaceted.

About the author

Franz Winter is professor and chair at the Department of Religious Studies at the University of Graz in Austria. His research interests include, among other areas, Asian religions, the history of Western esotericism, contemporary religion and spirituality culture, and new religious movements (in

Europe, the United States, and Asia). A recent major publication is the *Handbook of East Asian New Religious Movements*, coedited with Lukas Pokorny and published with Brill, which was awarded an accolade in the category of social sciences at the International Convention of Asia Scholars in 2019.

Suggestions for further readings

In this book
See also chapters 25 (What are Technopagans?), 64 (Do Pagans avoid technology?), and 65 (What is WitchTok?).

Elsewhere
Benedikt, Michael, ed. Introduction to *Cyberspace: First Steps*, 1–26. Cambridge: MIT Press, 1992.

Cowan, Douglas. *Cyberhenge: Modern Pagans on the Internet*. New York: Routledge, 2005.

Lewis, James R. "Becoming a Virtual Pagan: 'Conversion' or Identity Construction?" *Pomegranate: The International Journal of Pagan Studies* 16(1) (2014): 24–34.

Berger, Helen A., and Douglas Ezzy. "The Internet as Virtual Spiritual Community. Teen Witches in the United States and Australia." In *Religion Online: Finding Faith on the Internet*, edited by Lorne L. Dawson and Douglas Cowan, 175–188. New York: Routledge, 2004.

McSherry, Lisa. *The Virtual Pagan: Exploring Wicca and Paganism through the Internet*. Boston: Frederick S. Weiser, 2002.

46
Is Christmas a pagan festival?

Alessandro Testa

No, Christmas is neither a Pagan nor a pagan festival. It is one of the most heartfeltly celebrated Christian festivities across the planet and an essential component in the Christian liturgical year, forming part of a festive system that begins with Advent in December and ends with Epiphany in January. It is, moreover, also interconnected with more mundane end-of-the-year celebrations—and not only in the some 35,000 Christian denominations around the world. Just like Carnival and Halloween, in spite of the multitude of late modern declensions it can take and takes, it is an immediately recognizable festival. It is one that developed in the forms that are today considered typical and canonical relatively recently—in the past three centuries. As anthropologist Claude Lévi-Strauss wrote in a now classical study (1952), "Noël est essentiellement une fête moderne et cela malgré la multitude de ses caractères archaïsants" (Christmas is essentially a modern festivity and that in spite of a multitude of archaising aspects).

"Christmas Day" varies between Western and Eastern Christianities. In most of the West, it is celebrated on the twenty-fifth of December, which marks the beginning of the core festive period of twelve days between Christmas and Epiphany (an interval known in the English-speaking world as Twelvetide). This period is one of the most important festive periods—if not *the* most important one—in the entire West.

That said, if Christmas per se is, as its name suggests, quintessentially Christian, this does not mean that all its constitutional and symbolic components originated during Christian times. Some are actually older and can therefore be considered "pagan" (in the broad sense of originating from or being associated with pre-Christian religions and rituals). The first of such elements I would like to recall is the visit of the Magi to Bethlehem. The Gospel of Matthew tells about these powerful and wise men from the East, who were, presumably, magicians. This is an interesting and literally "pagan" element at the core of Christmas (intended here as the tale of the Nativity of Jesus), for there was logically no Christianity or Christendom when Jesus was born—Jesus himself was a Jew, born and raised in a Jewish context.

As with many other Christian traditions, it is, however, their origins (historical or mythical) that carry a higher quotient of paganness. In fact, well-known are the hypotheses according to which the origin and day of Christmas were influenced by or meant to substitute previous pagan end-of-year festivals such as the Roman Saturnalia and/or the solstice celebration for the syncretistic god of the sun, the Dies Natalis Solis Invicti (the Birth Day of the Invincible Sun). Although there is a general acknowledgment of the importance of these celebrations in the development of what would later become the historical Christmas—celebrations that for a time indeed even coexisted with early Christianity during the late antiquity—no consensus exists among scholars as to the actual extent of this influence and how exactly this amalgamation happened.

Strictly connected with the idea of the birth or return of the sun is the omnipresent and quintessentially Christmas element of light, which associates this festival with many other winter solstice celebrations around the world. Candles and lamps (and today electric lights) are traditional decorative and symbolic elements of Christmas. These, too, are well-documented in pre-Christian traditions, not only in Europe.

Lights decorate what has grown to become the universal symbol of this festivity: the Christmas tree. Originally a German Protestant tradition that developed during the early modern period, the iconic Christmas tree we know today crystallized in its current form, just like many other things Christmassy, in the nineteenth century. It has, in time, acquired the status of an enchanted object. The magic of the Christmas tree comes, on the one hand, from its being the umpteenth manifestation of the widespread pre- and not-Christian symbolism and cult of trees. (This does not mean that a historical filiation exists between these cults and Christmas; there is, however, no denying the universal but culturally specific symbolic importance of trees in human cultures and religions.) On the other hand, the magic of the Christmas tree also lies in its representing an enchanted sort of *coincidentia oppositorum*, being an element of nature in utmost cultural settings (squares and hearths), cut but alive, (ever)green in winter, and illuminated in the darkest days of the year.

Christmas lights and trees come together with another widespread symbol of the festival: Santa Klaus, or Christkindl, or the other national avatars of the gift-bringer (Père Noël, Babbo Natale, Saint Nicholas, Ježíšek, etc.). Santa Klaus, for instance, is often associated with "paganism," sometimes explicitly and in striking forms, as when he joins together with the demonic Krampus of the Alpine areas or the less scary devils accompanying him during Advent in Western Slavic Catholic countries. One such association with paganism was analyzed by Claude Lévi-Strauss (1952, 1579), who writes, in a beautiful page about the French Père Noël,

> He wears a scarlet suit: he is a king. . . . He is a venerable old man; hence he embodies the benevolence and the authority of the elders. . . . This supernatural being is immutable, everlastingly fixed in his form and defined by an exclusive function and by an eternal return. More god-like than human-like, he is the object of worship by the children, and just like a god he rewards the good and reprimands the evil. He is the divinity of a specific age class of our society. (My translation)

About the author

Alessandro Testa is associate professor at the Faculty of Social Sciences, Charles University, Prague. He specializes in the history of religions, social anthropology, and the ethnology of Europe. His latest publications include *Rituality and Social (Dis)Order* (2020), *Politics of Religion* (with Tobias Köllner, 2021), and *Ritualising Cultural Heritage and Re-Enchanting Rituals in Europe* (2023).

Suggestions for further readings

In this book
See also chapters 13 (Do all Pagans follow the same festivals?), 47 (Is Carnival a pagan festival?), and 48 (Are Halloween and Easter pagan festivals?).

Elsewhere
Larsen, Timothy, ed. *The Oxford Handbook of Christmas*. Oxford: Oxford University Press, 2020.

Lévi-Strauss, Claude. "Le Père Noël supplicié." *Les Temps Modernes* 77 (1952): 1572–1590.

47
Is Carnival a pagan festival?

Alessandro Testa

Carnival has existed in Europe as a recognizable festival for nearly one thousand years (and for about four hundred years in former overseas European colonies, especially Latin America). However, while it doubtlessly emerged as a festival connected with Lent (the period of fasting preceding Easter) and therefore as a festival within the Christian liturgical and festive calendar, it likewise doubtlessly fed upon previously existing ritual celebrations that were spread all around Europe but especially in the Latin areas that had known Roman rule in ancient times. Unsurprisingly, the earliest documented Carnival is that of Rome itself (twelfth century).

Several festivals of Roman religion provided, in fact, the symbolic and performative elements as well as the ritual blueprint for the historical Carnival that would emerge during the High Middle Ages and develop during the following centuries. For instance, the influence of ancient Roman festivals such as the Saturnalia, the Lupercalia, and the archaic tradition of Mamurius Veturius—which were variously characterized by masquerades, ritual inversions, excesses, scapegoat-like rituals, and end-of-year celebrations—is rather manifest in Carnival. The church was fully aware of this and for centuries condemned first the aforementioned historical predecessors of Carnival, then Carnival itself.

The reprimands, condemnations, and often episodes of veritable repressions perpetrated by the Christian clergy against Carnival and carnivalesque culture in general are well-documented. They are scattered across the entire history of this popular European tradition, although several exceptions are known in which the festivity was actually tolerated or even endorsed by the clergy and the Christian rulers. Generally, however, clerics and literate pious men during medieval and early modern times explicitly considered Carnival a "pagan" or, alternatively, Satanic or diabolical tradition: describing the Florentine Carnival in the fifteenth century, Girolamo Savonarola wrote that "oggi tutto quello che facevano anticamente li pagani facciamo noi" (today we are doing everything as the pagans did), and already in the fourteenth century, canons from Sorbonne University were discussing the pagan nature of Carnival and similar festivities. Later observers abound: in the seventeenth century, a certain Heinrich Lubbert from Lübeck published a book titled *The Devil of Carnival* (*Faaß-nachts-Teuffel*), whereas a few decades before, the French erudite Jean Savaron had published a *Treatise against the Masks* (*Traité contre les masques*) in which, centuries before Sir James Frazer, the origins of Carnival were explicitly traced back to the Roman Lupercalia, whose spirit, according to Savaron, was still alive in the Carnival of his time. Earlier and later examples of premodern erudite interpretations of Carnival as pagan could be easily multiplied.

Nevertheless, at the popular level, this characterization seems to have been mostly unknown by the European popular classes that so eagerly indulged in Carnival celebrations throughout the centuries. Well nested within the liturgical calendar and in line with the prescription of the church concerning the Lent and Easter periods (fasting could not but be preceded by binging, one might say), Carnival survived as a spectacularly vivacious and changing phenomenon up until the nineteenth century, when it started to lose its vitality and capacity to adapt to modernity. A long phase of fatigue set in, lasting for part of the modern times and until the ritual and folkloric revival of the contemporary era. Lately, Carnival has proven to be an extremely adaptable and changing phenomenon, and today, a few decades after that cultural climate of both revivalism and counterculture that emerged during and after the 1960s, Carnival is again a vital festival, in its European as well as globalized forms.

Moreover, in recent times, the "pagan" characterization of Carnival has been often brought forth explicitly as a form of cultural reappropriation of the liberating force of public rituality, and that at the expense of the millennium-long hegemony of the church over all things ritual and festive. This has been happening for some time now, in spite of the fact that the greatest majority of contemporary Carnivals are either not old enough to be direct descendants of pre-Christian rituals or actually the products of recent reenactment and revival. In these cases, the "paganness" of Carnival should be considered symbolic and discursive rather than historical and factual. In fact, not everything that is transgressive, "Dionysiac," and excessive and that makes use of animal disguises and other masking practices is pagan, especially not when such traditions were invented in the 1960s, 1970s, or 1980s to accommodate the then (and still) growing neo-Romantic European taste for the primitive, the mysterious, the transgressive, and the magical.

About the author

Alessandro Testa is associate professor at the Faculty of Social Sciences, Charles University, Prague. He specializes in the history of religions, social anthropology, and the ethnology of Europe. His latest publications include *Rituality and Social (Dis)Order* (2020), *Politics of Religion* (with Tobias Köllner, 2021), and *Ritualising Cultural Heritage and Re-Enchanting Rituals in Europe* (2023).

Suggestions for further readings

In this book

See also chapters 46 (Is Christmas a pagan festival?) and 48 (Are Halloween and Easter pagan festivals?).

Elsewhere

Testa, Alessandro. *Rituality and Social (Dis)Order: The Historical Anthropology of Popular Carnival in Europe*. New York: Routledge, 2020.

Testa, Alessandro. *Ritualising Cultural Heritage and Re-Enchanting Rituals in Europe*. Durham: Carolina Academic Press, 2023.

Glotz, Samuël. "Les dénominations du Carnaval." *Tradition Wallonne* 4 (1987): 371–489.

48
Are Halloween and Easter pagan festivals?

Jenny Butler

Halloween and Easter are two festivals in the Christian calendar that have some elements of the celebrations and observances relating to traditions predating Christianity. The name Halloween is derived from "All Hallows Eve," which was the name in Britain for the evening before All Saints' Day. By the late eighteenth century, this had been shortened to "Hallows Eve" and then "Halloween." This is why the spelling sometimes has the apostrophe—Hallowe'en—as it represents the word "evening."

All Saints' Day falls on November 1 and is when Roman Catholics venerate the saints who are believed to be in heaven. All Souls' Day, also called the Commemoration of All the Faithful Departed, falls on November 2 as a day of remembrance of the dead and specifically as a time when Catholics pray for the souls in purgatory, where it is believed sinners rid themselves of sin by making amends or reparations so that they can continue onward to heaven; prayers are understood to help them on their way.

Some have argued that the placement of All Saints on November 1 was an attempt by Christians to supplant the already-existing festival associated with the dead. However, the history is not so clear-cut. All Saints was observed by Christians at different times and in accordance with different calendars in different places. November 1 was made the official date by the Catholic Church in the eighth century when Pope Gregory III dedicated a chapel inside St Peter's Basilica in Rome to all the saints and all Christian martyrs. All Souls' Day has been observed on November 2 since the eleventh century and was instituted by Abbot Odile, a Benedictine monk, as a day to pray for deceased monks of his order, but it broadened out to the custom of a mass being said for all souls in purgatory.

As with other Christian festivals and holy days, elements of older "pagan" practices mixed in with the Christian observances. In Celtic regions, the festival of Samhain marked the start of winter. The form of the festival name, *samain* in Old Irish, is thought to mean "summer's end" because, for the Celts, this may have been the end of the "bright half" of the year and the entrance into the "dark half." In modern Ireland, Samhain is the Irish-language name both for the festival of Halloween and for the month of November.

Since there are no extant accounts from the Celtic peoples themselves and few reliable sources that tell of their festivals and celebrations, we are reliant on archaeological and literary sources in attempting to glean some information about pre-Christian times. The literary sources are medieval manuscripts written by Christian monks. Also, we are trying to learn about pagan cultures through a Christian lens, and this is problematic. However, the medieval sources do inform us of some things about religious and cultural observances prior to Christianity.

The Early Irish literature, for instance, contains many references to Samhain and its connection with the otherworldly. It is said that at this time, *síd* mounds of the otherworldly people, the *aos sí*, open up. The word *sí* was translated as the English word "fairies," which, along with many kinds of spiritual beings, are associated with Samhain. There are mythical connections between Samhain and feasts and gatherings at sites such as the Hill of Tara and Tlachtga, also known as the Hill of Ward, both located in County Meath in Ireland. In the folklore of the Celtic regions, Samhain is connected to magic and the spiritual world. Since medieval times, there have been documented traditions of Samhain being a festival associated with the dead. However, we cannot know how pre-Christian peoples understood this festival or how they might have celebrated it.

Although All Saints and All Souls didn't derive from a pagan festival, some still argue that they were moved close to the observance of Samhain so that they would give Christian significance to the older festival. However, in folk customs of the Celtic regions, there are aspects that do not seem easily reconcilable with the Christian belief system or doctrines, such as the concept of the "returning dead" (deceased relatives coming back to their homes) and the traditions of guising (or disguising oneself in costumes), making scary faces on jack-o'-lanterns, and practicing divination on Halloween night. Therefore, we can say that Halloween is a festival of many layers, Christian and pagan.

As with All Hallow's Eve, rather than replacing a specific pre-Christian festival, Easter is the result of older traditions mixed in and continued as part of the Christian celebration. It is a movable feast because it is determined by the lunar calendar. In 325 CE, the Council of Nicaea, which was the first Christian church council, made the decision that Easter would fall on the first Sunday after the paschal full moon, meaning the full moon that appears on or after the spring or vernal equinox, which is in March in the Gregorian calendar.

On the spring equinox, there is balance between light and darkness; winter is ending, and there are signs of new plant growth, buds on the trees, and animals being born. Celebrations of fertility and new life at springtime were absorbed into Christianity, including customs connected to bunnies, chicks, and eggs, all symbols of new life. Various cultures have traditions of decorating eggshells or hard-boiled eggs—such as the decorated eggs on Nowruz, the Persian New Year, which falls on the spring equinox. Rabbits and hares abound in European folklore, and in Western Germany, there is the Osterhase ("Easter hare"), an egg-laying hare for whom children would make nests so she could lay her colored eggs in them. In the 1700s, when Germans emigrated to Pennsylvania and other parts of New England, this morphed into the American tradition of the Easter Bunny, depicted as a rabbit who wears clothes and hides chocolate eggs for children to hunt for.

Older understandings fused with Christian significance and symbols. In medieval times, eggs were forbidden for Christians during Lent, a period of forty days of fasting, prayer, and almsgiving (charity) that begins on Ash Wednesday and ends on Holy Thursday, and thus would have been a treat once Easter Sunday came. In Germanic languages, the name for the spring festival was *Ostern*, perhaps from Ēastre (or Eostre), a name for the Anglo-Saxon fertility goddess, thought to come from an older word meaning "dawn" or "east." Easter in English derives from this name, as does the contemporary Pagan name for the spring equinox, Ostara.

There is a complex relationship between Christianity and Indigenous and traditional religious and cultural practices around the world whereby some older aspects were incorporated into the Christian tradition. While festivals such as Easter are undeniably Christian, they have a pagan flavor.

About the author

Jenny Butler is a lecturer in the Study of Religions Department at University College Cork and a principal investigator at UCC's Environmental Research Institute. She researches in the areas of contemporary Paganism in Ireland and esotericism and Irish history.

Suggestions for further readings

In this book
See also chapters 46 (Is Christmas a pagan festival?) and 47 (Is Carnival a pagan festival?).

Elsewhere

Butler, Jenny. "Neo-Pagan Celebrations of Samhain." In *Treat or Trick? Halloween in a Globalising World*, edited by Malcolm Foley and Hugh O'Donnell, 67–82. Cambridge: Cambridge Scholars, 2009.

Dowden, Ken. *European Paganism: The Realities of Cult from Antiquity to the Middle Ages*. Abingdon: Routledge, 2008.

Hutton, Ronald. *Stations of the Sun: A History of the Ritual Year in Britain*. Oxford: Oxford University Press, 2006.

Lee, A. D. *Pagans and Christians in Late Antiquity: A Sourcebook*. Abingdon: Routledge, 2016.

Santino, Jack. *The Hallowed Eve: Dimensions of Culture in a Calendar Festival in Northern Ireland*. Lexington: University Press of Kentucky, 2009.

Pagan discussions

49
Do Pagans practice sacrifice?

Jefferson Calico

The practice of sacrifice is a persistent and important part of the repertoire of Pagan devotion. It has also been frequently misrepresented in popular culture in ways that trivialize or sensationalize the practice to scandalize non-Pagan audiences.

Many Pagans may prefer the language of offerings to that of sacrifice, but both terms refer to the practice of giving something to a divine being. That could be as simple as pouring a sip of a drink as a libation or burning a stick of incense or as complex as choreographing grand public ceremonies. Offerings are gestures of reverence and love, cries of need, acts of communication, symbols of goodwill and reconciliation. Contemporary Pagan offerings are motivated by a variety of values and beliefs. Polytheist Pagans might make sacrifices during a *blót* to the Gods whom they venerate. Animist-oriented Pagans may give offerings to the spirits of place in natural settings. Ancestor-oriented Pagans might honor departed family members and important kin by leaving food on an ancestral altar.

The practice of sacrifice emerges from the Pagan experience that the world is full of powerful divine beings. Cultivating relationships with these beings contributes to our wholeness and thriving. The basic intention of offerings is to build, maintain, and at times, mend relationships between humans and the many divine beings that exist around us. Pagans seek to relate to these beings in ways that acknowledge their distinctive personhoods and build mutually beneficial connections. Through sacrifice, Pagans participate in a reciprocal exchange, a gifting cycle that binds the Gods and their human worshippers together in a flow of life-energy and blessing.

Pagans use ritual to consecrate the offering, setting it apart for its divine recipients. For Heathens, almost every act of worship involves a ritual of sacrifice called *blót*. The most common offering given in a Heathen *blót* consists of mead or honey wine consecrated with the prayers and intentions of the worshippers and poured out as a libation offering to the Gods.

A ritual of sacrifice may involve symbolically damaging or destroying the offering. This sacralizes the object, rendering it useless in the material world but valuable and available in the spirit world. Just as the libation offering is poured out onto the ground, other sacrifices might be burned, bent, broken, or buried. Offerings might also be eaten—consumed and enjoyed by the religious community in feasts or social rites of solidarity, celebration, and communion. Pagans often make noncorporeal offerings. They sacrifice their time by devoting it to the Gods in unpaid religious duties, give their money by donating to causes that correspond to a deity's sphere of interest or power, and offer their labor in acts of service and volunteerism for others in their communities.

Of course, the practice of sacrifice has changed over time and has been significantly influenced by the context of the contemporary Western world. Worshippers might make use of digital technology to give virtual offerings, like lighting an electronic candle in an online shrine. Pagans increasingly bring an ecological awareness to the practice of sacrifice. Environmentally sound and sustainable offerings might use biodegradable containers instead of plastic, avoid polluting and littering, and carefully consider how offerings impact the health of local fauna, flora, and soil.

Popular culture continues to spread damaging misconceptions about Pagan religiosity with sensationalized depictions of human and animal sacrifice. While human sacrifice may have taken place in the ancient past, all contemporary Pagans reject this practice as abhorrent. In part because of their own experiences of marginalization, Pagan communities are mindful of the importance of protecting and expanding human rights. Indeed, this extends to the value of other-than-human life. Almost all Pagans consider animal sacrifice to be both unethical and unnecessary given contemporary moral concerns about animal cruelty and consent and the postagrarian context of most modern people's lives. Only a minority of reconstructionist Pagans (primarily small groups of Heathens) have begun to practice animal sacrifice on a limited basis in private settings for very significant religious and communal occasions. These Pagan communities are usually directly connected to local farming economies and are committed to the ethical treatment of farm-raised animals in their religious practice.

Giving offerings is an important dimension of religious life for many, though not all, Pagans. It provides a sense of connection to spiritual beings. It enacts and engages Pagan practitioners in supernatural ecologies of reciprocal relationships with more-than-human beings. Over the years, Pagans have creatively and carefully constructed systems of ritual for these acts of offering and sacrifice.

About the author

Jefferson Calico is a teacher, writer, and religious studies scholar working in the Appalachian region of the upper South. His book *Being Viking: Heathenism in Contemporary America* was published by Equinox Publishing Ltd. in 2018.

Suggestions for further readings

In this book
See also chapters 22 (What is Heathenry?) and 51 (What explains the enduring bias against Pagans?).

Elsewhere
Calico, Jefferson. "Animal Sacrifice and the Blót." In *Being Viking: Heathenism in Contemporary America*, 307–333. Sheffield: Equinox Publishing Ltd., 2018.

Keltoi, Ocean. "How Does Worshiping the Gods Work?" April 28, 2022. YouTube video. https://youtu.be/D2pCGqtfxZc.

The Oak Witch. "How to Dispose of Spells and Offerings in an Eco-Friendly Way." May 20, 2021. YouTube Video. https://youtu.be/HREFfvJacaI.

50
Are Satanism and Paganism the same?

Ethan Doyle White

The simple answer is that Satanism and Paganism are different things. Modern religious Satanism encompasses diverse worldviews that center on Satan, also known as the Devil or Lucifer, as a figure worthy of worship or at least considerable respect. Modern Paganism represents a family of new religions that are actively inspired by the pre-Christian traditions of Europe, West Asia, and North Africa that were rendered extinct by the rise of Christianity and related Abrahamic religions. Conceptually, the two things are quite separate.

The situation is nevertheless more complex than first appearance may suggest. Both modern Paganism and modern Satanism arose within Christian-majority societies, and both set themselves against this dominant religious framework by embracing imagery and identities that have historically been regarded as antithetical to Christianity. Modern Pagans place great value on the religious traditions that Christianity (as well as Judaism and Islam) supplanted; most practitioners embrace the term "Pagan" as a self-designation—the very term that Christians since at least the fourth century have used to pejoratively categorize all those not worshipping their God of Abraham. Satanists, similarly, embrace a figure who has long been regarded as the great bogeyman of Christian theology. Openly setting themselves in conceptual opposition to Christianity is something that modern Satanists and modern Pagans share but is not something found among many other new religions, such as Scientology, Theosophy, or Rastafari.

Moreover, both Satanists and certain types of modern Pagans are heavily inspired by the historical imagery surrounding witchcraft. In early modern Christendom, witches were regarded as "devil worshippers," and thus witchcraft imagery has obviously influenced modern Satanism. However, the single largest modern Pagan religion, Wicca, also draws heavily on this same witchcraft imagery. Early Wiccans such as Gerald Gardner and Doreen Valiente believed that those persecuted as witches in early modern Europe were actually adherents of a pre-Christian religion, one that had survived into the mid-twentieth century as Wicca. Thus, Wiccans typically call themselves "witches"; their celebrations, Sabbats, are influenced by the historical witches' sabbaths; and their Horned God owes a great deal to early modern depictions of a horned devil.

It is almost certainly because Wiccans have drawn so heavily on the iconography of Satanic witchcraft that outsiders to the religion have often confused Satanism and Wicca. This conflation of the two has proved particularly strong among certain Christians, and here it has probably been influenced by the belief that all non-Christian religions are ultimately created by the Devil. For some Christians, therefore (of varied denominations), it does not matter if Wiccans do not literally believe they are worshipping Satan, for the Devil is the one manipulating them away from the "true religion" of Christ.

Confusion between Satanists and Wiccans, as well as confusion between Satanists and other modern Pagans and occultists, can have serious repercussions. The 1980s and 1990s saw what was often called the Satanic Panic or Satanic ritual abuse hysteria, whereby a coalition of Christians, feminists, therapists, and elements of law enforcement promoted the idea that there was an international conspiracy of Satanists engaged in the widespread ritual abuse and murder of children. Further investigation found that the claims were largely baseless, but various people were prosecuted or otherwise fell under suspicion in the United States and Britain. Given this context, it is unsurprising that many Wiccans and other Pagans have been very keen to insist that they are not Satanists, often doing so by maintaining that they do not even believe in the Devil, let alone worship him.

Demarcating modern Paganism and modern Satanism as wholly distinct phenomena is further confused by a small number of groups that straddle the two categories. From at least the 1990s, some self-described witches have maintained that the Horned God is, in fact, Lucifer—an entity they claim is real, benevolent, and distinct from Christian ideas of Satan. Another crossover is the Order of Nine Angles, a politically extreme group that emerged in 1970s England and claims to venerate the deities of pre-Christian Britain while calling its practices "Traditional Satanism." Also confusing matters is the Temple of Set, established in California in 1975; although a breakaway from the Church of Satan, its founders claimed that Satan's real identity was Set, a deity from ancient Egypt, thus moving them into modern Pagan territory. Perhaps the best way of understanding these sorts of Satanist/Pagan crossovers is by regarding modern Paganism and modern Satanism not as unified movements but as diffuse milieus with some areas of overlap.

About the author

Ethan Doyle White has a PhD in medieval history and archaeology from University College London and has written extensively on modern Paganism and related forms of esotericism. His publications include *Wicca: History, Belief, and Community in Modern Pagan Witchcraft* (Sussex Academic Press, 2016), *Pagans: The Visual Culture of Pagan Myths, Legends and Rituals* (Thames and Hudson, 2023), and *The New Witches of the West: Tradition, Liberation, and Power* (Cambridge University Press, 2024).

Suggestions for further readings

In this book
See also chapters 38 (What does the pentacle symbol mean to Pagans?), 51 (What explains the enduring bias against Pagans?), and 52 (Is there antipathy between Pagans and Christians?).

Elsewhere
Doyle White, Ethan. "Between the Devil and the Old Gods: Exploring the Intersection between the Pagan and Satanic Milieus." *Alternative Spirituality and Religion Review* 9(2) (2018): 141–164.

Introvigne, Massimo. *Satanism: A Social History.* Leiden: Brill, 2016.

51
What explains the enduring bias against Pagans?

Franz Winter

As a matter of fact, Pagans always were and still are looked upon suspiciously by mainstream society, as they are conceived as part of a separate realm within the religious landscape. The movements themselves emphasize this specific positioning with the use of, at least traditionally, highly contested terminology, such as "witch" or "wizard," which they try to redefine in contrast to commonly accepted patterns. A firsthand explanation for this bias would be that the early Christian application and usage of the terminology was related to an active refusal of those designated with it, often leading to severe suppression. This is beyond doubt a major aspect of the general framing of the term "pagan" itself, starting with the use of the designation as introduced and fostered by Christian authors and officials as early as the fifth century. Evidently, it was used in regard to non-Christians in order to establish boundaries with a clear overtone of inferiority (a comparable phenomenon would be the history of the Latin term *secta*, "sect," which came to be used in a negative sense after its application in the Christian context). These pejorative connotations remained a defining characteristic of the word until the early modern attempts to revive the alleged pagan traditions by redefining its meaning. It is only in the twentieth century that people designated themselves as "Pagans" in a positive way.

Taken from this angle, Pagan movements make up part of the wide arena of alternative religious movements that emerged through the centuries and were always portrayed as the "other" by the mainstream religion—namely, Christianity.

Some traits of the movements themselves fostered this image. This starts with the self-perception as a revived and refurbished version of pre-Christian traditions (with a variety of differing frames). Another aspect would be the importance of secrecy within Pagan movements. Although nowadays, most of their teachings are well-known and practically accessible to everyone (as most of the material is widely circulated on the internet), the self-perception of many Pagan movements has a lot to do with the idea of having access to a hitherto unknown, hidden knowledge that is guarded by a few and revealed to those who are participating. Naturally, this provokes suspicion.

Another obvious reason for the general societal bias was (and probably still is, although to a lesser degree) the gender issue: Pagan movements were highly attractive for women, as they provided the opportunity to form communities outside the commonly accepted frames of traditional religions. Some of these movements even stressed this specific trait by asserting a special role for female sexuality that is introduced as a key to accessing higher realms of knowledge and wisdom. From the outside, this led to a general overrating of the role of sexuality in these movements that was a further *signum* of their problematic position in the societal context. Other features commonly ascribed to Pagans are also still widely used and make up part of a very long negative description history, such as their assumed penchant for ritual sacrifices (which include, as a worst-case scenario, human beings) and their relations to "devil worship" linking them to marginalized areas such as Satanism and occultism.

When taking into consideration the above-mentioned instances, a probable answer to the question of why Pagan movements were often treated suspiciously is their role as a kind of counterprogram to commonly accepted societal and cultural patterns. Every movement that breaks with these rules faces a counterreaction. A lot has changed in recent times, though, and this, quite naturally, has a lot to do with the changing religious landscape and the obvious loss of influence when it comes to the Christian tradition. However, there is still a certain reluctance to accept Pagans fully. This is also obvious with new negative frames that became more valid in the perception of Pagan movements just recently. One important aspect in this regard would be a highly critical evaluation of their political stance, often pointing to their alleged fondness for right-wing, even fascist content. Although there is a specific history of references to Pagan traditions that is intrinsically related to the history, for instance, of National Socialism in Germany, this should not be regarded as a general characteristic of—or used as an easy knock-down argument against—those movements.

About the author

Franz Winter is professor and chair at the Department of Religious Studies at the University of Graz in Austria. His research interests include, among other areas, Asian religions, the history of Western esotericism, contemporary religion and spirituality culture, and new religious movements (in Europe, the United States, and Asia). A recent major publication is the *Handbook of East Asian New Religious Movements*, coedited with Lukas Pokorny and published with Brill, which was awarded an accolade in the category of social sciences at the International Convention of Asia Scholars in 2019.

Suggestions for further readings

In this book
See also chapters 49 (Do Pagans practice sacrifice?), 50 (Are Satanism and Paganism the same?), and 52 (Is there antipathy between Pagans and Christians?).

Elsewhere
Clunies Ross, Margaret, ed. *The Pre-Christian Religions of the North: Research and Reception*. 2 vols. Turnhout: Brepols, 2018.

Hoff Kraemer, Christine. "Gender and Sexuality in Contemporary Paganism." *Religion Compass* 6(8) (2012): 390–401.

Overend, Joanne, ed. *Nature Religion Today: Paganism in the Modern World*. Edinburgh: Edinburgh University Press, 1998.

von Schnurbein, Stefanie. *Norse Revival: Transformations of Germanic Neopaganism*. Boston: Brill, 2016.

52
Is there antipathy between Pagans and Christians?

Denise Cush

Yes, no, and all positions in between and beyond. Sadly, individuals and communities tend to define their identities in part by who they are not—the "others," who represent a threat, whether to physical safety or cherished values and ideas. In European history, Pagans and Christians have often been this "other."

Christianity began when the pagan Roman Empire was the resented colonial power in Judea. Jesus himself, normally tolerant of diversity in a way radical for his context (women, Samaritans, Roman centurions), when teaching about prayer, advised his followers not to "babble as the pagans do." In the first Christian centuries, Christians were persecuted and put to death for refusing to worship the emperor as a god. Once Christianity became accepted, later centuries saw missions to convert rulers and peoples from paganism to Christianity. Today, some Christians view Pagans as worshippers of false deities, immoral, predatory on young people, or evil/Satanic. They may be quick to believe false claims, such as when Pagans were accused of "Satanic ritual abuse" of children in the 1980s and 1990s.

Some contemporary Pagans define themselves in contrast to Christianity, viewed as dogmatic, patriarchal, sexist, intolerant of diversity in relation to gender and sexuality, negative about the physical body, and responsible for environmental disasters. They may point out the prevalence of child sexual abuse by Christian clergy. Reviewing history, Pagans may resent missionary, political, and military activity that imposed Christianity on pagan societies in Europe between the fourth and fourteenth centuries. They may identify with the witches and heretics put to death when Christians were in power in medieval and early modern times, though most now accept that these were unlikely to have been pagans.

However, when fears, stereotypes, and prejudices are put aside, more positive relationships are possible. "Pagan" and "Christian" are not monolithic categories, and there is much diversity within each tradition. Some Christians and some Pagans can find friendship and more in common than initially expected. Some Christians appreciate the divine (and human) feminine, the physical body, positive attitudes toward LGBTQ+ people, and openness to plurality and have a deep concern for the planet. There are Pagans who extend their pluralism to include Christians and can appreciate Christian commitment to the love of all (including enemies), forgiveness, and social action. There has been more mutual influence over the centuries than is sometimes admitted. Some Christian customs and rituals have elements deriving from the pagan contexts into which the religion was introduced, as well as Jewish antecedents. Some Pagan practice, especially within Wicca and Druidry, has been influenced by Christian precedents. There is a tendency to consider that the pagan came first (for example, with seasonal festivals), and there may have been deliberate policy on the part of Christian authorities to "baptize" existing celebrations in various contexts. However, as Wicca, Druidry, and the cycle of eight festivals are, at least in their contemporary forms, of twentieth-century origin, some rituals and customs may well be Pagan adaptations of Christian ones.

Recently, there have been more interfaith encounters between Christians and Pagans, as Pagan religions become more acknowledged and accepted. In 2010, the Druid Network was accepted as a registered charity. The Pagan Federation joined the Religious Education Council of England and Wales in 2011. Both were accepted as members of the Inter Faith Network UK in 2015, but many local interfaith groups had Pagan members well before this date. In the 1980s, Christian and Pagan women stood together at the Greenham Common protests. Although in the 1990s, shared worship was controversial, Philip Shallcrass organized the pioneering Avebury Gorsedd in 1993, and other shared ceremonies have taken place since, including at the "Conversation" between Pagans and Christians at Imbolc/Candlemas 2014 (see Cush 2015).

Christians and Pagans can agree on the importance of a deeper spiritual dimension to life, the recognition of religious experience (however interpreted), the power of ritual to enable transformation, and the power of myth to explore and express meaning. They can celebrate very similar festivals. They can both recognize that ethics are not essentially about rules but about love and compassion and increasingly agree on the importance of connecting with nature. They cooperate in working for environmental causes, as well as other practical concerns of equality and social justice.

Of course, Christian and Pagan worldviews are not identical, and there are many important theological differences in relation to fundamental ideas such as the nature of the divine and its relationship with the natural world, life after death, human nature, or the need (or lack of need) for salvation. Nevertheless, they can choose to become friends; discuss areas of agreement and disagreement honestly; share rituals; live together in peace, love, and understanding; and work together toward a better future for people and the planet.

About the author

Denise Cush is professor emerita in religion and education at Bath Spa University. She acted as "impartial chair" for an interfaith "Conversation" between Pagans and Christians in 2014. Her 2018 wedding included blessings from Christian, Buddhist, and Hindu celebrants as well as a handfasting conducted by a priestess from the Glastonbury Goddess Temple and a nonreligious civil ceremony.

Suggestions for further readings

In this book
See also chapters 51 (What explains the enduring bias against Pagans?) and 53 (Can a Christian also be a Pagan?).

Elsewhere
Cush, Denise, ed. *Celebrating Planet Earth, a Pagan/Christian Conversation: First Steps in Interfaith Dialogue*. Winchester: Moon Books, 2015.

Pearson, Joanne. *Wicca and the Christian Heritage: Ritual, Sex and Magic*. Abingdon: Routledge, 2007.

53
Can a Christian also be a Pagan?

Rhiannon Grant

For some people—for example, those who associate Paganism with practices clearly opposed by the Christian tradition, like worshipping multiple deities—the answer to this question will be simply "no." For others—including those who understand themselves to be both Pagan and Christian—the answer to this question will obviously be "yes." In order to understand both perspectives, as scholars, we might prefer to say, "It depends," then explore further on what factors exactly the answer depends. These factors include the requirements of belonging (or what it means to "be" a Christian or a Pagan), views on what matters in religion, and whether the question is addressed at the individual or community level.

Before assessing whether someone can be both Pagan and Christian, we should start by considering what it means to be either Christian or Pagan in the first place. For Christian communities, this may seem obvious. Most of the Christian tradition uses rituals, such as baptism and confirmation, to signal membership in the community, and many Christian churches also keep membership lists and other details. This forms one way of measuring whether someone is Christian or not. However, things rapidly become more complex. Is someone baptized in childhood who never attends church and holds no Christian beliefs really a Christian? Is an active participant in a small Christian group that does not practice baptism really a Christian? What about being culturally Christian or a solo believer with no community connections? And those questions only become more numerous and difficult when we turn to Paganism, where solitary practitioners are even more common, the range of sources for membership rituals is more diverse, and the question of what counts as "being a Pagan" even less clear-cut. This means that different communities will assess an individual's belonging differently. In practice, the person with the greatest knowledge of the relevant factors is the person themselves, and when people report that they are indeed both Pagan and Christian, sociologists and other scholars should take that self-identification seriously.

Respecting the individual's view on their religious identity does not solve all the conundrums associated with this question, though. Even for the person practicing more than one religion, there are theological and cosmological problems—in her book *Buddhist and Christian?* Rose Drew describes the ways in which people either try to solve or put aside issues like the conflict between the Buddhist belief in reincarnation and the Christian belief in resurrection. For someone who is both Christian and Pagan, there will be similar issues. One way people address this is to ask which aspect of religion matters most: belief, practice, community, or something else? A conflict at the level of belief, like a contradiction between monotheism and polytheism, might be resolved at that level (e.g., by saying that polytheistic deities are expressions of or metaphors for aspects of a monotheistic god), or set aside, with the focus moving to community or practice. If the focus is on practice, a person's church attendance and participation in a Wiccan coven are more important than their beliefs. If they have community connections—such as family members—in multiple traditions, one person may have some form of belonging in a very large number of religious communities.

This brings us to the final consideration—the interaction between the individual and the communities involved. It is entirely possible for the judgment about whether a person is both Pagan and Christian to be different from different perspectives. The same person might see themselves as being both Christian and Pagan and have that accepted by their Druid community but not by their Roman Catholic church. Someone else making that claim might have it accepted within a progressive or liberal Christian community but not by a group of strongly feminist goddess worshippers. Because of these complexities, in any particular case, there may not be a simple yes or no answer to the question, "Is this person both Christian and Pagan?"

Instead, it might be helpful to be more specific. In the field of people who might be both Pagan and Christian, there are, among other possibilities, people who follow the teachings of Jesus but incorporate nature spirituality into their worship, mainly believe in a Pagan theology but attend some church services, grew up in a Christian community and kept some aspects of their faith even after becoming Pagan, want to be Pagan but have to hide it from Christian family members, find inspiration from both Christian and Pagan sources, or identify as both Pagan and Christian in some way that needs more explanation.

About the author

Rhiannon Grant teaches for Woodbrooke Quaker Study Centre. She works with postgraduate students in all areas of Quaker studies, and her own research explores Quaker religious language and multiple religious belonging. She is a member of Central England Area Quaker Meeting and the Order of Bards, Ovates, and Druids.

Suggestions for further readings

In this book
See also chapters 16 (Can a Pagan follow more than one path or tradition?) and 52 (Is there antipathy between Pagans and Christians?).

Elsewhere
Bidwell, Duane. *When One Religion Isn't Enough: The Lives of Spiritually Fluid People*. Boston: Beacon, 2018.

Drew, Rose. *Buddhist and Christian? An Exploration of Dual Belonging*. Abingdon: Routledge, 2014.

Vincett, Giselle. "Quagans: Fusing Quakerism with Contemporary Paganism." *Quaker Studies* 13(2) (2009). http://digitalcommons.georgefox.edu/quakerstudies/vol13/iss2/6.

54
Can Paganism be applied to non-European religions, such as Shinto?

Douglas Ezzy

What does it mean to be "Pagan"? I argue that this term is best kept for Western Paganisms, including both classical forms such as Greek paganism and contemporary forms such as Wicca, Druidry, and Heathenry. This defines Paganism in terms of geography, community, and history as well as belief and practice. I prefer to use the term "Paganism" to refer to these traditions and similar ones, as is the practice among most contemporary scholars.

Arguments that the term "Pagan" can be applied more broadly tend to focus on similarities in belief systems and, to a lesser extent, practice. These arguments tend to ignore the importance of geography, history, power, and community. For example, Michael York (2003) argues that both Chinese folk religion and Japanese Shinto, along with some Indigenous religions, can be counted as "pagan" religions. He distinguishes "pagan" religions (with a lowercase "p") from contemporary Western Paganisms, which he terms "Neopaganism." He sees pagan religion as a broader category that includes Neopaganism. York's definition of "pagan" emphasizes beliefs. From this perspective, he is able to claim some similarities between Western Neopaganism and some non-Western religious traditions.

According to Walter et al. (2021), claiming Indigenous religions as "pagan" could be seen as a form of colonialism. It could also be described as a form of cultural appropriation that occurs when "members of one culture take the cultural practices of another as if their own, or as if the right of possession should not be questioned or contested" (Jonathan Hart, cited in Welch 2002, 21). There is probably some merit to York's articulation of the similarities between contemporary Paganisms and Indigenous religious traditions. However, the history of oppression and colonialism experienced by Indigenous peoples makes it deeply problematic for Pagans to attempt to "claim" these traditions as "pagan"—a term primarily used to describe Western religious traditions. It looks like yet another example of white Westerners attempting to impose a particular way of understanding on Indigenous peoples.

Similarly, it is problematic to consider Japanese Shinto and Chinese folk religion as pagan. There is also some merit to York's argument that Japanese Shinto and Chinese folk religion share some similarities with contemporary Western Paganisms; however, the risk of defining them as "pagan" is that Westerners are perceived to be using frameworks of understanding derived from Western Paganisms and imposing these on Japanese and Chinese religiosity.

York's argument that these other religions are pagan is part of an attempt to describe Paganism as a "world religion." By showing that Paganism is as large as a "world religion," he seeks to make a stronger argument for it to be respected because of the number of people who follow it. The world religions paradigm is increasingly seen as problematic, in part because there is huge variety within religions depending on where and how they are practiced (Harvey 2013). It makes more sense to argue that religions should be respected in all their variety and diversity rather than to try to amalgamate them into larger and larger groups of dubious similarity.

So no, the term "Paganism" should not be applied to non-Western religions such as Indigenous traditions and Shinto. To do so is disrespectful to these religions, which should be valued in their own right. There probably are some similarities between various non-Western religions and contemporary Western Paganisms. However, there is also a long history of people from the "West" assuming they can interpret non-Western religions and, as a consequence, seriously misunderstanding them. This concern with Western imperialism and lack of respect is very significant. Being attentive to this means that it is best to avoid applying the term "Paganism" to Indigenous and non-Western religions.

About the author

Douglas Ezzy, PhD, is professor of sociology at the University of Tasmania, Australia. He is lead investigator of the Australian Research Council Discovery project "Religious Freedom, LGBT+ Employees, and the Right to Discriminate." He is a coinvestigator on the Canadian "Nonreligion in a Complex Future" project led by Professor Lori Beaman. His books include *LGBT Christians* (2017, with Bronwyn Fielder), *Sex, Death and Witchcraft* (2014), and *Teenage Witches* (2007, with Helen Berger).

Suggestions for further readings

In this book

See also chapters 24 (Is Druidry the Indigenous religion of Europe?), 55 (Can witch doctors and Africana spiritual traditions be regarded as Pagan?), and 56 (How much of Paganism is based on cultural appropriation?).

Elsewhere

Ezzy, Douglas. "Religions of Practice: The Case of Japanese Religions." *Journal for the Academic Study of Religion* 29(1) (2016): 13–29.

Harvey, Graham. *Food, Sex and Strangers: Understanding Religion as Everyday Life.* Durham: Acumen, 2013.

Walter, M., R. Lovett, B. Maher, B. Williamson, J. Prehn, G. Bodkin-Andrews, and V. Lee. "Indigenous Data Sovereignty in the Era of Big Data and Open Data." *Australian Journal of Social Issues* 56(2) (2021): 143–156.

Welch, Christina. "Appropriating the Didjeridu and the Sweat Lodge: New Age Baddies and Indigenous Victims?" *Journal of Contemporary Religion* 17(1) (2002): 21–38.

York, Michael. *Pagan Theology.* New York: New York University Press, 2003.

55
Can witch doctors and Africana spiritual traditions be regarded as Pagan?

Mary Hearns-Ayodele

The terms "witch doctor" and "pagan" share one major commonality: the definitions of both terms have been impacted by the intersectionalities of race, sex, and class within the dominant culture that writes about them. Both witch doctor and Pagan describe religio-spiritual practices and people who are positioned as being outside of a dominant religious culture that defines how people "should" behave religiously and where the ailing should seek succor to overcome illness in body, mind, and soul. When the perceptions of African-based precolonial religious beliefs are attached to these terms, the definitions grow in complexity.

During the colonial era, African spiritual traditions were often demonized by European missionaries and colonizers. These traditions were seen as threats to Christianity and to European colonialism. As a result, African spiritual traditions were often suppressed, and their practitioners were persecuted. The echoes of suppression are still felt today in the perception of Africana spiritual traditions on the continent and in the diaspora, such as Asamanism, Ifa, Odinani, Santeria, Umbanda, Candomble, Hoodoo, and Vodou.

In many parts of the world, including parts of the African continent, a witch doctor is a person who solves problems related to witchcraft. Their support is widely recognized as useful and instrumental in preserving a viable and healthy community, as witchcraft, when defined in an Africana context, is harmful to the community and causes disruption. The Africana definition of "witchcraft" differs markedly from the contemporary Eurocentric definition in several ways, and in Africana contexts, it is not seen as socially desirable or acceptable for various reasons as defined by the community in which it occurs.

However, this term has been used negatively toward traditional healers around the world to demonize and infer fraudulent activities based on superstition. It is important to note that without understanding the political undercurrent and while seeking to learn the language of colonizers, some traditional healers have taken the term "witch doctor" to describe themselves as part of attempting to communicate their purpose to outsiders to their culture and traditions.

Practitioners of Africana spiritual traditions (AST), which are grounded in the principles and practices of traditional African religions, will provide different answers depending on their personal practice and culture. In the global North, the emphasis on personal choice and individual freedoms can be seen as a political position that establishes that what a person defines for themselves is more valid than the values of the communities in which they live. In this way, we may see a person who identifies as both a Pagan and practitioner of AST.

Additionally, there are practitioners of Santeria and Vodou who center the health of their community as the source of their individual well-being and may not describe themselves as Pagan due to the individual contextualization that the term may hold for them. The question is not what they consider themselves but what the community considers itself, and one individual does not answer for the entire community. In a decolonial context, the community defines itself using its own terms, not the terms imposed on it by outsiders.

Whether or not African witch doctors or AST are considered "pagan" depends on who and how one defines the term. Historically, the term has been used generically to refer to people who do not follow the so-called Abrahamic religions of Judaism, Islam, or Christianity. However, when regarding practices that have syncretized any of the Abrahamic religions into their practices, as some AST do, the definition shifts. Moreover, when the communities and practitioners define themselves in their own decolonized terms, new word choices are added to the lexicon and the discussion is enhanced.

About the author

Mary Hearns-Ayodele is a prophetess, Africana folk medicine scholar, and doctoral student in philosophy and religion at the California Institute of Integral Studies (CIIS). Before coming to CIIS, she completed an MA in culture and spirituality (2004–2006) at Holy Names University. Her research interests include the intergenerational transfer of Africana folk healing practices.

Suggestions for further readings

In this book
See also chapters 19 (Are all witches Pagan?), 20 (Can anyone be called a "witch"?), 54 (Can Paganism be applied to non-European religions, such as Shinto?), and 56 (How much of Paganism is based on cultural appropriation?).

Elsewhere
Hazzard-Donald, Katrina. *Mojo Workin': The Old African American Hoodoo System*. Baltimore: University of Illinois Press, 2012.

Opokuwaa, Nana Akua Kyerewaa. *The Quest for Spiritual Transformation: Introduction to Traditional Akan Religion, Rituals and Practices*. Washington, DC: iUniverse, 2005.

Umeh, John Anenechukwu. *After God Is Dibia: Igbo Cosmology, Divination and Sacred Science in Nigeria*. Vol. 1. London: Karnak House, 1999.

Wells-Oghoghomeh, Alexis. "Decolonial Magic: Africana Religions in America and the Work of Ronald Hutton." *Magic, Ritual, and Witchcraft* 17(1) (2022): 13–20.

56
How much of Paganism is based on cultural appropriation?

Sabina Magliocco

In order to answer this question, we need to establish two things. The first is that all new religious movements are built on existing ideas adapted from other religions. Christianity, for example, began as a sect of Judaism; as it spread, it incorporated many features of late antique pagan cults and philosophical movements. Modern Paganism is no exception to this pattern: it emerged from nineteenth-century Romanticism and has incorporated influences from numerous other philosophies and religions, past and present.

The second task before us is to define cultural appropriation. Cultural appropriation can be defined as the unauthorized use of material from a subordinate culture by members of a dominant culture. While cultures have always influenced one another, and many of those exchanges were part of unequal power relationships, the concept of cultural appropriation is relatively new; it emerged only in the 1970s and became part of the wider cultural conversation in the early 2000s. It is part of the critique of Western colonialism and its damaging effects on colonized cultures. Cultural appropriation is always embedded in an unequal power relationship between the colonizer and the colonized and represents another way that Westerners exert power over colonized cultures. It presumes the existence of a system in which culture is commodified; the use, marketing, and sale of inauthentic forms of culture harm the bearers of the authentic item by trivializing it, turning it into a commodity, or in the case of artwork, making it more difficult for them to profit from it by flooding the market with cheap imitations.

Modern Paganisms, like other new religious movements, are built on existing cultural material, much of it preserved in literature, art, and folk traditions. Because they are primarily of European origin, they draw predominantly on European cultural productions, including Western esotericism and Greek, Roman, Celtic, and Norse mythology, as well as nineteenth-century Romantic reworkings of those narratives for popular audiences. There is often a strong component of ethnic revivalism in modern Paganisms: many Pagans seek to revitalize the religious traditions of their own pre-Christian ancestors in order to establish their ethnic identity. None of this is cultural appropriation.

Yet while modern Paganisms are not based on cultural appropriation, some Pagans do appropriate the cultural practices of colonized peoples. It is important to understand how and why this happens. Pagans often romanticize Indigenous spiritualities, seeing them as more "natural" and authentic in contrast to Western religions. This view, itself rooted in colonialism, can motivate Pagans to appropriate non-Western spiritual practices to enhance their own sense of authenticity or legitimacy. In other cases, little is known about certain aspects of pre-Christian European religious practice because so much of it was reworked or destroyed by Christianity. In these instances, modern Pagans may turn to non-Western religions for inspiration, finding practices that may be like ones observed by earlier European peoples. If they adopt these practices into their new traditions without the explicit permission and agreement of the people whose practices they are imitating, they are engaging in cultural appropriation. Finally, the wide diffusion of information through the internet and social media can make non-Western Indigenous traditions seem fashionable, attractive, and entertaining to Westerners. The fragmentation and individualization of religious practice, in which all spiritual observances are divorced from their original context and treated as commodities, encourage cultural appropriation over cultural appreciation.

The appropriation of spiritual practices is rooted in perennialism, a philosophical concept underlying many new religious movements that tends to see all world religions as sharing fundamental common features that point to one underlying universal truth. This idea is itself a product of colonialism; by emphasizing allegedly shared universal features, it flattens differences between religions and encourages appropriation of elements decontextualized from their original practice and meaning.

Nonetheless, cultural exchanges are often complex and resist stereotyping, especially when they involve personal interactions between individuals and groups. Some Indigenous teachers may share spiritual practices with outsiders despite opposition from other group members. In other cases, modern Pagans may incorporate the practices of surrounding colonized cultures, such as when elements of Mexican American observations of Dia de los Muertos find their way into North American Pagan remembrances of the dead on October 31. It is more difficult to label this type of exchange as appropriative, since cultures that coexist in the same geographic area inevitably influence one another.

A few varieties of Norse Paganism have instrumentalized the critique of cultural appropriation to further a racist or nationalist agenda. These groups insist that only members of a specific racial, ethnic, or cultural group can follow traditions practiced by their blood ancestors. While it is important to avoid cultural appropriation, such practices are equally noxious, as they are used to deliberately exclude members of marginalized communities.

About the author
Sabina Magliocco is professor of anthropology and chair of the Program in Religion at the University of British Columbia in Vancouver.

Suggestions for further readings
In this book
See also chapters 12 (Do Pagans have sacred sites?), 54 (Can Paganism be applied to non-European religions, such as Shinto?), and 55 (Can witch doctors and Africana spiritual traditions be regarded as Pagan?).

Elsewhere
Aldred, Lisa. "Plastic Shamans and Astroturf Sundances: New Age Commercialization of Native American Spirituality." *American Indian Quarterly* 24(3) (2000): 329–352.

Lupa, ed. *Talking about the Elephant: An Anthology of Neopagan Perspectives on Cultural Appropriation.* Stanford: Megalithica Books, 2008.

Sabina Magliocco. *Witching Culture: Folklore and Neo-Paganism in America.* Philadelphia: University of Pennsylvania Press, 2004.

Michael York. "New Age Commodification and Appropriation of Spirituality." *Journal of Contemporary Religion* 16(3) (2001): 361–372.

57
Do Pagans have particular political views?

Ethan Doyle White

Like any large and diverse group of people, modern Pagans exhibit political beliefs stretching across the ideological spectrum. Some Pagans consider their political views to be quite separate from their religious identity, while for others, their political ideology and activism are wholly intertwined with their religious commitments.

The impulse to revive the pre-Christian religions of Europe was largely bound up with the cultural and political nationalisms of the early twentieth century. Fascinated by folklore and legend, many European nationalists sought the origins of their respective national identities deep in the pre-Christian past. For this reason, there has always been a relationship between certain modern Pagan religions and nationalist stances commonly attributed to the political right. Early forms of what we now call Heathenry, the religion based on the pre-Christian traditions of linguistically Germanic peoples, were, for instance, promoted by ethnic nationalists like the Austrian esotericist Guido von List.

Ethnic nationalist Pagans often believe in an intrinsic link between a person's ancestral heritage and particular deities. This means that they typically exclude those who do not share their ethnic identity from their religious groups and rituals. Ethnic nationalist (or "folkish") Heathens, for instance, generally believe that Heathenry should be practiced only by people who are biologically descended from pre-Christian Germanic-speaking populations. Pagans holding to such views often point admiringly to other ethnic religions, such as those of certain Native American groups, that similarly restrict religious activities to members of an ethnic in-group. In a few cases, ethnic nationalist Pagans have embraced violent extremism; the American Heathen David Lane was, for instance, a leading member of the Order, a white supremacist militia that operated in the 1980s.

In contrast to these right-wing Paganisms, there are other Pagans whose beliefs are identified with the political left. This alignment between Paganism and left-wing politics emerged as a prominent force in the United States during the 1960s and 1970s, when Pagan religions proved attractive to many people involved in leftist causes such as second-wave feminism. It was there that Dianic Wicca emerged as a form of the Wiccan religion explicitly informed by feminist sentiment, something that fed into the broader Goddess movement that emphasized opposition to patriarchal society. Feminism has retained a strong presence within the Pagan milieu, although feminist Pagans continue to clash over issues like transgender participation in women's-only rituals.

It was from this left-feminist milieu that an American Pagan named Starhawk established the Reclaiming tradition in the late 1970s, a leftist grouping whose members performed rituals to combat the right-wing administration of US president Ronald Reagan. In more recent years, many Wiccans and other Pagans conducted rituals intended to restrict the right-wing administration of US president Donald Trump using magic. Meanwhile, many Heathens concerned about the ethnic nationalist presence in their religion have embraced overt antiracist and leftist political stances.

Pagan interest has also been attracted to political issues that are not intrinsically wedded to either the left or the right. Of these, environmentalism is the most prominent. The notion that Europe's pre-Christian religions were rooted in the worship of nature is long-standing, and since at least the 1970s, modern Pagans have increasingly regarded their traditions as "nature religions." For this reason, it is unsurprising that many have expressed concern about ecological degradation and a minority have become active environmentalists. In 1990s Britain, for instance, "Eco-Pagans" could be found engaged in direct action protests against road construction projects, ritually invoking their deities and nature spirits to assist in their efforts.

It should be borne in mind that many Pagans have not seen their political views as something integral to their religious identity or ritual activity. Gerald Gardner, the man who spearheaded Wicca in mid-twentieth-century Britain, was, for instance, politically conservative but did not expect all his fellow Wiccans to be. Since that time, many Wiccan covens, as well as other Pagan groups, have contained members with varied political opinions, all typically accepting the liberal democratic premise that a free society should allow its citizens their own political and religious views. Many recognize that as a small religious minority, Pagans largely rely on this social pluralism for their safety.

While acknowledging this political diversity, it is also noteworthy that certain ideologies predominate within the Pagan milieu. Since the late twentieth century, sociological studies have indicated that the Pagan population of the United States leans disproportionately to the left; the same is likely true of Pagan communities in other Western countries. In central and eastern Europe, conversely, more conservative and nationalistic views appear to predominate within the Pagan scene.

About the author

Ethan Doyle White has a PhD in medieval history and archaeology from University College London and has written extensively on modern Paganism and related forms of esotericism. His publications include *Wicca: History, Belief, and Community in Modern Pagan Witchcraft* (Sussex Academic Press, 2016), *Pagans: The Visual Culture of Pagan Myths, Legends and Rituals* (Thames and Hudson, 2023), and *The New Witches of the West: Tradition, Liberation, and Power* (Cambridge University Press, 2024).

Suggestions for further readings

In this book
See also chapters 22 (What is Heathenry?) and 58 (Is there a problem with fascism in contemporary Paganism?).

Elsewhere
Gardell, Mattias. *Gods of the Blood: The Pagan Revival and White Separatism*. Durham: Duke University Press, 2003.

Salomonsen, Jone. *Enchanted Feminism: The Reclaiming Witches of San Francisco*. New York: Routledge, 2002.

58
Is there a problem with fascism in contemporary Paganism?

Amy Hale

Possibly so, but first, it is important to define the word "fascism," as it is a slippery term that many people use incorrectly as a shorthand for authoritarianism. For this essay, I am defining fascism as a political and economic movement characterized by authoritarianism, militarism, and ultranationalism and organized around principles of hierarchy, tradition, and cultural or "racial" purity, where a strong dictator is believed to represent the "soul of the people." At the time of this writing, the relationship between contemporary Paganisms and fascist ideologies is an area of growing concern.

It is a common misconception that most contemporary Pagans are politically progressive, stemming from the increased popularity of Paganism during the period of the counterculture of the 1960s and 1970s. This glosses over the complex influences derived from both left- and right-wing political cultures that shaped the character of contemporary Paganism in the late nineteenth and early twentieth centuries. While the progressive counterculture did, in fact, contribute to the growth of Paganism in the 1970s, modern Paganism initially developed in a milieu that was culturally conservative—Wicca and Druidry are two obvious examples. Both of these groups' formative identities originally relied on narratives of tradition, nativism to varying degrees, and cultural preservation, which are values often identified with conservatism. Additionally, Paganism is often characterized by Romantic aesthetics and sensibilities, supporting the space for wider conservative discourses about tradition, nature, and the past. Thus, Paganism has historically demonstrated uncomfortable structural compatibilities with the ideals and values of some sectors of the counterculture of the radical Right. This convergence has become more pronounced in the years after the financial crisis of 2008 with the emergence of right-wing anticapitalist and antiglobalist critiques of neoliberalism alongside the existing left-wing critiques, which have contributed to a rise in the crossovers between Paganism, particularly reconstructionist traditions, and developing fascist ideologies.

Paganism has certainly had a relationship with historical Fascism. It is well documented that after World War I, members of the emerging Nazi regime in Germany and extreme right-wing thinkers in Italy, such as Julius Evola, idealized antimodern pre-Christian paganisms, imagining the revival of a golden age, pre-Christian society that was intensely hierarchical and patriarchal, incorporating rhetoric about racial and ethnic purity and "native" religious traditions. After World War II, Slavic reconstructionist Paganism adopted similar ultranationalist positions as it spread to Canada, the United States, and throughout Western Europe, ultimately becoming an important feature of religiosity in the post-Soviet landscape of Central and Eastern Europe. Additionally, inspired by the Nazi dalliance with Germanic religion, some branches of Heathenry since the 1970s have explicitly promoted white nationalism. This is still a problem of internal challenge within Heathen religious communities worldwide.

Yet why has there been an increase in intersections between some contemporary Pagan groups and extremist right-wing politics in recent years? Primarily, shifting ideological positions on the Right internationally have intersected with values and aesthetics that have broad appeal to some Pagans, especially those who are interested in reconstructing cultural religions and traditions. There are a number of distinguishing features of contemporary Paganism that are compatible with fascist and radical Right principles. Perhaps most important of these are the following:

- a socially marginalized identity
- discourses of Indigeneity
- an interest in the preservation of folk traditions and nativism
- antimodernism
- neotribalism
- environmental preservation

Interestingly, a number of these cultural foci are also part of countercultural leftist Paganism and, in general, characterize a radical response to societal and cultural pressures. Yet recently, these values have coincided with shifts in the international Right, posing a critique of neoliberalism and the dominance of Christianity in right-wing politics. In Europe and the United States, the Right is generally preoccupied with social hierarchies, traditional gender roles, nativism, and ethnonationalism rooted in anti-immigration and anti-LGBTQ sentiments. However, the alt-right and the New Right have combined these concerns with anticapitalism, antiglobalism, antimodernism, and environmentalism. This shift has attracted nativist Pagan religious groups that are developing alongside an increase in populist and place-based ethnonationalisms. In short, there is a growing movement of ethnonationalist Pagans trying to re-create an imagined golden age where everyone was in their proper homeland, worshipping their own gods, living in harmony with nature according to natural hierarchies.

Although it can be expected that any religious group will represent a range of political thought, the nature of Paganism as a countercultural religion of resistance suggests that its adherents may fall along lines of political extremes. While in the latter half of the twentieth century, most Pagans represented the Left, in the twenty-first century, the influence of the radical Right on Paganism internationally is much more dramatic and may be shaping the trajectory of Paganism itself.

About the author

Amy Hale (PhD in folklore, UCLA) is an Atlanta-based writer, curator, and critic. Research interests include contemporary magical history and subcultures, art, women, and Cornwall. She has written widely on artist and occultist Ithell Colquhoun, notably the biography *Ithell Colquhoun: Genius of the Fern Loved Gully* (Strange Attractor, 2020) and the collection *Sex Magic: Diagrams of Love* (Tate, 2024). She is the editor of *Essays on Women in Western Esotericism: Beyond Seeresses and Sea Priestesses* (Palgrave, 2022).

Suggestions for further readings

In this book
See also chapters 22 (What is Heathenry?), 57 (Do Pagans have particular political views?), and 59 (Are Pagans involved in the war in Ukraine?).

Elsewhere
Gardell, Mattias. *Gods of the Blood: The Pagan Revival and White Separatism*. Durham, NC: Duke University Press, 2003.

Strmiska, Michael F. "Pagan Politics in the 21st Century: 'Peace and Love' or 'Blood and Soil'?" *Pomegranate: The International Journal of Pagan Studies* 20(1) (2003): 5–44.

59
Are Pagans involved in the war in Ukraine?

Giuseppe Maiello

In the last decade of the twentieth century, after the collapse of the Soviet Union, a rapid development of Pagan groups occurred both in Russia and in Ukraine. Relations between Ukrainian and Russian Pagan groups were excellent, in part because the concept of "Slavic brotherhood" was almost always the basis of the ideology of these groups. The meetings between Pagan Russians and Ukrainians took place both on the level of individual contacts and on the level of leaders. They participated in rituals, honored Slavic deities, and drank mead together.

Like many other Pagan groups, especially from eastern Europe, many Russian and Ukrainian Pagans had a certain tendency toward ethnonationalism. Furthermore, although they referred to Slavic mythology, they also often made use of symbols used by the German Nazis, such as the swastika, the Black Sun, and the greeting with the right arm raised at an angle of about 120 degrees from the torso.

With the outbreak of the war in Donbas in 2014, Russian and Ukrainian Pagans further radicalized their positions by militarizing their organizations. The Azov Battalion, on the Ukrainian side, was the most well-known of these military groups with a significant presence of Pagan fighters. Among the armed factions of Pagans that received support from the Russian army, the Svarog Battalion was the most renowned.

Both battalions originally used similar symbology—that is, a mixture of Old Slavic and Old Germanic symbols. With the escalation of the conflict (starting in February 2022) and with the direct or indirect intervention of the great world powers in the war, Pagan rituals have been decreasing within the military groups. This is because, first of all, many of the fighting Pagans fall in battle or are mortally wounded or taken prisoner. Furthermore, on both sides of the warring parties, the use of Pagan symbols and rites by organized military contingents has begun to make the respective political representatives uncomfortable.

Russia, which entered directly into the conflict with the military occupation of territories still legally belonging to Ukraine, sees its intervention both as a defense against "Nazism"—and therefore its symbols—and as a defense of Christian orthodoxy. In the Russian propaganda videos, the symbols of swastikas tattooed on the bodies of the members of the Azov Battalion were therefore displayed prominently, but obviously it was not said that similar swastikas were probably also tattooed on the bodies of many fighters on the Russian side.

The Ukrainian side instead attempted to trivialize the fact that the fighters used symbols attributable to Nazism under their flags, also due to the fact that this symbolism is repudiated—if not outlawed—by Ukraine's allies (that is, the Western countries). The same Western mass media have tried, when possible, to avoid dealing with the topic of Pagan and Nazi symbology among Ukrainian soldiers.

Paganism, therefore, had, at the beginning of the conflict in Ukraine in 2014, a flowering both in terms of rituals and in terms of symbology. Currently, however, it is being put on the back burner for political reasons. The commands of both sides in the field prefer not to underline the fact that among the fighters, there are active Pagans, given that the rest of the original battalions have been incorporated into more substantial military bodies such as regiments and brigades.

About the author

Giuseppe Maiello is an associate professor and head of the Department of Social Sciences at the University of Finance and Administration in Prague, Czech Republic.

Suggestions for further readings

In this book
See also chapters 57 (Do Pagans have particular political views?) and 58 (Is there a problem with fascism in contemporary Paganism?).

Elsewhere
Aitamurto, Kaarina. *Paganism, Traditionalism, Nationalism: Narratives of Russian Rodnoverie*. New York: Routledge, 2016.

Smorzhevska, Oksana. "The Hero-Warrior in the Worldview and Practice of Contemporary Pagans in Ukraine." *Religio: Revue pro religionistiku* 31(1) (2023): 9–31.

60
Why do some polytheists reject the term "Pagan"?

Angelo Nasios

Today, Paganism represents a contemporary religious movement with followers spread across the globe. As a broad category, Paganism encompasses multiple traditions, including but not limited to Wicca, various forms of witchcraft, Druidry, Heathenry, Asatru, and Goddess worship. Likewise, "Pagan" identifies a member of Paganism or one of the traditions commonly acknowledged as part of Paganism. However, some people who are categorized as "Pagan" by scholars and other Pagans reject this classification for several reasons. This essay explores the historical differences between "paganism" and "Paganism" as major factors for the rejection of Pagan religious self-identification within Greek polytheistic communities. The Greek rejection of the Pagan categorization provides a good case study on the conflict between in-group (emic) and out-group (etic) narratives and classifications.

One way of examining the Greek rejection of the "Pagan" religious label is by considering the ancient context of the word "pagan" and its relation to the Greeks. While the modern spelling convention of capitalizing "Paganism" and "Pagan" refers to proper identities (and therefore requires capitalization), this was not the case historically. When written in lowercase forms—"paganism" and "pagan"—these terms represented a category of "otherness" created by Christians in late antiquity.

According to historian Maijastina Kahlos, "paganism" was never a religion, and there were no pagans as such before Christianity. Rather, Christians invented "paganism" both as a term and as a system to establish and negotiate the proper boundaries of Christian identity. For the ancients, "pagan" and "paganism" were not claimed identities. Instead, they were terms that only existed in relation and contrast to Christians. Therefore, historically, "paganism" is understood in relation and contrast to Christianity.

The use of the term "pagan" by Christian authors reflects the Latin-speaking conversation in the western half of the Roman Empire. In the east, where Greek was commonly spoken, Christians adopted the term "Hellene" to scorn their moderate Christian peers who were more accommodating and less polemical toward polytheists. In Christian polemics of the fourth century, "Hellene" and "pagan" were thus used interchangeably to construct Christian identity by dehumanizing the other.

An example of this is clearly seen in a polemic treatise by Theodoret of Cyrus, who wrote an extensive attack against the Greeks, known in English as *A Cure for Pagan Maladies*. The Greek title of the text is *Hellēnikōn Therapeutikē Pathēmatōn*, and the Latin title is *Graecorum Affectionum Curatio*. "Hellēnikōn" and "Graecorum" are the words that mean "Greek" but are being translated as "Pagan" in English. An alternative translation into English could easily be "A Cure for Greek Maladies." This unique history of the term in relation to the Greeks makes it off-putting to polytheists in Greece. It is almost impossible for them to accept the modern "Pagan" label due to its polemical history in which "pagan" and "Hellene" were interchangeable in translation within Christian polemics.

In addition to exploring the ancient origins of the use of the word "pagan" and its significance for modern Greeks, a second approach to understanding why Greeks reject the "Pagan" label involves examining the differences in identity structures between Pagans and Greeks. Ethnicity is the main conflicting factor in comparing them. For Greeks, ethnicity plays a significant role in self-perception, particularly in religious matters. Greek Orthodox Christianity has long been considered fundamental to Greek ethnic identity. Typically, a Greek becomes a polytheist due to an identity crisis prompted by an examination of the history of Christianization, which leads to questioning the Christian connection to their ethnic identity.

Becoming a polytheist is only but one of many paths out from an identity crisis. The reason polytheism is the path forward for those who do go that route is that polytheism aligns with the Greek ethnic identity in ways other religious identities do not. The identity crisis here was originally caused by a historical examination of Christianization, and as a result, a newfound sense of self emerged. This new self seeks to recover what is considered to have been lost or stolen from them—that is, their "true" religious identity that aligns with their ethnicity and collective history.

In contrast, the situation is vastly different for those who generally identify as Pagan, and the United States provides a useful comparison. In this case, the sociological process by which an American becomes Pagan can be explained by the market theory of religion. According to this theory, different religions meet the needs and demands of people. In other words, people become Pagan because Paganism meets their individual needs, with ethnicity not typically playing a role in their choice of religion (though personal ancestry could play a role for some). This stands in sharp contrast to the Greek context, where ethnicity is a foundational element of self-reflection concerning categories of identity such as religion. In other words, ethnicity has an engulfing quality for Greeks. It impacts other categories of identity and unifies the Greek experience of being polytheist, which isn't shared with the general population of Pagans practicing Paganism.

In conclusion, the rejection of the "Pagan" label by Greek polytheists has multiple underlying factors. The two most significant ones are rooted in the ancient Christian polemics against Greeks, which render the term "Pagan" offensive and incorrect, and in ethnicity, which plays a foundational role in Greek religious identification, though it is not characteristically a contributing factor in Pagan identification more broadly.

About the author

Angelo Nasios is an independent scholar with an MA in history. His interests and research focus on the history of religion—primarily Greek religion in late antiquity.

Suggestions for further readings

In this book
See also chapters 5 (What is the relationship between ancient and contemporary Paganism?) and 32 (Can a person have Pagan beliefs without being Pagan?).

Elsewhere
Kahlos, Maijastina. *Debate and Dialogue: Christian and Pagan Cultures c. 360–430*. London: Routledge, 2016.

Papadogiannakis, Yannis. *Christianity and Hellenism in the Fifth-Century Greek East: Theodoret's Apologetics against the Greeks in Context*. Cambridge: Harvard University Press, 2012.

61
Is Paganism empowering for women and LGBTQI+?

Giovanna Parmigiani

A variety of groups and movements are contained within the umbrella term "Paganism" today, including solitary practitioners. For this reason, it is not possible to make broad generalizations. While there are few Pagan movements that adhere to traditional, patriarchal, heteronormative, cisnormative, and white supremacist visions of the world, it is fair to say that, as in studies by sociologist Helen A. Berger (e.g., 2019), the vast majority of self-defined Pagan religions, spiritualities, and individuals are inclusive or tend to be more inclusive than the context in which they operate, regarding women and LGBTQI+ rights and experiences.

In order to contextualize and support this claim, I will briefly refer, below, to three interconnected bodies of scholarship on contemporary Paganisms that engage with these themes: Pagan the(a)ology, the historical connections between contemporary paganisms and political feminist movements and ideologies, and recent ethnographic insights on the "lived" aspects of contemporary Pagan practices. Although the themes I will cover below do not account for all Pagan traditions and Native Faith spiritualities and all their local and regional expressions, they nonetheless trace some of the main (historical and contemporary) currents and global influences within contemporary Paganisms.

First, while it is worth remembering that not all Pagan traditions are theist, polytheism is very frequently associated with contemporary Pagan spiritualities. Theistic Pagans, as opposed to followers of monotheistic religions, celebrate and worship expressions of the divine feminine—what is usually referred to as "the Goddess(es)." Some, like Wiccans, do so alongside their worship of the divine masculine. Other forms of Paganism, like the Reclaiming and Dianic witchcraft traditions, focus on the figure of the Goddess(es). These forms of spirituality are expressions of what is usually called "Goddess spirituality": a prominent branch of contemporary

Paganisms. Even though it is worth stressing, with Berger (2019, 141), that "worshipping the Goddess or goddesses does not necessarily make one a feminist," the aforementioned groups are generally body- and sex-positive and inclusive of queer, trans, and nonbinary individuals and groups. A notable exception to this is that of some conservative Dianic witches, as it emerged in the aftermath of the 2011 and 2012 PantheaCon, a former yearly Pagan convention, around the topics of trans-inclusivity. However, it is important to mention that there are a number of explicitly queer-oriented Pagan spiritualities and groups within contemporary Paganisms, such as the Radical Fairies and the Cult of Antinous.

Second, the connections between feminist activism and Pagan spiritualities have been historically attested (see, e.g., Clifton 2006; Feraro 2015). The importance of these themes in contemporary Pagan movements, though, goes beyond these geographical regions. Given the cultural and political prominence of English-speaking countries and their online presence, Pagan feminist ideas and practices have spread beyond the United Kingdom and North America, in what could be considered a "global" Pagan arena. Authors like Starhawk (Miriam Simos), for example, a trans-inclusive Pagan ecofeminist and activist, have had their works translated into several different languages. This, together with the active online presence of Pagan feminists and leaders, has contributed to their becoming (directly or indirectly) reference points for many Pagan practitioners both in the United States and worldwide—often complementing other specific Pagan, spiritual, or religious affiliations.

Third, beyond Anglophone contexts, some recent ethnographic work on the "lived" aspects of contemporary Paganisms show that women and LGBTQI+ individuals and groups see Paganism and Pagan communities as generative and healing spaces that allow them "to contest gender stereotypes outside the Pagan community" (Lepage 2017, 601) and to imagine alternative, empowered, and empowering ways of being in the world.

About the author

Giovanna Parmigiani is a lecturer on religion and cultural anthropology at Harvard Divinity School and a research associate at the Center for the Study of World Religions at Harvard University. Her focus of interest is on the relationships between religion, politics, and gender. She writes on magic, contemporary Paganisms, alternative spiritualities, and conspiracy theories, with *The Spider Dance* forthcoming from Equinox Publishing Ltd.

Suggestions for further readings

In this book
See also chapters 30 (How do Pagans conceive of gods?), 62 (Is Paganism "queer"?), and 70 (Are contemporary Pagan religions indicative of a new form of religiosity?).

Elsewhere
Berger, Helen A., Leigh S. Shaffer, and Evan A. Leach. *Voices from the Pagan Census: A National Survey of Witches and Neo-Pagans in the United States*. Columbia: University of South Carolina Press, 2003.

Berger, Helen A. *Solitary Pagans: Contemporary Witches, Wiccans, and Others Who Practice Alone*. Columbia: University of South Carolina Press, 2019.

Clifton, Chas. *Her Hidden Children: The Rise of Wicca and Paganism in America*. Lanham, MD: AltaMira, 2006.

Feraro, Shai. "Connecting British Wicca with Radical Feminism and Goddess Spirituality During the 1970s and 1980s: The Case Study of Monica Sjöö." *Journal of Contemporary Religion* 30(2) (2015): 307–321.

Lepage, Martin. "Queerness and Transgender Identity." *Studies in Religion* 46(4) (2017): 601–619.

62
Is Paganism "queer"?

[M] Dudeck

The term "queer" first entered the English language in the early sixteenth century, then used to describe someone strange, odd, peculiar, eccentric, suspicious, or "not quite right." Now "queer" is used as an umbrella term in contemporary culture and critical thought to describe nonnormative/nonbinary gender identities and diverse sexualities. "Queer" as a construct intentionally resists categorization through its blanketed resistance to all forms of normativity, with several theorists defining "queer" as whatever is at odds with the normal, the legitimate, or the dominant.

It is, therefore, reasonable to suggest that prior to biblically inspired prohibitions against same-sex desire and gender variance, behaviors we now refer to as "queer" would have expressed themselves in a variety of means through the lived reality of pre-Christian Europe. Up until now, historians, archaeologists, and anthropologists have avoided using contemporary queer terminologies to describe the sexual and gendered characteristics of the ancient world, but rapid changes in the body politic are rewriting long-established codes.

Recent articles published in mainstream newspapers such as the *Guardian* and the *Smithsonian* bear headlines such as "Mysterious Iron Age Burial May Hold Remains of Elite Nonbinary Person" or "1,000-Year-Old Remains in Finland May Be Non-binary Age Leader." These headlines describe a pagan burial site referred to as the Suontaka Grave, in Finland, where the remains of an Iron Age leader whose gender has baffled archaeologists for decades lie in queer archaeological ambiguity. This chieftain, who clearly enjoyed significant social status in their pagan community, was buried alongside a variety of objects mixed and matched from traditional male and female burials. The question has led scholars to rethink nonnormative gender positionalities and to imagine that paganism in Europe prior to Christianity may have been (proto)queer.

In 2013, a survey of neo-Pagans in England, Wales, Canada, Australia, and New Zealand revealed a total of 48.8 percent of women and

44.5 percent of men identified as "nonheterosexual," which is nearly half of the total population of modern Pagans. Like many new religious movements emerging since the Second World War, Paganism is countercultural, counterhegemonical, and in some cases, heretical, appealing in particular to queer religious outcasts searching for spiritual connection after having been intentionally excluded, ostracized, and abused by dominant institutionalized religions.

Queers occupy a unique cultural minority—in that we appear in virtually every culture, regardless of race, belief, geographic location, or cultural norm. Unlike other cultural minorities bound to geography, heritage, and a shared myth system, queers are often searching for mythological ancestors, and neo-Paganism provides access for us to invent our own histories with the speculative remains of a world before the incrimination of desire and the birth of compulsory heterosexuality. Many of the pre-Christian gods and heroes, witches, wizards, and supernatural entities bear queer birthmarks that give us this sense of historicity, even if it's only legend. For example, Odin the One-Eyed, All-father of the Norse pantheon, was both a war god and sorcerer and the most powerful practitioner of *seid*, a form of magic practiced almost exclusively by women. If a man practiced *seid*, he could be accused of *ergi*, a form of unmanliness with connotations of what we today, in the Western cultural and historical context, term homosexuality. Cernunnos, the proto-Celtic Horned God (now a central figure in modern witchcraft), is regularly portrayed in art and archaeology with an erect penis surrounded by other men with erect penises, hinting at homosexual ritual.

In *Another Mother Tongue* (2016), author Judy Grahn suggests terms such as "faggot," "poof," and "flaming"—used to describe homosexuality and gender variance in men—are all fundamentally connected via the mythological theme of "fire." Grahn proposes an inherent queerness to fire-stealing myths where handsome, young, athletic men steal fire from the goddess and, burned by the feminine, bring civilization to humanity. These myths provide a vital function to queer refugees from the margins of organized religion: as queer scholar José Muñoz (2009, 1) states, "queerness exists for us as an ideality that can be distilled from the past and used to imagine a future."

About the author

[M] **Dudeck**, PhD (Edinburgh), is an artist and cultural engineer who invents their own queer religion as art and a scholar of new religious movements exploring the role of art in the construction of belief systems.

Suggestions for further readings

In this book

See also chapters 30 (How do Pagans conceive of gods?), 61 (Is Paganism empowering for women and LGBTQI+?), and 70 (Are contemporary Pagan religions indicative of a new form of religiosity?).

Elsewhere

Evans, Arthur. *Witchcraft and the Gay Counterculture.* Boston: Fag Rag Books, 2018.

Grahn, Judy. *Another Mother Tongue: Gay Words, Gay Worlds.* Boston: Beacon, 1984.

Muñoz, José Esteban. *Cruising Utopia: The Then and There of Queer Futurity.* New York: New York University Press, 2009.

63
Why is witchcraft popular among teenagers?

Denise Cush

Every so often, over the last few decades, there has been a flurry of media interest in teenagers, especially young women, identifying as witches. This usually refers to an interest in Wicca or other forms of ritual magic within a general contemporary Pagan worldview and to teenagers within "Western" culture. However, with increasing access to the internet and social media, teenage witches of the contemporary Pagan sort may now be found worldwide in diverse cultures.

Identifying as a "witch" is a minority position, so calling this phenomenon "popular" is an exaggeration. Nevertheless, teenage witches (and other young Pagans) deserve to be taken seriously. There was something of a peak in media interest from the late 1990s to the early 2000s, coinciding with the films *The Craft* (1996) and *Practical Magic* (1998) and a UK Channel 4 documentary *Teenage Kicks: The Witch Craze* (2002). Results of academic research from that period were published from 2007 onward. The main development since then is that practicing or would-be witches are more likely to access information and communities digitally, including via TikTok. There were also "teenage witches" in the 1960s, 70s, and 80s, some of whom are today's grown-up Wiccans/Pagans.

Though every young person has their own story, it is possible to make some generalizations from research about the elements of the witch/Pagan worldview that appeal to these teenagers. The positive valuation of female power in the images of the witch, priestess, or Goddess/goddesses attracts young feminists. The positive attitude toward the body and sexuality is welcome at an age when these can be major issues. The sacredness of nature provides depth to concerns about the future of the planet. The life-affirming ethics, emphasizing freedom and personal responsibility, is preferable to imposed rules and regulations. The stress on personal convictions and intuition leads young witches to feel that finding the Pagan/witch community confirms existing beliefs and values.

With several generations now of Wiccans and other contemporary Pagans, a few teenage witches have been raised in Pagan families and are thus familiar with traditions and terminology from home. Others may be familiar with Pagan motifs as they are becoming more common in wider society. Information and communities are more readily available than ever from digital sources but also books (the Pagan Federation lists twenty-nine for teenagers), shops, stalls, and festivals ("witchfest" conferences and markets are proliferating).

Interviews with teenage witches—whether female, male, or nonbinary—reveal that a witch identity/practice helps with self-esteem and confidence. The practice of ritual magic is empowering in that it gives a sense of control over events and personal destiny in a difficult world, whether understood as drawing on external or internal resources. Many have a strong desire to change the world and themselves for the better and see ritual magic and a witch/Pagan lifestyle as a way to do this. Some find this a way to express and cope with a feeling of being different, including LGBTQ+ teenagers who find the Pagan/witch community welcoming. There can be a link with alternative youth cultures, such as goth (allegedly experiencing a revival). Some gained an initial interest in witches/magic featuring in children's books, magazines, teen fiction, adult novels, poetry, myths and legends, films, TV series, or digital sources, leading to further exploration. Teenage witches claim to be media literate and to know the difference between entertainment and "real witchcraft." Many are very well-informed and able to articulate their worldview and explain their practices.

Practice may be solitary, with a small group of friends, or as part of an online community, though some older teenagers might join an organized coven. Rituals may be taken from books or other media or self-created, but they usually include familiar features such as circles, candles, incense, symbols such as pentagrams, and the practice of concentration / meditation / mental discipline as well as "spells." Most recognize the eightfold festival wheel common to many Pagan groups. Theologically, young witches may be bitheist (goddess and god), polytheist or pantheist, sometimes atheist (though rarely), or occasionally, theist.

Most are serious, idealistic young people who want to improve themselves and the world around them. Being a witch can be a form of protest, resistance, and transformation, providing self-confidence, a sense of control, an ethical outlook, pride in identity, and a shared vocabulary with which to articulate spirituality. It can also be fun.

About the author

Denise Cush is professor emerita in religion and education at Bath Spa University. She admits to having been a primary school witch and retaining an interest ever since, as well as an interest in Buddhist, Hindu, and Christian traditions and pluralist religious education.

Suggestions for further readings

In this book
See also chapters 7 (Are most Pagans solitary practitioners?), 65 (What is WitchTok?), and 66 (How do Pagans use fiction and film?).

Elsewhere
Berger, Helen A., and Douglas Ezzy. *Teenage Witches: Magical Youth and the Search for the Self.* New Brunswick, NJ: Rutgers University Press, 2007.

Cush, Denise. "Consumer Witchcraft: Are Teenage Witches a Creation of Commercial Interests?" *Journal of Beliefs and Values* 28(1) (2007): 45–53.

Cush, Denise. "Teenage Witchcraft in Britain." In *Religion and Youth*, edited by Sylvia Collins-Mayo and Pink Dandelion, 81–87. Burlington, VT: Ashgate, 2007.

Johnston, Hannah E., and Peg Aloi, eds. *The New Generation Witches: Teenage Witchcraft in Contemporary Culture.* Burlington, VT: Ashgate, 2007.

Walker, Josh. "TikTok Has Become the Home of Modern Witchcraft (Yes, Really)." *WIRED*, November 1, 2020. https://www.wired.co.uk/article/witchcraft-tiktok.

64
Do Pagans avoid technology?

Chris Miller

To give a brief, simple answer: no. Pagans use technology just as much as any other community. However, it is worth reflecting on why someone might ask this question to begin with. The assumption that Pagans would avoid technology stems from some of the beliefs of and perceptions about Paganism, which this chapter aims to explore. This chapter will end by reaffirming that Pagans do not avoid technology by pointing out various ways that Pagans engage with it.

Concerning the first factor behind this assumption, Paganism is often described as a nature-based or earth-centered religion. Many practitioners observe Sabbats celebrating the annual cycle of seasons, or esbats centered on the lunar cycle. Rituals encourage Pagans to connect with nature, whether through an underlying narrative, using natural symbols, or simply gathering outdoors. These religious beliefs about the importance of nature carry over into social outlooks. For instance, one survey found that Pagans are more likely than the average American to self-identify as environmentalists. Considering this nature-focused outlook, it seems only logical to think that such people are less likely to stay inside and surf the web.

Second, Paganism is often seen as an ancient religion. Some practitioners see themselves as carrying on a long-standing lineage, while others look to ancient or prehistoric traditions for inspiration. This results, for example, in worshipping gods from the ancient Greek pantheon, modeling rituals after the Druids of the British Isles, or incorporating Norse runes into one's daily life. At first glance, it might seem anachronistic that someone who celebrates the solstice at a prehistoric site like Stonehenge would use their phone's GPS to find directions.

Finally, hobbies that are popular among Pagans might also fuel assumptions about avoiding technology. Again, reflecting the religion's nature-centered outlook, many Pagans enjoy outdoor activities such as hiking or gardening. Many Pagans also attend "living history" or Renaissance fairs, dressing, speaking, and acting in the fashion of people from centuries past. Other common hobbies include traditional crafts such as embroidery, brewing mead, and wood carving. These activities reflect a fascination with history and love of nature but are not generally associated with being tech-savvy.

Acknowledging the rationale behind this assumption, I want to reiterate that Pagans do not avoid technology. As highlighted above, though certain outlooks among Pagans promote more traditional pastimes, these are not necessarily incompatible with technology. Though Pagans may enjoy gardening or ancient history, this does not preclude one from also using electronics.

Granted, as with any diverse group, there is inevitably variation. Some Pagans may still use a landline instead of a cell phone or try to periodically "unplug" from technology. Further, there is a range of competence or familiarity among practitioners. However, most Pagans use technology just as much as the average person. Indeed, there is even some evidence that Pagans are early adopters. Surveys conducted in the late 1990s found that many Pagans were employed in skilled professions that required technological proficiency, suggesting that Pagans have long possessed skill and comfort with computers. Pagans have continued to develop alongside technology. For instance, in the early 2000s—during the most primitive era of social media—there were thousands of Pagan forums on sites like Yahoo! and MSN. Two decades later, when the COVID-19 pandemic forced groups to hold their meetings online, many Pagans proudly shared that they had already been conducting virtual rituals for years. These and similar examples across time show that Pagans are as tech-savvy as any group, and in some cases, they may even be ahead of the curve.

In conclusion, there is no creed or belief that precludes Pagans from using technology, and they do so in all the typical ways that other people use technology: watching shows on Netflix, making FaceTime calls, using Google Maps for directions, and many other tasks. In addition to these "mundane" uses, Pagans also use technology for what we might call "religious" purposes. This includes conducting research using digital archives, performing virtual rituals over Skype or Zoom, or using social media for community organization. Since Pagans use their phones and computers for magical and nonmagical purposes, some practitioners even recommend cleansing one's devices regularly with crystals or incense. These are just some of the ways that Pagans "enchant" technology—both literally and metaphorically—and use it for religious purposes, reinforcing that Pagans (on the whole) do not avoid technology.

About the author
Chris Miller is a postdoctoral fellow with the Nonreligion in a Complex Future project, hosted at the University of Ottawa.

Suggestions for further readings
In this book
See also chapters 25 (What are Technopagans?), 45 (Do Pagans use the internet for their religion?), and 65 (What is WitchTok?).

Elsewhere
Cowan, Douglas E. *Cyberhenge: Modern Pagans on the Internet*. New York: Routledge, 2005.

Snook, Jennifer. *American Heathens: The Politics of Identity in a Pagan Religious Movement*. Philadelphia: Temple University Press, 2015.

Renser, Berit, and Katrin Tiidenberg. "Witches on Facebook: Mediatization of Neo-Paganism." *Social Media + Society* 6(3) (2020): 1–11.

65
What is WitchTok?

Mary Hamner

Much of the growth in witch, occult, and contemporary Pagan communities is the result of the popularity of these movements on social media. Increasingly, platforms like Instagram, TikTok, and YouTube are where a growing number of new Pagan and witchcraft practitioners first learn about these traditions and practices and where they continue to engage in order to learn and develop. Users share photos and videos of themselves, their personal tools and altars, books and journals, artwork, nature imagery, and more, applying hashtags that make their content searchable to other users. Popular hashtags vary by platform. Larger, more general tags (#witch, #witchcraft, #pagan) may yield millions of results, while others pertaining to more specific factions within witchcraft and Pagan communities (#traditionalwitchcraft, #gardnerian, #greenwitch) may include posts numbering only in the hundreds. Over time, hashtags themselves become communities within the bounds of a shared platform, with influencers, popular users, content trends, shared templates, and taboos of their own. WitchTok is an example of such a community. Accessible through the use of the #witchtok hashtag on TikTok, WitchTok also became a popular shorthand for the entirety of content posted and circulated by witchcraft practitioners and enthusiasts of all kinds on the growing platform, regardless of which hashtags they use.

Every social media platform favors some types of content over others (for example, short-form video versus still images or long text versus short text) and thus tends to attract distinct user groups, often along age lines. TikTok, with its short videos, easy editing tools, emphasis on music, and comparatively relaxed oversight, is particularly popular with teens and young adults (though it should be noted, there is a substantial number of older users, and the platform is also popular with businesses, musicians, writers, and visual artists). Because of this, the content that circulates on the platform reflects the styles of young people and sometimes has little overlap with the content that circulates on platforms favored by other demographics.

Over time, the result is a body of jargon, memes, texts, trends, and social concerns that are unique to each site. This can create fragmentation in wider communities (for example, religious communities) that we might otherwise assume to be cohesive. Witches and Pagans who primarily rely on one platform are likely to be consuming different information—from the books they purchase to the social issues they find most pressing—than witches and Pagans on another platform. This has potentially had an impact beyond the internet, shifting Pagan festival attendance and also influencing metaphysical publishing sales. How significant these shifts will be over time remains to be seen.

WitchTok represents not just an online community but also a tension between younger practitioners and their more established older counterparts. On other social media platforms, WitchTok has been a topic of derision and is allegedly an environment rife with misinformation and melodrama. It is common to see witches and Pagans on other platforms warning newcomers against using TikTok to learn about magic and the occult. Whether or not these warnings are justified is highly debatable, especially when we consider the anxieties that often surround the introduction of new technologies, new communities, new practices, and new leading voices. It is likely that at least some of the criticism of TikTok among older, more experienced, or otherwise more established witches and Pagans is rooted in typical generational suspicions. Witnessing the inevitable replacement of trusted authors and teachers, coping with naturally shifting vocabularies, and navigating an ever-expanding set of potential identities is always unmooring for preceding generations, and these types of changes cause controversy in any large group we might examine, whether online or off. In this sense, WitchTok makes a convenient scapegoat. It is also true, however, that TikTok—with its massive user base and rapidly cycling content—allows for particularly speedy information exchange and often wider distribution. All media, both digital and traditional, leaves room for misinformation. WitchTok, for both good and ill, merely functions faster than other mediums and with potentially further-reaching consequences.

About the author

Mary Hamner is at the University of North Carolina at Chapel Hill specializing in religion and culture. Her research interests include religion and social media, ethnography, secularism, and contemporary witchcraft. She publishes about Wicca and witchcraft and maintains a social media presence under the name Thorn Mooney.

Suggestions for further readings

In this book
See also chapters 45 (Do Pagans use the internet for their religion?) and 63 (Why is witchcraft popular among teenagers?).

Elsewhere
Hoover, Stewart M. *The Media and Religious Authority*. University Park: Pennsylvania State University Press, 2016.

Katz, Roberta, Sarah Ogilvie, Jane Shaw, and Linda Woodhead. *Gen Z, Explained: The Art of Living in a Digital Age*. Chicago: University of Chicago Press, 2021.

66
How do Pagans use fiction and film?

Carole M. Cusack

The majority of modern Pagans are people who have consciously decided to revive the worship of ancient and medieval deities that at some point in history had died out—for example, ancient Egyptian gods or medieval Scandinavian gods.

Pagans often engage with the reinvention of an imagined past, though there are differing attitudes as to how creative or forensically grounded in history and archaeology these reinventions can be. Thus, reconstructionist Pagans are deeply immersed in original languages (Classical Greek, Latin, and Old Norse, for example) and are concerned with celebrating only festivals and rituals for which there is textual or archaeological evidence. So-called eclectic Pagans draw on a broader range of sources in the revival of (primarily) Indigenous European religion and may combine rituals and iconography from a range of different polytheistic pantheons (Greek, Norse, Slavic, and Celtic, for example). The reality is, even when Pagans engage with historical sources in reconstructing their religion, they are making real-world phenomena from things that exist only in texts and are, out of necessity, using imagination and creativity to bring these "dead" traditions to life.

Yet there are also Pagans who engage with the invention of new deities and religious forms, often based on popular fictions, including novels and films. I would argue that this process is not so different from animating an ancient source text or illustration on the wall of an archaeological site; however, from approximately 1950 to 2000, there was a commonly held belief that modern Paganism was a survival of the pre-Christian religions of Europe and that the witches tried and executed in the early modern era were, in fact, Pagans dedicated to the worship of the Horned God. At the close of the twentieth century, that idea had comprehensively been demolished by Ronald Hutton, whose marvelous book *Triumph of the*

Moon (1999) revealed that modern Paganism was a twentieth-century creation of a small circle of like-minded esotericists and fringe cultural figures, chief of whom was retired civil servant Gerald Brousseau Gardner (1884–1964), the founder of Wicca. In light of this discovery, the practice of invented religions—many of which overlapped with Paganism or became branches of it—gained credibility.

Discordianism, an invented religion that worshipped Eris, the Greek goddess of strife (*Discordia* in Latin) was founded in a twenty-four-hour bowling alley in East Whittier, California, in 1957 by Kerry Thornley (Omar Khayyan Ravenhurst), Greg Hill (Malaclypse the Younger), and a few friends. Five years later, in April 1962, Tim (Oberon) Zell and Lance Christie founded the Church of All Worlds (CAW), a real-world instantiation of a church founded by Martian-born Valentine Michael Smith in Robert A. Heinlein's bestselling science fiction novel *Stranger in a Strange Land* (1961). These are the two longest-running invented religions; both are now definitely part of Paganism. Eris, as a classical goddess, was a Pagan focus for Discordians from the beginning of the religion; with CAW, the integration with Paganism came in 1968, when Zell became friends with Frederick McLaren Adams, founder of two influential Pagan groups, the Fellowship of the Hesperides and Feraferia. Zell then integrated Wiccan practices such as the Wheel of the Year ritual calendar, and later, the goddess for CAW was identified with Gaea, Earth.

While Pagans used fiction and film to craft new religions, there was a synergy between the emergence of alternative religions and the popular culture of the 1960s and 1970s. For example, Robin Hardy's exceptional film *The Wicker Man* (1973) is a Pagan classic, though its source text, David Pinner's novel *Ritual* (1967), was sympathetic to the views of the Christian inspector David Hanlin (Sergeant Neil Howie, played by Edward Woodward in the film). In *The Wicker Man*, Howie's nemesis is Lord Summerisle (played by veteran horror actor Christopher Lee, in a career-defining performance), who admits to deliberately reviving Paganism to increase the prosperity of Summerisle, a link with the actual practice of modern Pagans. Another inspirational text was devout Catholic J. R. R. Tolkien's trilogy *The Lord of the Rings* (1954), which, despite being imbued with Christian theology, inspired the Elven movement (which grew out of an early Tolkien religious group, the Elf-Queen's Daughters, founded in 1972) and has been adopted as scripture by two groups studied by Markus Altena Davidsen of Leiden University—Tië eldaliéva (the Elven Path) and Ilsaluntë Valion (the Silver Ship of the Valar), who seek contact with the godlike elves via ritual and contemplation.

It could be argued that Jediism, a religion based on George Lucas's *Star Wars* films, is Pagan in spirit, though often Daoism and Eastern spiritualities are the framework used to analyze it. There are also Pagans who are deeply engaged with the religious and spiritual traditions of a range of novels, films, online games (*World of Warcraft* or *Age of Mythology*, for example), and mythologized sites in the real world (UFO contact sites, Neolithic monuments, and so on). Religion is a human cultural product, and modern Pagans recycle and repurpose many different cultural products in the crafting of their religion.

About the author

Carole M. Cusack is professor of religious studies at the University of Sydney, Australia. Her research focuses on new religious movements, contemporary religious trends, religion and popular culture, and Western esotericism. She edits several journals.

Suggestions for further reading

In this book
See also chapters 44 (What is Chaos Magic?) and 67 (Is Paganism make-believe?).

Elsewhere
Cusack, Carole M. "Invented Religions." In *The Bloomsbury Companion to New Religious Movements*, edited by George Chryssides and Benjamin E. Zeller, 291–294. London: Bloomsbury, 2014.

67
Is Paganism make-believe?

[M] Dudeck

Between 1917 and 1921, archaeologist and anthropologist Margaret Murray (1863–1963) popularized "the witch-cult hypothesis," wherein she claimed to have found evidence from selective inquisition records for a pan-European, pre-Christian religion existing prior to the witch trials, going all the way back to the Stone Age. Murray wasn't the originator of this concept, but she legitimated it in academic circles, and in 1929, she was invited to provide the entry on "witchcraft" for the fourteenth edition of the *Encyclopaedia Britannica*, wherein she propagated her witch-cult theory intentionally excluding any alternate theories or counterarguments, providing the authoritative definition of witchcraft until it was updated in 1969. This forty-year period of influence helped give birth to and shape modern witchcraft, Wicca, and contemporary Paganism authoritatively—allowing for the witch-cult hypothesis to be presented to the public as fact before it was discredited as pseudoscience. This also inspired author, amateur anthropologist/archaeologist, and "father" of Wicca Gerald Gardner (1884–1964) to build on Murray's thesis, adding that he himself had been initiated in one of the last of the English covens practicing "the Old Religion." This corroborated Murray's argument, but Gardner was unable to evidence it, as the coven had sworn him to secrecy, a secrecy they affirmed was necessary following the Witch Trials.

Prior to Murray and Gardner, several scholars and visionaries in Britain began to imagine and produce their own experimental forms of proto-Paganism, evidenced by the artistic reinterpretation of historical documents or the strategic excavation of rituals and folklore. Doctor-turned-clergyman (considered by some to be the father of British archaeology) William Stukeley (1687–1765) was an advocate of British Israelism, an argument that claimed the Druids were originally from the direct line of Abraham and descended from "an oriental colony" of Phoenicians who had settled in Britain between the mythic end of Noah's flood and the biblical time of Abraham. He theorized that the ancient Druids were in fact a monotheistic priesthood akin to modern Christians. Several known forgeries also abound within the English database of Paganism—including most notably *The Works of Ossian* by James MacPherson (1736–1796) and *The Druid's Prayer* by Edward Williams, a.k.a. Iolo Morganwg (1747–1826), who forged bardic rituals and Druidic religious texts. However, many modern Pagan practitioners, aware of the forged or fictional status of many of the sacred texts of their so-called ancient religion, openly admit that Paganism is an invention but, out of the religions available, find an authentic spiritual expression in what is ostensibly an intergenerational work of historical fiction that generates belief systems and ritual practices.

Invented religions, as both a concept and category, conjure problems and provocations rooted in the configuration of the two terms combined (invention + religion). Invented religions are paradoxical, as religion remains entangled with notions of collective transcendence and communitas that appear to eclipse the historical and individualist pretexts "invention," as a concept, is built atop. It was only in the Renaissance that the term "inventor" began to be used to describe the actions of artists, engineers, architects, and alchemists producing "original works." This is also a point in history, with the rise of Humanism, where "having genius" gave birth to "being a genius"— prior to this, particularly in ancient Rome, the individual artist or author was never considered the originator of their material; rather, they were seen as a trained vehicle that could transmit effectively the genius of the universe moving through them. Inventing a religion is a task that, historically, is the product of many protagonists over multiple generations, so the very notion of an "invented religion" initiates a reconsideration of what a religion is, who has the authority to preside over or establish religions, and if religions can be created or authored by human beings at all.

Paganism occupies a unique place in this dialogue, as it is at once a historical term used to describe a vast range of religious activities over an equally vast range of historical times (from prehistory to the present day) while also referring to a series of new religious movements that have been remixing and reinventing histories in an effort to produce new belief systems. Thus, the threshold between make-believe and make-belief is blurred by Paganism because its spectrum consists of those who, in good faith, believe in the fictions remixed out of remnants of the past (and are indifferent to the evidence of factuality of these claims) and those for whom the fictional nature of their scripture is part of its appeal. Paganism is, therefore, very much a product of make-believe—but then aren't all historical religions?

About the author

[M] **Dudeck**, PhD (Edinburgh), is an artist and cultural engineer who invents their own queer religion as art and a scholar of new religious movements exploring the role of art in the construction of belief systems.

Suggestions for further readings

In this book

See also chapters 44 (What is Chaos Magic?) and 66 (How do Pagans use fiction and film?).

Elsewhere

Cusack, Carol. *Invented Religions: Imagination, Fiction & Faith*. Surrey: Ashgate, 2010.

Lewis, James R., and Hammer Olav. *The Invention of Sacred Tradition*. Cambridge: Cambridge University Press, 2007.

Studying and teaching Pagan religions

68
How do scholars study Paganism?

Chris Miller

Pagan studies describes an academic field devoted to researching Pagan groups, practitioners, ideas, and activities. The field dates back to roughly the 1980s, when a handful of scholars who studied these topics connected through conferences, eventually producing books, journals, and edited volumes. At present, the field comprises perhaps little more than one hundred scholars worldwide who work within broader disciplines, including archaeology, anthropology, and theology. Each approach brings different questions and methods to the study of Paganism. A historian traces how covens develop in one area over time. A folklorist explores how old stories continue to resonate with modern Pagans. A sociologist analyzes the rise (or decline) of different identities. Amid this variety, some approaches are obviously more common than others. This chapter will outline some of the most common methods that scholars adopt to study Paganism.

One of the most popular approaches in Pagan studies is ethnography, which involves a researcher observing (or immersing themselves within) a community. Common sites for ethnography can include Pagans throughout one city, a single coven, or a Pagan festival, and data collection can span days, months, or even years. Research activities include watching rituals, attending social events, or accompanying someone running errands. Ethnography is often complemented by interviews, which allow scholars to ask more direct and in-depth questions.

A more specific form of ethnography is participant observation, which describes simultaneously *watching* and *engaging in* an event. One does not just observe a ritual but actively contributes and participates. However, ethnographers must balance this immersion with traditional scholarly tasks such as writing field notes. A related approach is called autoethnography. Since many who study Pagans are also practitioners, research can involve reflecting on how one was shaped by a given experience. In autoethnography, the focus is not *exclusively* on the researcher, but one's experiences—and how they compare with others—become a topic of discussion.

Another popular (though challenging) research method is the use of surveys. Pagans represent a small proportion of most populations and are not well-represented in censuses or general surveys. For this reason, most scholars adopt what is called "snowball sampling." This involves, for example, someone announcing that they have a survey for Pagans to complete, then asking people to forward the survey to others who might be interested. Like a snowball rolling down a hill, this gradually increases the number of respondents. Snowball samples are never random, since respondents are all connected—everyone knew someone who knew someone who knew the researcher. However, using this strategy, scholars can gain large numbers of respondents and discover the demographics of Pagans, as well as their experiences, preferences, and outlooks.

Since Pagans draw inspiration from prehistoric and ancient history, historical and archival research are also popular methods. Researchers may excavate archaeological materials and ask how Pagans interpret those artifacts or read old correspondences to decipher the root of some ritual. Additionally, although often labeled a new religion, some Pagan traditions are nearly one hundred years old. Scholars may, therefore, explore the historical development of Pagan figures, groups, and practices.

Another range of approaches can be termed "textual studies." Referencing the amount of reading some Pagan traditions require, many call Paganism "the religion with homework." Practitioners read spell books, instructional guides, and also works of fiction, and scholars study Paganism by analyzing this material. Selecting a text, one can analyze any changes over time, examine its symbolism, or ask why it is important to Pagans. "Texts" do not even need to be religious. In exploring young adult fiction novels, for instance, one can analyze what themes a book expresses or its reception among Pagans.

Bringing this religion into modern times, Pagans also use technology for many purposes. Researching Paganism in digital spaces can involve observing a website long-term, analyzing responses to a hot-button issue, or surveying what materials Pagans access online. These approaches allow scholars to explore emerging forms of community and practice among Pagans.

This chapter has highlighted several possible ways to study Paganism, though this list is hardly exhaustive. Additionally, most projects draw on several methods concurrently. For instance, before conducting a survey, you might interview Pagans and ensure that your questions are appropriate or conduct some historical research to understand the answers you may receive. Finally, studies of digital media highlight that scholars constantly integrate new field sites and techniques to acquire and analyze data. As Pagan studies continues to evolve, these diverse methods enrich our understanding of Pagan communities.

About the author

Chris Miller is a postdoctoral fellow with the Nonreligion in a Complex Future project, hosted at the University of Ottawa.

Suggestions for further readings

In this book
See also chapters 1 (What is Paganism?), 3 (What is the difference between "Pagan," "pagan," "Paganism," and "neo-Paganism"?), and 54 (Can Paganism be applied to non-European religions, such as Shinto?).

Elsewhere
Blain, Jenny, Douglas Ezzy, and Graham Harvey, eds. *Researching Paganisms*. Toronto: AltaMira, 2004.

Davy, Barbara Jane. *Introduction to Pagan Studies*. Toronto: AltaMira, 2007.

Reid, Síân Lee, and Shelley Tsivia Rabinovitch. "Witches, Wiccans, and Neo-Pagans: A Review of Current Academic Treatments of Neo-Paganism." In *The Oxford Handbook of New Religious Movements*, edited by James R. Lewis, 514–533. New York: Oxford University Press, 2008.

69
Should Pagan religions be taught in schools?

Denise Cush

Yes—but it does depend on context: the type and location of the school, whether there is a Pagan presence in the school or community, and what you mean by "teaching."

Whether any religions at all are taught in schools varies considerably around the world and depends on whether the schools are publicly or privately funded. The state-funded education systems in some countries (e.g., the United States, France, China) are considered "secular" in the sense of keeping religion out of schools, so there is no subject called "religious education." Some religious material may feature in other subjects like history. Other countries have religious education (RE) in their curricula, where the teaching is "confessional" or "denominational," so pupils are nurtured within "their own religion" (the religion of their family/community). Either one tradition is deemed the national religion and taught to all (often with exemptions for nonadherents), or pupils are divided into separate classes for recognized religions/worldviews. The third option is "nonconfessional" or "integrated" RE, where all pupils are taught together and a range of traditions is explored. Pioneered in Sweden and the United Kingdom in the late 1960s, this teaching aspires to be academic: objective, critical and pluralist, and secular in the sense of impartiality toward worldviews. There is more scope for teaching Pagan religions in this third model.

The following discussion relates primarily to state-funded schools in England "without a religious character," although much may be transferable to other settings. Since the 1980s, I have advocated teaching Pagan religions in English RE and included Paganism in teacher training courses. The 2018 report of the Commission on RE suggested that Paganism might be included in RE, as well as other neglected traditions.

In England (and Wales), Pagan religions have gradually gained a wider public profile over the last fifty years, including in academic study, interfaith groups, chaplaincy work, and various media. For several decades now, Pagans have become primary teachers (for children aged five to eleven) or RE specialists in secondary schools (for students aged eleven to eighteen). Other teachers, though not identifying as Pagan, may have had the chance to study Pagan religions at university. The Pagan Federation was accepted as a member organization of the RE Council of England and Wales in 2011.

Children from Pagan families and older students identifying as Pagan are present in some of our classrooms, and their traditions and personal worldviews deserve the respect and interest from both teachers and fellow pupils that would be afforded to others—they should not feel excluded. As Pagan ideas and practices have osmosed into wider society, non-Pagan pupils may well share some knowledge of Pagan symbols, festivals, and practices or find them "relatable." Some research with young people, even those identifying as Christians, reveals a move toward an immanent sense of the divine.

Pagan religions have long been present in some of the myths and stories from different cultures told to children and in topics such as the history of the Romans, Egyptians, or Vikings. It is important that myths are presented to pupils not as silly or disproved ancient science but as conveying truths and values of a different kind, to which Pagans and non-Pagans can relate. Witches and Druids, however characterized, do appear in popular children's literature. Pagan motifs are entangled with Christian, secular, and commercial ones in festivals celebrated—especially Christmas/Yule, Easter/Ostara, and Halloween/Samhain—and should be explored. Local customs such as wassailing seem increasingly to reflect Pagan as well as environmental concerns and imagery.

Pagan examples can be very helpful for illustrating and illuminating such topics as ritual, symbolism, images, transformative experiences, sacred places, rites of passage, and ethical, social, and political influences of and on religion as well as the very concept of religion itself.

There may be negative reactions arising from ignorance of or prejudiced perspectives on Pagan religions that need to be handled calmly and sensitively. The diversity of Pagan traditions needs recognizing even when lack of time means generalizations are inevitable. Any new content in RE requires training and resources—but both can now be found online. At present, there are more resources for Pagan families than for schools, but these can be used or adapted by discerning teachers.

In short, teachers and schools must decide for themselves whether to include Pagan content, but exploring traditions that emphasize caring for the earth and one another and an ethic of harming none may benefit all, whether Pagan or not.

About the author

Denise Cush is professor emerita in religion and education at Bath Spa University. She was a member of the Commission on Religious Education for England (2016–2018) and has published on Buddhist, Hindu, Christian, and Pagan traditions as well as pluralist religious education.

Suggestions for further readings

In this book
See also chapters 2 (Is Paganism a religion?), 51 (What explains the enduring bias against Pagans?), and 52 (Is there antipathy between Pagans and Christians?).

Elsewhere
Commission on Religious Education (CoRE). *Religion and Worldviews: The Way Forward. A National Plan for RE*. London: REC, 2018. https://www.religiouseducationcouncil.org.uk/projects/core/.

Cush, Denise. "Paganism in the Classroom." *British Journal of Religious Education* 19(2) (1997): 83–94.

Cush, Denise, with Mike Stygal. "Pagan" (subject knowledge for teachers). RE:Online, 2016. https://www.reonline.org.uk/knowledge/pagan/.

Pagan Federation Community. "Resources and Activities for Children and Families." 2023. https://www.pfcommunity.org.uk/resources-for-children-and-families/.

RE:Online. "Voices from Pagan Worldview Traditions." 2020. https://www.reonline.org.uk/wp-content/uploads/2020/08/Voices-from-Pagan-Worldview-Traditions.pdf.

70
Are contemporary Pagan religions indicative of a new form of religiosity?

Denise Cush

From the 1960s onward, from elite academia to alternative youth culture, there has been a gradual growth in contemporary Western culture (and beyond) of a new form of religiosity (and interest in studying it) characterized by a stress on the experiential and an eclectic but selective use of religious traditions old and new. Often called "mystical" in the 1960s and early 70s, later decades saw labels like "New Age" or "spirituality" discussed, including the phrase "spiritual but not religious." Writing in the early 2000s, Heelas and Woodhead spoke of a "spiritual revolution," and although their research showed that this new religiosity was still very much a minority position in a typical English town, they predicted that this would be different by 2035. This amorphous and contested but recognizable trend seems recently to be becoming unremarkable and ordinary. Other recent research has focused on the increasing number of people who identify as "nonreligious." This can mean the definitely atheist secular humanist, who would be as dismissive of Pagan religions as of Abrahamic, but also includes many whose worldviews would fit the new kind of religiosity, although they reject the label "religion" as having negative associations.

Generalizing, this new religiosity could be characterized by the following tendencies:

- The main source of authority is the experience of individuals or informal communities rather than the hierarchies, institutions, and rulebooks associated with traditional religious organizations. This is not necessarily *individualistic*, as connection with others is also important.

221

- The organization tends toward networking, in person or online.
- Centrally defined creeds, doctrines, and metaphysical truth claims are not as important as the emotional, creative, and experiential aspects of religion, including rituals, stories, and mythology.
- The sources drawn on are eclectic, facilitated by increasing social diversity, travel, and communications technology.
- It recognizes the plurality of worldviews and lifestyles, which goes beyond the mere tolerance of other paths.
- It has contextual rather than rules-based ethics, emphasizing freedom and human (and other-than-human) flourishing.
- Attitudes are socially liberal (reflecting contemporary concerns with equality, diversity, and human rights), welcoming to feminists and those identifying as LGBTQI+.
- It sees the divine as immanent within nature, linking with environmental concerns.
- There is freedom to be creative in crafting new rituals to suit individual circumstances.
- Some are less comfortable with being described as "religious" and may see themselves as spiritual or nonreligious or reject the religious/nonreligious binary distinction (Cush 2023).

Many contemporary Pagan religions appear to share some or all of the above characteristics, and perhaps they represent the most coherent and describable exemplars. Many Pagans would stress personal experience and reject dogmatism, advocating "a life lived by following your heart, believing what your soul knows to be true before you were told what to believe" (Pagan woodcut in author's possession). It is common to celebrate the diversity of religious paths. Prudence Jones (a former president of the Pagan Federation in the United Kingdom) called this "strong pluralism." They appreciate the importance of ritual, myth, story, poetry, and creativity and subscribe to ethics based on love and freedom, as in the Wiccan phrase "And it harm none, do what thou wilt." With powerful and positive images of the female, such as the Goddess(es), priestesses, and witches, feminists feel at home, as do those identifying as LGBTQI+, who may have experienced rejection in other traditions. Groups tend to be connected networks. The focus on the sacredness of nature is seen as definitive of Paganism. Several ancient traditions are drawn on, deities from different pantheons may be included in practice, and terms such as "karma" may be used. Groups feel free to create their own ceremonies and even deities. Beyond those who identify as Pagan, there is a wider constituency of those who are "a bit Pagan" who may include Pagan motifs in their own worldview. As Peter Nynäs argues, in our new context, "people combine spiritual and religious positions with secular values into authentic and unified outlooks on life" (2018, 57).

One main difference is that the majority of Pagans are happy for their worldview to be called a religion and indeed have campaigned to be included in the category and thus more accepted socially and legally and afforded equal respect and rights as other religions. Some Pagan groups are hierarchically organized and may have esoteric rituals or teachings not shared with outsiders. Others may have distinct gender roles or be critical or dismissive of other traditions. Most important would be the claim that Paganism is not a new form of religiosity but the ancestral religion of humanity, exemplified both in ancient polytheist or pantheist traditions and contemporary Indigenous traditions. Some (notably, Heathen groups) are keen to stress their continuity with ancestral traditions, but other Pagan groups accept that although drawing on the past, revering prehistoric ancient sites, and sometimes using archaic-sounding language, their worldview is basically of recent, re-created, or reconstructed origin. The Pagan Federation respects both these positions in seeing Paganism as "an age-old current surfacing in a new form suited to the needs of the present day" (Pagan Federation, 2024). We might conclude that many contemporary Pagan religions are part of a new form of religiosity wider than Paganism but also respect and draw on ancient traditions in their own distinctive ways.

About the author

Denise Cush is professor emerita in religion and education at Bath Spa University. She has published on Buddhist, Hindu, Christian, and Pagan traditions as well as pluralist religious education.

Suggestions for further readings

In this book
See also chapters 1 (What is Paganism?), 2 (Is Paganism a religion?), and 8 (What is a Pagan worldview?).

Elsewhere
Cush, Denise. "But Are You Religious Yourself? Being Non-Binary between 'Religious' and 'Non-Religious.'" *Professional REflection / RE Today* 40(2) (2023): 53–58.

Heelas, Paul. "The Spiritual Revolution: From 'Religion' to 'Spirituality.'" In *Religions in the Modern World*, edited by Linda Woodhead, Paul Fletcher, Hiroko Kawanami, and David Smith, 357–377. London: Routledge, 2002.

Heelas, Paul, and Woodhead, Linda. *The Spiritual Revolution: Why Religion Is Giving Way to Spirituality*. Oxford: Blackwell, 2005.

Nynäs, Peter. "Making Space for a Dialogical Notion of Religious Subjects: A Critical Discussion from the Perspective of Postsecularity and Religious Change in the West." *Journal of Constructivist Psychology* 31(1) (2018): 54–71.

The Pagan Federation. "Introduction to Paganism." 2024. https://www.paganfed.org/paganism/.

Index

Abrahamic religions, 30–31, 125, 129, 160, 176
ADO (Ár nDraíocht Féin), 73
Adyar, 47
Aegir (see: Norse tradition)
Aesir, 69, 70 (see also: Norse tradition)
Albanese, Catherine, 31–32
All Saints' Day, 151–152 (see also: Halloween)
alternative healing modalities, 60 (see also: healing)
alternative religious movements, 4, 90, 163, 208
alternative spirituality, 64, 131
amulets, 12
ancestors, 37–39, 69, 73, 107, 109, 110, 124–125, 157, 179–180, 196
 of blood, 109
 of place, 109
 of spirit, 109
 of tradition, 109
 veneration of, 69
ancient Baltic religion, 85
ancient Druidry, 75 (see also: Druids)
ancient Egypt, 97, 207
ancient Greece, 135
Ancient Order of Druids, 81 (see also: Druids)
ancient Paganism, 15–16, 81
ancient Rome, 81
ancient Slavic "paganism," 127
androgyny, 98
animism, 98, 127
animists, 106
anthropology, 14, 55, 103, 215
Antinous (Greek god), 98, 193
antiracism, 70, 182
archetypes, 16, 54, 115
archival research, 216
Aristotle, 113
Artemis, 116

Artese, Leo, 93
Asamanism, 175
Asatru (Ásatrú), 55, 57, 70, 109, 189
astrology, 35, 103–104, 129
athame, 127 (see also: chalices)
atheism, 107
Atheopaganism, 106–107
authoritarianism, 184
autoethnography, 215–216
Avebury, 38
Awen (creative force), 44, 73
ayahuasca, 92–93

Babbo Natale, 146
Bardas, The, 72–73
bards, 44, 73, 75–76
barrows, 110
BDO (British Druid Order), 73, 109
Beltane, 41 (see also: festivals)
Benedikt, Michael, 143
Berger, Helen A., 192, 193
Besant, Annie, 47 (see also: Theosophy)
bhakti devotionalism, 55
Blavatsky, Helena Petrovna, 46–47 (see also: Theosophy)
blood ancestors, 109, 180
blót, 69, 157 (see also: Norse tradition; sacrifice)
body/soul split, 125
Böhme, Jakob, 46
Bonewits, Isaac, 92
Book of Shadows, 44
Book of the Law, The (*Liber AL vel Legis*), 135 (see also: Crowley, Aleister)
British Israelism, 210
Buddhism, 47, 61, 72, 101

Cabot, Laurie, 91
calling the quarters, 115
candles, 25, 146, 199
Candomblé, 175

INDEX

cardinal directions, 78
carnival, 145, 148–149 (see also: festivals)
casting the circle, 28
Çatalhöyük, 38
Catholicism, 61, 105, 130
Celtic tradition, 61, 92
   deities, 97, 207
   festivals, 28
   languages, 116
   myths, 13, 178
   people, 3, 109, 151–152
   revivalists, 76
   sources, 43, 73
censuses, 7, 18–19, 21, 216 (see also: surveys)
ceremonial magic, 52
Ceridwen, 43, 92
Chaldean oracles, 12
chalices, 79, 122, 127
chaos magic, 138–140
charge of the Goddess, 44
charity registration, 6, 75
Christianity, 81–82, 85, 100–101, 132, 145–146, 151–153, 160, 163, 166, 175–176, 178–179, 185, 189–190, 195
Christkindl, 146
Christmas, 146, 219
Church of All Worlds (CAW), 52, 208
Church of Satan, 161
Clan of Tubal Cain, 52
clergy, 104, 119, 148, 166, 210
   pagan ministers, 7, 119, 219
climate change, 98 (see also: environmentalism)
Cochrane, Robert, 52
collective consciousness, 101
collective transcendence, 211
Colman Smith, Pamela, 130 (see also: tarot)
colonialism, 64, 109, 172, 175, 179
comparative mythology, 55
consciousness, 3, 33, 35, 47, 98, 100–101, 110, 124, 136
consensual relationships, 127 (see also: sex magick)
consensus reality, 139
contested identities, 70
core shamanism, 92 (see also: shamanism)
cosmology, 12, 69
Council of American Witches, 33
Council of Nicaea, 152
counterculture, 133, 184

covens, 21, 52, 57, 66–67, 79, 143, 170, 182, 199, 210, 215 (see also: Wicca; witchcraft)
creeds, 6, 202, 222
Crowley, Aleister, 16, 43 (see also: Thelema)
crystals, 202
cultural appropriation, 172, 178–179, 180
cultural reappropriation, 130, 149
Cunningham, Scott, 21
cycle of life, 124

Daoism, 139
Davidsen, Markus Alten, 208
Davis, Erik, 78
de Martino, Ernesto, 105
deep ecology, 113 (see also: environmentalism)
deities
   androgynous, 98
   Celtic, 97, 196, 207
   Slavic, 81–82, 187, 207
demographics, 204, 216
Descent of Inanna, 16
Dia de los Muertos, 179
diabolical tradition, 148
Diana (Herodias), 16
Dianic witchcraft, 92, 182, 192–193
Dievas, 84
Discordianism, 138, 208
disenchantment of the world, 13, 132
divination, 34, 122, 130, 152
   astrology, 35, 103–104, 129
   tarot, 25, 34, 129–130
divine, the, 3–4, 24, 28, 35, 44, 54–55, 73, 97, 98, 125, 167, 192, 219, 222
divine feminine, 97, 192
divine ontology, 55
DNA, 109, 208
do what thou wilt, 222 (see also: Thelema)
"Drawing Down the Moon," 116 (see also: Wicca)
dreams and visions, 34, 101, 116
Drew, Rose, 170
Druid Network, the (TDN), 6, 71, 75, 92, 167 (see also: Druids)
Druidry, 6–7, 27, 44, 58, 72–73, 75–76, 91–92, 97, 109, 110, 115, 119, 167, 172, 184, 189
Druids, 6, 13, 44, 52, 72–73, 75–76, 92, 109, 167
   OBOD (Order of Bards, Ovates, and Druids), 73, 76

Druids' groves, 21
Durga, 55
dying and rising god, 16

Earth Mother, 84
Easter (Ēastre, Eostre), 149, 151–153 (see also: festivals)
eclectic Pagans, 4, 22, 57–58, 139, 207, 221–222
ecology, 69, 113 (see also: environmentalism)
Eco-Pagans, 182 (see also: environmentalism)
Eisler, Riane, 93
Eisteddfod, 73 (see also: Druids)
Elven movement, 208
elves, 69, 208
Elysium, 101
enchanted worldview, 135
enlightenment, 23, 129, 186
environmentalism, 10, 30–33, 34–35, 97, 113, 158, 166–167, 182, 185–186, 219, 222
Epiphany, 145
esbats, 201
esotericism, modern Western, 121
eternal punishment, 100
ethics, 27, 106, 112–113, 118, 167, 198, 222
ethnicity, 31, 37, 51, 63, 75–76, 82, 85–86, 97, 179–180, 181–183, 190–191
ethnography, 215, 216
ethnology, 81, 103
European Court of Human Rights, 86, 90
Evans, Dave, 138
evil, 63, 82, 113, 147, 166
 definition of, 113
evocation, 116
Evola, Julius, 185

fairies, 38, 116, 152, 193
Farrar, Janet and Stewart, 43–44, 52, 82, 84, 104, 127, 153
Fascism, 184–185
Faur, Mirella, 91
feminism, 97, 182
Feraferia, 208
fertility, 14, 33, 67
festivals, 9, 15, 19, 25, 27–28, 40–41, 61, 84, 115, 146, 148, 151–153, 167, 199, 207, 219
 Beltane, 41
 Samhain, 41, 78, 110, 151–152, 219 (see also: Halloween)

film and TV, 199, 208
financial crisis of 2008, 184
folkish Heathens, 70, 181
folklore, 14, 25, 38, 84, 152, 181, 210
folkloristics, 103
forests, 34–35, 66, 78, 116
Frazão, Marcia, 91
Free Masonry, 73
freedom of religion, 88
Freneau, Philip, 33
Frigg, 54

Gabija, 84, 85
Gaea, 208
Gaelic language, 116
Gaia, 34–35
Gardner, Gerald, 27, 44, 51–52, 57, 63, 66–67, 91, 136, 160, 182, 204, 208, 210 (see also: Wicca)
gender identification, 85, 98, 164, 166, 182, 185, 191, 195–196, 223
ghosts, 104
gnomes, 115
Gnosticism, 100, 139
God Is Red, 75
goddess figurines, 43
Goddess movement, 38, 182
Golden Bough, The, 16
Golden Dawn, Hermetic Order of the, 52, 73, 130
good, 82, 104, 106, 113, 147, 205 (see also: evil)
Gorsedd (of the Bards of Wales), 73, 137
Gospel of Matthew, 145
Grace, Lisa, 64
Grahn, Judy, 196
Graves, Robert, 43
Greek Orthodox Christianity, 190, 191, 208
Greek tradition, 3, 15–17, 135, 172
 ancient Greeks, 34
 deities, 51, 82, 98, 201
 language, 107, 207
 modern Greeks, 189–191
 myths, 101
 philosophy, 133
 sources, 12–13, 43, 81, 178, 189–190
Greenham Common, 167
groves, 21 (see also: Druids)
Guardians of the Watchtowers, 115
guising, 152

Halloween, 110, 145, 151, 152, 219 (see also: Samhain)
Hanegraaff, Wouter, 135
hard polytheism, 54–55 (see also: polytheism)
Harner, Michael, 92
hashtags, 204
healing, 51, 60, 100–112, 122, 193
Heathenism, 70, 97, 110 (see also: Norse tradition)
Heathenry, 16, 27, 69–70, 109, 171, 181, 185, 189 (see also: Norse tradition)
Heinlein, Robert A., 52, 208
Hellenism (see: Greek tradition)
henotheism, 98
herbalism, 51
Hermes, 82
Hermetic Order of the Golden Dawn (see: Golden Dawn, Hermetic Order of the)
Herodias, 16
Hesperides, Fellowship of the, 208
hierophany, 133
high magic, 133
high priestess, 52, 143
Hinduism, 47, 55, 101
history of religions, 55
homosexual deities, 98
homosexuality, 98, 196
Hoodoo, 175
Horned God, 66, 97, 161, 196, 207
Hultkrantz, Åke, 100–101
human rights, 86, 89, 90, 158, 222
human sacrifice, 158 (see also: sacrifice)
humanism, 13, 211
Hutton, Ronald, 18, 44, 72, 207

Icelandic Eddas, 43, 123, 199 (see also: *Poetic Edda*; *Prose Edda*)
Icelandic sources, 43, 69, 125
Ilsaluntë Valion (Silver Ship of the Valar), 208
incense, 110, 157, 202
Indigenous, 10, 18, 31, 37, 38, 63–64, 66, 75–76, 93, 109, 153, 172–173, 179, 207, 223
Indigenous religion, definition of, 75
individualism, 97
inquisition records, 210
Inter Faith Network UK, 7
interconnectedness, 4, 121–122
interfaith groups, 167
interpretatio Romana, 55
invented religions, 208, 211

inverted pentacle, 122
invocations, 12, 116
Irish sources, 76, 152
Isis, 54
Isis Unveiled, 46 (see also: Blavatsky, Helena Petrovna)
Islam, 3, 13, 43, 101, 160, 176
Italian American witchcraft, 51
Italian Renaissance, 13, 130
Itzachilatlan, Sacred Fire of, 93

jack-o'-lanterns, 152
Jediism, 208
Ježíšek, 146
Jotuns, 69
Judaism, 3, 43, 61, 101, 160, 176
Julius Caesar, 75
Jungian psychology, 115
Juno, 54, 101

Kahlos, Maijastina, 189
Kali, 55
Khors, 81, 82
KIA ZOS system (see: chaos magic)
Knight, Sirona, 79
Krampus, 146

Laima, 84
Lakshmi, 55
Lane, David, 181
LaVey, Anton, 136
Leland, Charles, 43, 66
Lent, 148–149, 153
Lévi-Strauss, Claude, 145–147
Levy, Carminha, 92
LGBTQI+, 167, 185, 192–193, 199, 222
Liber AL vel Legis (see: *Book of the Law, The*)
Lir, 54
Lithuania, 84–86, 88–89
Loki, 82
Lubbert, Heinrich, 149
Lucifer, 161–162
Lugh, 115
Lughnasadh, 115 (see also: festivals)
Lupercalia, 148–149

Mabinogion, 43
MacPherson, James, 211
magi, 145
magic, 16, 134, 139, 140
 definition of, 135–136

magick, 127–128, 135–136
ritual, 198–199
magical circle, 16, 115
magical papyri, Greek and Demotic, 12
magick, 127–128, 135–136
sex magick, 127–128
Mahadevi, 55
mainstream religion, 163
Mamurius Veturius, 148
Manx, 70
market theory of religion, 190
masquerades, 148
material culture, 15, 55
materialist worldview, 104, 106–107
Mathers, Samuel Liddell MacGregor, 135
Mauss, Marcel, 132
Mc Lir, Manannán, 116
McSherry, Lisa, 143
mead (drink), 157, 187, 202
meditation, 25, 55, 58, 79, 110, 116, 125, 128, 199
Mediterranean cultures, 12
Mesopotamia, 16
militarism, 184
Mists of Avalon, The, 92
Mithraism, 16
Mokosh, 81
monism, 47, 55
monotheism, 4, 10, 97, 170
moon, 25, 41, 84, 129, 152
moon goddess, 66
moral codes, 112
Morganwg, Iolo (Edward Williams), 72–73, 76, 211
mother goddess, 33, 82
Murray, Margaret, 66, 210 (see also: witches: witch-cult hypothesis)
music, 73, 76, 79, 92, 124, 204
mystery cults, 17

National Socialism (Nazism), 70, 164, 185, 187, 188
nativism, 184, 185
natural philosophy, 135
natural world, 3–4, 12, 28, 30, 33–35, 44, 79, 98, 106, 121, 136, 167
naturalism, 106
nature spirits, 97, 98, 182
Nemetios, Marcílio, 92
neoliberalism, 184, 185
Neolithic monuments, 209 (see also: stone circles)
Neopaganism, 172
Neoplatonism, 12–13, 46, 54, 100, 121
Neptune, 54
New Age, 61, 91, 129, 130, 133–134, 138, 221
New Forest, 66
Nichols, Ross, 27
Ninguém, Marcos, 93
Norse tradition
language, 101, 207
mythology, 82, 97, 125, 178, 180
Paganism, 70, 180, 201
numinous reality, 54

OBOD (Order of Bards, Ovates, and Druids), 73, 76 (see also: Druids)
occulture, 140
Odinani, 175
offerings, 15, 38, 107, 110, 116, 117, 157, 158 (see also: ritual magic: ritual sacrifices; sacrifice)
Olcott, Henry Steel, 46, 47 (see also: Theosophy)
old religion, the, 67
online games, 209
online rituals, 79, 142
Order of Nine Angles, 161
ordination, 119
Ordo Templi Orientis, 52
ørlög, 69
orthopraxy versus orthodoxy, 27
Ostara, 153
Ostern, 153
otherworld, 101, 125, 152
Otto, Bernd-Christian, 136, 138

Pagan Federation, 6, 22, 109, 167, 199, 219, 222–223
pagan folk rock, 97
pagan revival, 97
pagan studies, 215, 217
pagan worldview, 24–25, 28, 167, 198
Paganism, definition of, 3–4, 9, 10, 22, 30, 46, 60, 109, 132, 163, 171
African, 175, 176
in Brazil, 91–93
lowercase versus uppercase, 10, 101, 114, 172, 189
Telluric, 100
versus Neopaganism, 172
panentheism, 98

PantheaCon, 191
pantheism, 98
participant observation, 215
paschal full moon, 152
pendants, 122
pentacles, 121–122
pentagrams, 121, 199
Père Noël, 146–147
perennialism, 54, 179
persecution, 11, 66, 109
Persian new year (Nowruz), 153
personal responsibility, 198
Perun, 81
Pettazzoni, Raffaele, 103
Pico della Mirandola, Giovanni, 46
pilgrimage, 38, 55, 92
Pinner, David, 208
planetary unconscious, 35
Plato, 113
Pliny the Elder, 75
pluralism, 55, 113, 167, 218, 222
Poetic Edda, 69, 125
poetry, 44, 67, 73, 76, 116, 119, 222
polytheism, 16, 33, 54–55, 60, 98, 106, 170, 190, 192
popular culture, 44, 97, 130, 140
Poseidon, 54, 116
priestess, 27, 35, 52, 85, 116, 143, 198, 222
Prieto, Claudiney, 92
Procopius of Caesarea, 81
Prose Edda, 69
protection, 6, 79, 89, 122
   from computer viruses, 79
Protestant Reformation, 107
pseudoscience, 210
psychedelic movement, 138
psychic censors, 139
psychological archetypes, 16
punk rock, 138

quantum physics, 139
Queen Elizabeth II, 73
queer, 61, 193–195
   definition of, 195–196
Quintino, Claudio (Crow), 92

Radegast, 82
radical othering, 70
Rasos (festival), 84
Rastafari, 160
reappropriation, 103

reclaiming tradition, 182
reconstructionism, 16, 92, 158, 185, 207
redemption, 100
reincarnation, 67, 101, 124–125, 170
relativism, 113
religion
   definition of, 27
   religious affiliation, 18, 119, 193
   religious education (RE), 7, 44, 167, 218
   religious identity, 170, 181–182, 190
   religious orthodoxy, 98
   religious practice, 3, 18, 55, 61, 73, 88, 127, 158, 179
   religious tradition, 3, 31, 47, 61, 72–73, 75, 121, 130, 160, 172–173, 179, 185, 221
   of resistance, 186
Renaissance, 13, 46, 201, 211
Restall Orr, Emma, 92
reverence for nature, 4, 28, 73, 128 (see also: environmentalism)
rites of passage, 17, 219
ritual magic, 198–199
ritual abuse, 161, 166
ritual creativity, 103
ritual efficacy, 104
ritual liturgy, 67
ritual practices, 107, 211
ritual sacrifices, 164 (see also: sacrifice)
ritual sex, 127–128, 166 (see also: sex magick)
rituals, virtual, 78–79, 118, 143, 158, 202
Rökkatru, 70
Rokkr, 69
Roman Empire, 190
Roman tradition
   deities, 13, 15–17, 146
   festivals, 146, 148–149
   language, 101
   sources, 13, 15
Romanticism, 133, 178
Rome, 10, 15, 55, 148, 151, 211
Romuva, 84–86, 88–90
runes, 25, 201 (see also: Norse tradition)
Russia, 88, 187, 188

sabbats, 161, 201
sacred circles, 28
sacred places, 219
sacred sexuality, 127, 128
sacred sites, 37, 38
sacred wisdom, 57

INDEX 231

sacred world, 143
sacrifice, 15, 31, 69, 81, 157, 164
   human, 158, 164
Saint Nicholas, 146
Saint Vitus, 82
salamander, 115
salvation, 100–101, 168
Samhain, 41, 78, 110, 151–152, 219 (see also: Halloween)
Santa Klaus, 146
Santeria, 175–176
Santo Daime, 93
Satanic panic, 67, 166
Satanic tradition, 148
Satanism, 122, 160–161, 164
Saturnalia, 146, 148
Savaron, Jean, 149
Savonarola, Girolamo, 148
science, 81, 107, 130, 132–133, 135–136, 219
Scientology, 160
Secret Doctrine, The, 46 (see also: Blavatsky, Helena Petrovna)
secularism, 19, 61, 64, 67, 100, 107, 112, 133, 136, 218–219, 221–223
seiðr (seid magic), 69, 169 (see also: Norse tradition)
Septimus, Savu, 92
sex magick, 127–128
sexual ecstasy, 35
sexual liberation, 97
sexuality, 127–128, 164, 166, 196, 198
Shallcrass, Philip, 167
shamanic journey, 125
shamanism, 19, 57, 91–93, 138, 139
Shelley, Percy Bysshe, 33
Sherwin, Ray, 138
Shinto, 31, 172–173, 187
sigilization, 139
sigils, 25
Sigrblot, 40 (see also: sacrifice)
Simargl, 81–82
simurg, 81–82
Sinnett, Alfred Percy, 47
Slavic deities, 81–82, 187, 207
Slavic Paganism, 81–82, 185
Slavic tradition, 61, 147
Smith-Waite-Rider Tarot, 130 (see also: tarot)
social media, 44, 66–67, 79, 179, 198, 202, 204–205
soft polytheism, 55, 106 (see also: polytheism)

solitary Druids, 73 (see also: Druids)
solstices, 40–41, 73, 84, 101, 146, 201
source, the, 125
Southern Hemisphere, 40
Spare, Austin Osman, 138–139
spells (casting), 12, 58, 79, 133–135, 199, 216
spirits, 38, 69, 82, 97, 101, 110, 115–117, 124, 157–158, 182
spiritual revolution, 221
Spiritualism, 47
spirituality, 4, 37, 60, 63, 75, 92, 98, 101, 112, 118, 121, 128, 131, 165, 170, 192, 199, 221
Starhawk (Miriam Simos), 182, 191
state recognition, 86, 89
Stone Age, 210
stone circles, 25, 37, 110 (see also: Neolithic monuments)
Stonehenge, 19, 38, 41, 73, 201
Strabo, 75
Stranger in a Strange Land, 52, 208
Stregheria, 51
Stribog, 81
Strmiska, Michael, 85–86
Stukeley, William, 210
substance abuse, 118
sumbel, 69
Summerlands, 125
sun, 24, 82, 129, 133, 146
sun astrology, 129 (see also: divination)
Suontaka Grave, 195
supernatural, 38, 69, 79, 98, 106–107, 112, 133, 135, 136, 147, 158, 196
superstition, 176
surveys, 18–19, 21, 81, 119, 195, 201–202, 216 (see also: censuses)
survival of consciousness, 110
Svantovit, 82
swastika, 187–188
sylphs, 115
symbols, 81, 98, 103, 115, 116, 121, 153, 157, 187–188, 201, 219
syncretism, 104

Taliesin, Book of, 76
tantra, 16
tantric Shaktism, 55
Tara, Hill of, 152
tarot, 25, 34, 129–130
technology, 15, 78–80, 139, 158, 201–202, 216, 222

232 INDEX

technopagans, 78, 80–81, 142
Telesco, Patricia, 79
Temple of Set, 161
temples, 15–16, 37, 55, 161
textual studies, 216
Thelema, 135, 139
Theodism, 70
Theodoret of Cyrus, 190
Theosophical Masters, 46
Theosophy, 46–47, 48, 160
Thomas, Keith, 132
Tië eldaliéva (the Elven Path), 208
TikTok, 22, 198, 204, 205 (see also: social media)
WitchTok, 204, 205
Tlachtga, Hill of, 152
Tolkien, J. R. R., 208
traditional healers, 176
traditional religions, 37, 86
trances, 51, 101, 116, 135, 139
trickster archetype, 82
Trinkūnas, Jonas, 84
Trinkūnienė, Inija, 85
Triumph of the Moon, The, 207–208
true will, 135–136 (see also: Thelema)

UFO contact sites, 209
Ukraine, 187–188
Umbanda, 91, 175
Urglaawe, 70

Valhalla, 125 (see also: Norse tradition)
Valiente, Doreen, 44, 52, 67, 160 (see also: Wicca)
Vanatru, 70 (see also: Norse tradition)
Vanir, 69 (see also: Norse tradition)
Vargas, Haroldo Evangelista, 93
Vedic astrology, 129 (see also: divination)
Veles, 82
veneration of nature, 3, 98 (see also: environmentalism)
Viking Age, 70 (see also: Norse tradition)
visualization, 25, 115–116
Vodou, 175–176
völkisch, 70 (see also: Norse tradition)
volunteerism in Paganism, 158
Von List, Guido, 181

Waite, Arthur Edward, 130 (see also: tarot)
wassailing, 19, 219

Wheel of the Year, 27, 40, 107, 208 (see also: festivals)
White Goddess, The, 43
white nationalism, 185
Wicca, 3, 4, 16, 19–22, 51–52, 55, 58, 60, 63–64, 66–67, 69, 91–92, 97, 115, 122, 127–128, 167, 182, 184, 198, 210
Alexandrian, 52, 57, 67
Gardnerian, 52, 57, 67
Williams, Edward (Iolo Morganwg), 211
witchcraft, 13–14, 19, 22, 27, 31, 34, 51, 52, 57, 60–61, 63–64, 66–67, 69, 79, 91–92, 107, 119, 160–161, 175, 189, 192, 196, 199, 204, 210
definition of, 52, 57, 63, 67, 175, 210
Dianic, 92, 182, 192–193
folk witch, 67
green witch, 67
Italian American witchcraft, 51
secular witch, 67
traditional witch, 37
Witchcraft Today, 67
witches, 44, 64, 66, 175–176, 199
definition of, 175, 210
folk, 67
green, 67
secular, 67
traditional, 37
witch doctors, 175–176
witch trials, 13, 210
witch-cult hypothesis, 66–67
Witches' Bible, A, 43
witches' sabbaths, 161 (see also: festivals)
witchfest, 199
wizards, 163, 196
Works of Ossian, The, 211
world soul, 35
World Wide Web, 143
worldview, pagan, 24–25, 28, 167, 198
wyrd, 69

Yarovit, 82
Yggdrasil, 69 (see also: Norse tradition)
YouTube, 130, 204 (see also: social media)
Yule, 40, 219

Zell, Tim (Oberon), 208
Žemyna, 84
Zhiva, 82
ZOS KIA system (see: chaos magic)

www.ingramcontent.com/pod-product-compliance
Lightning Source LLC
Chambersburg PA
CBHW060948230426
43665CB00015B/2113